Historic Ulster Churches

To Canon John Barry with gratitude
for three decades of inspiration

Historic Ulster Churches

Simon Walker

The Institute of Irish Studies
Queen's University Belfast

First published in 2000
The Institute of Irish Studies
Queen's University Belfast

British Library Cataloguing-in-Publication Data.
A catalogue record for this book is available from the British Library.

This book has received support from the Cultural Diversity Programme of the
Community Relations Council, which aims to encourage acceptance and understanding
of cultural diversity. The views expressed do not necessarily reflect those of the
NI Community Relations Council.

Cover illustrations
Front: Tamlaghtfinlagan (C of I) Church, County Londonderry
Back: Window by Helen Moloney at Creeslough Catholic Church, County Donegal
Both photographs are by the author, Simon Walker

ISBN 0 85389 767 0

Typeset in Garamond 10 pt
Designed by Page Setup, Belfast
Printed by W & G Baird Ltd, Antrim

Contents

Acknowledgements

I WOULD sincerely like to thank the following people, without whose help this book would not have come about:

Mrs Joy McCormick; Rev Canon John Barry; Mr Peter Rankin; Mr Alan Matchett; Mr Anthony Merrick; Mr Peter O Marlow; Ms Gail Pollock; the trustees of the Ulster Historic Churches Trust – the Venerable Alan Harper, Dr Evelyn Mullally, Dr Philip Robinson, Rev Robin Roddie, Mr Lawrence Weir, Rev Trevor Williamson and Mrs Primrose Wilson; the Cultural Diversity Group of the Community Relations Council; the staff of the Representative Church Body Library of the Church of Ireland; the staff of the Presbyterian Historical Society Library; the staff of the DOENI Environment and Heritage Service. I wish to express my gratitude to Dr Jonathan Bardon for writing the introduction and to Mrs Margaret McNulty and Ms Catherine McColgan of the Institute of Irish Studies for their assistance during the production stages. Thanks are also due to the clergy of the various churches for permitting me access to their buildings and also very often for the supply of useful information.

In particular I would like to record my thanks to the Chairman of the Ulster Historic Churches Trust, Very Rev Dr Hugh Kennedy, who has been a constant source of advice, and whose own detailed knowledge of Ulster churches of all denominations has been of considerable help in my research.

Simon Walker
June 2000

Preface

THIS BOOK represents work carried out, for the most part, between September 1996 and August 1997 under the auspices of the Liam McCormick Research Fellowship on Historic Churches, funded by the Cultural Traditions Group (now the Cultural Diversity Group) of the Community Relations Council. The fellowship was named, at the instigation of the Ulster Historic Churches Trust, in recognition of the remarkable ecclesiastical work of the architect Liam McCormick (1916–96).

At a time of significant change in Northern Ireland it is worth looking at the diversity of religious traditions in Ulster and the variety of interesting church buildings which they utilise. Churches constitute important and familiar landmarks in our physical and spiritual landscape. The author is aware that Ulster's historic churches may lack the magnificence of the great churches and cathedrals of Europe, bedecked with the accumulated treasures of many centuries: a cyclical pattern of peace and conflict has seen churches rise, only to be destroyed. Given these difficult circumstances, the continuity of Christian worship in so many places is to be celebrated just as much as our ecclesiastical architectural heritage. This is an ongoing story and the change and variety of our church architecture reflects the religious diversity to be found in Ulster. *A Tapestry of Beliefs* (Belfast, 1998), identifies at least twenty-four Christian denominations in Northern Ireland. Some of these are very new to the province and speak of the manner in which Christianity continues to develop. The physical and spiritual needs of these religious communities are reflected in the architectural surroundings they have provided for their worship, ranging from the simple tin gospel hall to the modern open-plan church.

In Ulster we still have much of interest in terms of historic church buildings and many with which we are already familiar may still be able to yield a few surprises. It is often stated that a church is not the structure of bricks and mortar, but rather the body of Christians that meets within the walls. This is true and indeed our church buildings are physical reflections of the spiritual aspirations of the people of God. As well as serving as living centres of worship, churches present us with a physical record of those who served God in the past. Very often monuments removed from older ruined churches and re-erected in a newer place of worship recall the continuity of a Christian community.

Every town and village in Ulster possesses at least one church, and to the congregations that gather within these walls each holds an important place in local affection and Christian witness. The difficulty in compiling a survey of these churches is which to include and which to omit. Individuals will point to features of a particular church, cherished by them, which are worthy of note in architectural or historical terms. The churches selected represent only a fraction of the fascinating ecclesiastical building stock of our province, but there has been an attempt to provide a representative sample (where possible) of historical periods, architectural styles and denominations. With the exception of those which provide examples from the medieval period, cathedrals have not been dealt with in great detail, due to the existence of other published works such as Peter

Galloway's *The Cathedrals of Ireland* (Belfast, 1992). The churches are presented chronologically in terms of their architectural development, although this is far from rigid given that some of our churches are an amalgam of architectural forms. The book has been the subject of personal research but has also relied on secondary sources including the published work of other architectural historians.

An effort has been made to paint a visual picture of each church by physical descriptions, along with historical information relating to its building and congregation, but the atmosphere often defies description. A visit to an empty church can conjure up a sense of the past; the craftsmanship and care which went into the construction of the building, the generations of devoted worshippers and a consciousness of the Gospel shared over the centuries.

There is much to look for when visiting a church, such as monuments, stained glass, organs and bells. Given that Ulster is rich in artistic and literary talent, our churches are sometimes rendered more interesting by associations with gifted or outstanding individuals. When enjoying our ecclesiastical heritage we also need to be aware that we are all custodians of this legacy and should strive to maintain this. Sadly, in studying our churches, we meet with examples that have either vanished or are in jeopardy. When a church reaches the end of its life as a place of worship new uses need to be found which maintain the integrity of the building, but which render it useful to the wider community. Simply to board up a disused church, or worse still, to demolish it, is to deny to the people of today that which was so carefully preserved in the past. In terms of worship, where a church has ceased to exist in the inner city, a new congregation may be flourishing in the suburbs. Churches are perhaps the most difficult buildings to find new uses for, and their conversion demands imagination and sensitivity.

Church buildings are, unfortunately, not only placed in jeopardy by the decrease of congregations, but also sometimes by the cancer of sectarianism which plagues our land. Indeed, some of the churches featured in this book have been subjected to sectarian attacks as part of the ongoing civil conflict. To be 'historic' a church does not have to be particularly old, for yesterday's events already constitute today's history. This book begins with the medieval period and takes us up to our own time, searching the past, and trying to discover what interesting places of worship our generation will hand on to be the heritage of the future. Of recent churches included here are those designed by the late Liam McCormick, that master of modern church architecture. In an attempt to look at the history and development of our churches, his work represents an important chapter in the story.

Every church has features that are unique to it, and indeed every religious denomination has its own mode of conducting worship, and very often this is reflected in the churches they have built for themselves. While there are diversities among our traditions here in Ulster, there are also many common denominators, and it is hoped that this book will help to engender an appreciation of the varied facets that make up our ecclesiastical built heritage. Indeed, the primary purpose for the construction of our churches, the worship of Almighty God, is the strongest bond uniting our religious traditions. If this book can help, even slightly, through a survey of historic churches, to diminish misunderstanding and religious intolerance then it will have served a useful purpose.

Simon Walker
June 2000

Foreword

IN IRELAND, still less in Ulster, there are few cathedrals or churches on a scale comparable to those in Great Britain or in the rest of Europe. But in their local Irish or Ulster context, our churches, so often understated, play just as important a role as do the great medieval and classical flowerings further afield.

In suggesting and advising upon this book, the trustees of the Ulster Historic Churches Trust have had to steer a course between, on the one hand, architectural excellence and historic interest and overall merit, and on the other giving a fair representation to all the principal Christian denominations. The trustees felt that in a book such as this, which is intended to spread an allied, if somewhat different gospel, namely that of the cherishing of good church buildings, those of Ulster's churches which are already well written about elsewhere should not necessarily feature here.

Churches are a part of the fabric and backdrop against which all our lives are lived, church-going or not. All our communities, town or village or rural, focus on and are enriched consciously or sub-consciously by churches, of our own and of our neighbours' denomination. We hope that this book is one not only about churches, listed or unlisted, important or not so important, but also about the place which church buildings occupy in our built environment and so in all our lives. It is not only buildings, as architecture and repositories of quality and excellence, seen and analysed as if in isolation in a showcase, but also buildings as buildings for the contribution which they make to what is Ulster – the cultural diversity of our different traditions, our historical sources and reference points. We, and our buildings, are in so many ways a case of 'the whole being greater than the sum of the parts'.

To some of us, the First Fruits Gothic of earlier nineteenth-century Church of Ireland churches may be one of the few sorts of 'old' architecture for which we have a genuine affection. Apart perhaps from High Church or architectural purists, or brutal modernists, such churches can be almost always entirely seemly and satisfactory places in which to worship. 'Less is more' is exemplified well by their understated simplicity – a simplicity often profound in its paring down to essentials. The spirit can soar where all is seemly – it can so easily be otherwise when the grimness of ecclesiologically-correct detail or, worse, detail provided by those who have not understood the architectural vocabulary, keeps on jarring and bringing down to earth.

In the field of modern architecture, it has not been easy to make a choice of which churches of the last fifty years to include. For many of us a number of modern churches not mentioned here seem quite justifiably to be seemly and admirable: they often make strong and satisfactory contributions in their several localities. In many cases such churches have been omitted not out of lack of regard for their architecture but rather from limitations of space and the confines of the brief. In the case of less architecturally emphatic or pretentious church buildings, gospel halls and mission halls and small meeting houses, these are undoubtedly as much a part of the religious landscape of Ulster as are any other churches, but in few cases, judged objectively, do they qualify for inclusion on the basis of merit as architecture.

Sadly, many of our churches have suffered grievously in the last thirty years of Ulster's history. While 'religion' may indeed have a connection with the reasons for strife and hatred, the churches in which the religion is practised have seldom deserved the trials to which they have been put, both directly in desecration of their fabric and indirectly through damage nearby. The patina of age, which once lost, no amount of the most painstaking reconstruction can replace, is at the mercy not only of the damage caused by political vandals but often regrettably equally of the zeal, so well-intentioned but likewise so ill-directed, of those who dearly love 'the place of God'. There is a message to be got across to all of us who may think we should see old wood cleaned to look like new, floors and staircases refaced to remove the wear of ages, slates and stonework and window frames without a trace of lichen or moss, churchyards with pre-cast edging ship-shape between marble chippings and new asphalt. The provision of disabled access and toilets, where they can be accommodated, also requires judgement and sensitivity.

And there is another vandalsim at work – lack of respect for original, architectural integrity, particularly of church interiors. While Vatican II is often the easy scapegoat for Catholic churches, no denomination is blameless. In many churches and often at the instigation of a forceful or vocal clergyman, person or group in congregation or parish, areas of focus in churches – apse or chancel or altar or central pulpit with choir below – are being rearranged, certainly in ways which the original builders could not have conceived or countenanced and often without the benefit of any advice from those with a knowledge of or a feeling for the style of the period of building involved. It is a common misconception that anyone who can see is an equal judge of a picture: anyone who can see is certainly entitled to judge, but not everyone is an equal judge. So in buildings, training, visual education, an 'eye' are necessary attributes: ill-informed alteration can spoil all for ever.

It is the hope of the trustees that this book will be of interest to many, and that it will give all of us a new understanding of church building in Ulster and its evolution over the centuries.

Rev Hugh P Kennedy, DD
Chairman, Ulster Historic Churches Trust
August 2000

Abbreviations

Those publications which are referenced only once in the text are detailed in full. For all the others the following abbreviations apply:

ASCD   *Archaeological Survey of County Down* (Belfast, 1966).

Barry   Barry, J, *Hillsborough: a Parish in the Ulster Plantation* (Belfast, 1982).

Brett (Antrim) Brett, CEB, *Buildings of County Antrim* (Belfast, 1996).

Brett (Belfast) Brett, CEB, *Buildings of Belfast, 1700–1914* (London, 1967).

Builder   *The Builder*, 1843–

Craig   Craig, MJ, *The Architecture of Ireland* (London, 1982).

Curl   Curl, JS, *Classical Churches in Ulster* (Belfast, 1980).

de Breffny   de Breffny, B and Mott, G, *The Churches and Abbeys of Ireland* (London, 1976).

Dixon   Dixon, H, *An Introduction to Ulster Architecture* (Belfast, 1975).

Dukes   Dukes, FE, *Campanology in Ireland* (Dublin, 1994).

Evans   Evans, D, *An Introduction to Modern Ulster Architecture* (Belfast, 1977).

Harris   Harris, W, *The Antient and Present State of the County of Down* (Dublin, 1744).

Hurley   Hurley, R and Cantwell, W, *Contemporary Church Architecture* (Dublin, 1985).

Killen   Killen, WD, *History of the Congregations of the Presbyterian Church in Ireland* (Dublin, 1886).

Larmour   Larmour, P, *Belfast: an Illustrated Architectural Guide* (Belfast, 1987).

Lewis   Lewis, S, *Topographical Dictionary of Ireland* (London, 1837).

Loane   Loane, E, 'Architectural Drawings by Thomas Cooley in the Public Library, Armagh', unpublished undergraduate thesis, Dublin, 1983.

McBride   McBride, S, 'Bishop Mant and the Church Architecture Society: influences on the nineteenth century ecclesiastical architecture of Ulster', unpublished paper presented to the Church of Ireland Historical Society, May, 1997.

McCullough   McCullough, N and Mulvin, V, *A Lost Tradition: the Nature of Architecture in Ireland* (Dublin, 1987).

O'Laverty   O'Laverty, J, *An Historical Account of the Dioceses of Down and Connor* (Dublin, 1878).

OSM   Day, A and MacWilliams, P, (eds), *Ordnance Survey Memoirs of Ireland*, 40 vols (Belfast, 1990–98). The volume number is indicated in brackets.

Potterton   Potterton, H, *Irish Church Monuments 1570–1880* (Belfast, 1975).

RCB   Representative Church Body of the Church of Ireland.

RSUA   Royal Society of Ulster Architects.

Rankin   Rankin, P, *Irish Building Ventures of the Earl Bishop of Derry* (Belfast, 1972).

Richardson   Richardson, DS, 'Gothic Revival Architecture in Ireland', unpublished doctoral thesis, Yale University, 1974.

Rowan   Rowan, A, *North West Ulster* (London, 1979).

Sheehy   Sheehy, J, *JJ McCarthy and the Gothic Revival in Ireland* (Belfast, 1977).

UAHS   Ulster Architectural Heritage Society surveys. Area indicated in brackets.

Introduction

Jonathan Bardon

IN AD 82 Gnaeus Julius Agricola, governor of Britain, assembled a flotilla in the Solway Firth with the intention of conquering Ireland. However, the invasion was not to be: a legion of Germans stationed in Galloway rose in mutiny and there was disturbing news that the Picts were becoming restless. Ireland was never to become part of the Roman Empire and an iron-age culture – unaffected by castella, straight roads, villas and planned towns – was to flourish for centuries more in the island long after it had been tamed and altered elsewhere. Nevertheless, modern archaeologists are demonstrating that Roman influence was far greater than has been previously realised: freebooting bands of legionaries carried out raids or hired themselves out to local kings as mercenaries, and regular trade links were established. Constantine gave toleration to Christians throughout the Empire in 313 but it may have been another century before Christianity got a foothold in Ireland. The first evangelists were shadowy figures – they included Camelacus, Auxilius, Iserninus and Palladius – who spread the gospel over much of Leinster and Munster. Palladius was sent to be the first bishop to the Irish by Pope Celestine in 431, with a brief to stamp out any signs of the Pelagian heresy there. In 434 Prosper of Aquitaine wrote in his *Contra Collatorem* that Celestine 'having ordained a bishop for the Irish, while he labours to keep the Roman island (Britain) Catholic, has also made the barbarian island (Ireland) Christian'.

Prosper was wrong in thinking that all of Ireland had become Christian: the northern half – known to the Irish as *Leth Cuinn* (Conn's half) – remained pagan. The man who spearheaded the evangelisation of the north was

Patrick, who wrote the first documents in Irish history. The inventions of medieval propagandists in Armagh make it difficult to be certain about many details of Patrick's life and the patron saint's very humility frustrates the enquiry of historians. Patrick gives no clues about the location of his British home, when he came to Ireland or where he preached.

'I, Patrick, a sinner, the simplest of country men…', he begins, 'was taken away into Ireland in captivity with ever so many thousands of people'. This was probably some time early in the fifth century when Goths, Franks and Vandals were surging across the Rhine and the Roman Empire was falling apart. Angles, Saxons and Jutes were beginning to flood into eastern Britain and from the west came Irish raiding parties in search of silver and slaves. Patrick, then aged sixteen, was one of those seized: he was a Romanised Briton whose father was a deacon and grandfather a priest. His home could have been Wales, or Cumbria, or the Solway Firth area, or somewhere by the Bristol Channel. It seems certain now that the six years he spent as a slave were not on the slopes of Slemish but somewhere near the 'western sea', the Atlantic. There in his extreme loneliness his faith was renewed so that 'the spirit seethed within me'. He escaped and walked 200 miles eastwards and, with the aid of pirates, got across the Irish Sea and back home. There he had a vision in which a man brought him a letter and as he read it he seemed to hear the voice of the Irish: 'We beg you, holy boy, to come and walk among us once again, and it completely broke my heart and I could read no more'.

Resolved to return, he took holy orders and – in a mission clearly co-ordinated by a British church not yet overwhelmed by the English – he began to preach to the Irish. Patrick is the only early missionary to have left a written record: the *Confession*, a reply to critics in Britain, and the *Letter to Caroticus*, a letter excommunicating a British prince. To Caroticus he expresses his anger and grief that British Christians could kill his Irish converts

'

newly baptised, in their white clothing – the oil still
shining on their heads – cruelly butchered and
slaughtered by the sword … greedy wolves, they
have glutted themselves with the congregation
of the Lord, which was indeed increasing splendidly
in Ireland, with the closest care, and made up
of the sons of Irish raiders and the daughters of
kings who had become monks and virgins of
Christ – I cannot say how many! So may the
wrong done not please you! And even into Hell
may it give you no pleasure!

'

Yet there is no other record of anyone being martyred for acceptance of Christianity. Patrick's mission was undoubtedly sustained by a vigorous evangelical British church and the new religion was particularly successful among the ruling class. The places associated with St Patrick are in the northern half of Ireland and include Saul, Armagh, Downpatrick, Slemish, Lough Derg, Templepatrick and Croagh Patrick.

St John's Point Church, County Down, as it might have looked in the 10th century.

The early Christian church in Ireland adapted to the old beliefs and traditions that were to survive for centuries after Patrick's time. Pools and wells, where the pagan Irish cast in their valuables to please Celtic gods such as Lugh the Long-Handed, Daghda, Manannan and Nuadu, became holy wells – examples include Struell Wells near Downpatrick and St Brigid's Well in Carnmoney churchyard. St Brigid was probably the christianised goddess Brigantia and it is significant that that her saint's day, 1 February, falls on the Celtic festival of *Imbolg*, which marked the start of the lambing season. Other places once important as ritual sites which later became Christian centres include Armagh, Tory Island and Derry. 'Derry', used both as a prefix and a suffix, is an anglicisation of *daoire*, meaning an oak grove and many of these were sacred, becoming sites for churches and monasteries. The Gaelic year began with *Samhain*, now Hallowe'en, a time when the spirits flew free between the real world and the other world; the whole Christian church adapted to this Celtic festival by making the following day All Saints' Day. The early church went in for public confession: the Irish preferred private confession, eventually persuading the whole Western church to accept it; it was left to some Protestant sects to revive public confession many centuries later.

The Roman system of church organisation, with parishes based on towns and dioceses centred on cities, was not well suited to Irish society – there were no towns at all: a king or noble lived in a *dun* or fort, while others dwelt in a *rath*, *lios* or *caiseal*, a ringfort or homestead with circular walls to keep out marauding wolves. The north African monastic system was preferred. Just as their pagan forebears had set aside land for the upkeep of druids and sorcerers, so now local kings gave generous grants of land to the church and vied with each other to be patrons of monasteries. Early monasteries were generally constructed of thatched wood and wattle and only a few traces of them survive. In upland and rugged areas stone was used from the outset and, as monasteries developed in importance, stone was more widely employed. In time monasteries became Ireland's closest equivalents to urban settlements. The largest, including Bangor, Armagh and Derry, became great centres of learning and craftsmanship: some texts from the classical world survive only because of the industry of Irish scribes; monks put on vellum the sagas and tales of the past, including the *Tain Bo Cuailgne*; exquisite lyrical verses were penned in margins; and La Tène styles were awesomely elaborated and developed to decorate reliquaries, shrines, church vessels, high crosses and illuminated manuscripts.

The cultural influence of Irish monasteries on much of the rest of Europe was extraordinary in the seventh and eighth centuries. Intrepid pilgrims were the first human beings to reach and settle in Iceland and the Faroe Islands; the evangelisation of the Picts and the English was largely the work of Colmcille and Aidan and their followers; Columbanus, Gall and other missionaries did much to help the revival and extension of Christianity in Frankish kingdoms and beyond; and Irish monks and scholars won admiration for their learning in the court of Charlemagne. Then in 795 the Vikings raided Rathlin: Ireland's long immunity from foreign invasion had come to an end.

Ireland was divided into dozens of kingdoms frequently in conflict with one another. The plundering and burning of monasteries often accompanied these wars. The Viking incursions, however, vastly increased the scale of destruction: the community of Bangor was scattered, for example, and even inland centres, such as Armagh, were vulnerable to Norse raiding parties.

Antrim round tower.

Though later built primarily as belfries, round towers were erected at sites such as Drumbo and Antrim as look-outs and refuges. The era of Irish influence overseas came to an end.

The Northmen get a bad press because the record was made by the monks. The Vikings built Ireland's first towns (mainly south of Ulster and Strangford, Olderfleet and Carlingford were little more than toe-holds). From the late ninth century they became Christians (which may explain Nendrum's immunity) and Sitric Silkenbeard was the founder of Christ Church cathedral in Dublin. Vikings who stayed became absorbed into Irish society and their Urnes and Ringerike styles had a powerful influence on indigenous art. Much of the earlier zeal and asceticism had disappeared from the church and there were periodic drives to institute reform. The most tenacious reformer was St Malachy who became Bishop of Connor in 1124. According to St Bernard, in his popular biography, Malachy understood 'that he had been sent not to men but to beasts. Never before had he found men so shameless in regard to morals, so dead in regard to rites, so stubborn in regard to discipline, so unclean in regard of life. They were Christians in name, in fact pagans'.

After a few years, we are assured, 'hardness vanished, barbarity ceased … Roman laws were introduced'. Though eventually driven out of his diocese, Malachy became Archbishop of Armagh: in effect, he and other reformers were striving to end the peculiarities of the Celtic church, to introduce communities such as the Cistercians from the European mainland and to get Ireland to conform by, for example, giving proper authority to bishops.

The first Norman invaders landed in the south-east in 1169 and soon afterwards followed Henry II, the most powerful monarch in western Europe. Henry had the papal approval of *Bull Laudabiliter* to justify his conquest and part of his remit was to complete church reform. Despite spectacular early successes, the Normans never conquered the whole island and in Ulster succeeded in taking little more than the coastlands of Antrim and Down. English and French influences were strong in the east and south, while traditional practices and building styles survived best in what Dublin Castle described as the 'land of war'. John de Courcy's foundation, Inch Abbey, was the first church in Ireland to be built in the new Gothic style and to build it and other foundations close by, English masons were brought over.

The Scots invasion of 1315–18, the Black Death, expensive campaigning in Scotland, Wales and France, the use of Scots mercenaries by Irish lords and the adoption of new military techniques brought about a severe contraction of the territory controlled by the Crown. By the middle of the fifteenth century the English Lordship of Ireland was confined to coastal towns and an area around Dublin known as the Pale. Carrickfergus, for example, was described in 1468 as 'a garrison of war … surrounded by Irish and Scots, without succour of the English for sixty miles'. Gaelic chiefs and descendants of the Norman conquerors were independent warlords and direct patrons of the church, founding friaries such as Bonamargy, Assaroe and Donegal. Particularly in areas never brought under the Crown's control there was strong resistance to conformity: here clergy frequently married and the church was run by hereditary families.

The Battle of Bosworth Field in 1485 and the return of stability in England under the Tudors inaugurated the recovery of the Crown's authority in Ireland. In parts of the island ruled from Dublin Castle monastic lands were confiscated by Henry VIII. The Anglican Church became Protestant in the reign of Edward VI and again when Elizabeth came to the throne in 1558. The Reformation made little impact in Ireland even among unswerving supporters of English rule. The Queen found it impossible to enforce conformity and no serious attempt was made to convert the Irish to Protestantism. In the eyes of not only the native Irish but also of the 'Old English', the reformed faith was the religion of those who conquered and humiliated. The tragedy for Ireland, and for Ulster in particular, was that the Elizabethan conquest of Ireland from end to end took place at a time of fierce religious conflict in Europe. That conquest was bloody and terrible and was not completed until 1603.

James I confiscated church lands for the Established Church in Ulster and, after the Flight of the Earls in 1607 and Sir Cahir O'Doherty's rebellion in 1608, launched a grandiose project to colonise the north with Protestant British settlers. In his scheme for the 'Plantation of Ulster' not only were colonists obliged to build parish churches but also extensive 'proportions' were set aside for the maintenance of the Established Church. In addition, all owners of land had to pay a tithe for the upkeep of the clergy. The colonisation of Antrim and Down was very successful but in the six counties in the official scheme – Londonderry, Armagh, Tyrone, Fermanagh, Cavan and Donegal – the Plantation fell far short of the expectations of both the Crown and the settlers. Planters found that the province was not depopulated as they had been led to believe and were everywhere surrounded by resentful native Irish who made frequent hit-and-run raids on their settlements. Friars trained on the European mainland

instilled the dispossessed with the ideals of the Counter Reformation. The contrast between Protestantism and Catholicism in Ulster was considerable: not only were most of the Scots Calvinist Presbyterians but English planters tended to be Puritans and the Irish Established Church was more distinctly low church than its English counterpart.

During the reign of Charles I, Lord Deputy Thomas Wentworth imposed swingeing fines on those Catholics and Presbyterians who failed to conform. At first Anglican bishops were pleased to accept Presbyterian ministers as parish clergy and to pay them accordingly. Wentworth, however, insisted on removing such ministers and all Scots over the age of sixteen in Ulster were required to take the 'Black Oath', abjuring the Scottish National Covenant, or face severe penalties. Sir John Clotworthy, a planter in both Antrim and Londonderry, played a key role as a Westminster MP in bringing about the condemnation and execution of Wentworth in 1641.

Political instability in England encouraged a furious native Irish insurrection in Ulster in 1641. Thousands of colonists were slaughtered or driven out. The following year a Scots army led by Major General Robert Monro exacted a fearful revenge. This army set up the first presbytery on Irish soil on 10 June 1642. Meanwhile the English Civil War had begun and Ireland continued to be convulsed by warring and destruction. In 1649 Cromwell visited his wrath on the island: Catholics were massacred at Drogheda and Wexford, and Presbyterians were routed at Lisnagarvey, Belfast and Londonderry. Catholic worship was made illegal and mass had to be said in remote places. Despite a brief attempt to stamp out the Presbyterian system, the Commonwealth from 1655 gave all Protestant ministers fixed allowances paid for out of taxation.

The restoration of Charles II inaugurated a new era of tolerance and it was the frenzy of those who believed in a 'Popish Plot' in London, not Ireland, which led to the execution of the Catholic primate, Oliver Plunkett. Presbyterian ministers received the *regium donum*, 'gift from the king', and the Catholic Earl of Antrim was restored to his estates. A fresh period of conflict followed the 'glorious revolution' of 1688 ending with victories for the planters at Derry and Enniskillen and for William III at the Boyne and Aughrim. A tolerant Dutch Protestant, William approved of the moderate terms agreed by his commander at Limerick, but he was overruled by the parliaments at both Dublin and Westminster. The first penal law against Catholics was passed in 1695 but it was in the reign of Queen Anne that the most draconian legislation was introduced.

The Penal Laws were directed primarily at Catholics of property and the most effective legislation prevented them from buying land and excluded them from lucrative public posts and from the legal profession. The religious clauses proved most difficult to enforce: Catholics were not prevented from worshipping as they had been during the Commonwealth but monks, nuns, friars and higher clergy were to leave the country; pilgrimages were forbidden; priests could not wear clerical garb in public; and churches could not have bells, steeples or crosses. In fact, pilgrimages continued and bishops and archbishops reappeared. Presbyterians also suffered disabilities, including exclusion from public office, and lost the *regium donum* for a time. Tensions between Anglicans and Presbyterians often ran high, fuelled by the influx of around 90,000 Scots in the 1690s during a devastating famine in Scotland.

The Church of Ireland, because of its privileged position, had the lion's share of ecclesiastical buildings. It had taken over all medieval churches and cathedrals not in ruins; it had the income from its huge estates; and the tithe from tillers of the soil. In the settled conditions of the eighteenth century new churches were erected in many parishes and some wealthy clerics, such as Archbishop Robinson of Armagh and Frederick Hervey, the 'Earl-Bishop' of Derry, put their own private incomes into church buildings. Presbyterian meeting houses, built in a sober style, appeared all over the province – Belfast, though it had only 19,000 citizens by the end of the century, had three meeting houses beside each other in Rosemary Street. With the exception of the Teelings in Lisburn and some families in Newry, there were very few

The original St Patrick's Catholic Church, Donegall Street, Belfast, which was consecrated in 1815. As in the case of St Mary's, it was built with substantial financial help from Protestants.

Catholics of wealth in Ulster, particularly when an Earl of Antrim conformed to the Established Church. It was poverty, as much as penal legislation, which prevented the building of Catholic chapels capable of surviving to the present. St Mary's chapel in Belfast, opened with a Volunteer parade in 1784, was largely paid for by Protestant subscription. All the significant Penal Laws had been repealed by 1793 with the exception of that which prevented Catholics from sitting in Parliament.

Presbyterians undoubtedly could have got penal restrictions removed earlier had they been united. Most gave their allegiance to the Synod of Ulster, formed in 1690, but there were those who subscribed to the doctrine as stated in the Westminster Confession and those who refused to do so. As the eighteenth century progressed a growing number of Presbyterians supported the view that doctrine could not be imposed and could only be accepted by personal conviction: they were known as 'New Lights' and their critics as the 'Old Lights'. In addition there were Covenanters and Seceders, congregations of traditionalists. The Society of Friends, or Quakers, much persecuted in the seventeenth century, were given tolerance by stages from 1715 onwards; they were most numerous in Lisburn and Lurgan. Legislation to encourage Protestant 'strangers' to come to Ireland helped to introduce new sects such as the Moravians who, led by John Cennick, pioneered popular evangelicalism in County Antrim in the middle of the century. John Wesley made the first of twenty-one visits to Ireland in 1747: his greatest success was among members of the Church of Ireland who chafed against worldliness and lack of passion. When Wesley died in 1791 there were 15,000 members of Methodist societies in Ireland, most of them in the north, particularly in the counties of Armagh and Fermanagh.

Killinchy Presbyterian Church, built in 1739.

Presbyterians in Antrim and Down felt secure enough to challenge the rule of the Anglican elite, the 'Protestant Ascendancy', and eagerly absorbed radical ideas coming in from America, Scotland and France. They supported the demand for Catholic Emancipation, formed the Society of United Irishmen and many rebelled against the Crown in 1798, an insurrection which led to the Act of Union. West of the River Bann, the ancient rivalries between Catholics and Protestants remained strong and a fierce sectarian war raged in mid-Ulster during the 1780s and 1790s, culminating in the Battle of the Diamond in September 1795 and the formation of the Orange Order. The spectacular growth of Belfast in the nineteenth century drew in thousands from central and western Ulster to work in the mills, docks, engineering shops and shipyards in a migration accelerated by the collapse of the domestic textile industry and the potato famine. Immigrants chose where they lived with care and fierce riots erupted along the invisible and unstable frontiers separating Protestant and Catholic enclaves. Similar enclaves and disturbances developed in Portadown and Derry. Uncertainty about Ireland's political future helped to inflame sectarian passion where it had been quiescent before, for example in the affray at Dolly's Brae near Castlewellan in 1849.

Disputes over orthodoxy continued in the Presbyterian church, the champion of adherence to the Westminster Confession being the Rev Dr Henry Cooke and his principal opponent being the Rev Dr Henry Montgomery. In 1830 Montgomery and seventeen ministers, denounced as 'Arians', withdrew from the Synod of Ulster and eventually formed the Non-Subscribing Presbyterian Church. The majority stayed with Cooke and became part of the General Assembly of the Presbyterian Church in Ireland in 1840. In part these divisions were political: Cooke was opposed to Catholic Emancipation and Daniel O'Connell's campaign for repeal of the Act of Union and was determined to drive liberals out. He declared that he was publishing the 'banns of marriage' between Anglicans and Presbyterians to defend the Union.

The Evangelical Revival in Ireland can be dated back to the activities of the Moravians in the 1740s and the visits of John Wesley, though some would go back as far as the Six Mile Water Revival in the reign of Charles I. In the nineteenth century the revival was sustained and all Protestant churches were affected. It reached a crescendo in 1859 when, the *Ballymena Observer* remarked, the revival was 'advancing wave after wave, like some restless tide upon the strand; each surging swell marking its

The Methodist, George Whitefield, preaching at a timber yard in Lurgan, County Armagh in 1751.

onward progress to a predestined limit, but no human eye can see the boundary'.

Meanwhile, a Catholic renewal was well under way. Emancipation had been won as a result of popular action led by O'Connell in 1829 but the Ascendancy long maintained not only ownership of most of the land but also a near monopoly of senior public appointments. At the beginning of the century the Catholic church's organisation was particularly weak in Ulster, partly because there were so few Catholics there with substantial property and influence. During the Evangelical Revival many Catholics in the north converted to protestantism, partly because the great majority of schools were run by Protestant churches. The years after the Famine in the 1840s saw a real increase in living standards across the island and it was in the second half of the nineteenth century that new Catholic churches were erected across the land. At the Synod of Thurles in September 1850, Paul Cullen, Archbishop of Armagh and later Cardinal, launched a comprehensive programme to strengthen the church. Particular attention was paid to Ulster where folk religion was prevalent and church attendance rates were lower and illegitimacy rates were higher than in the rest of Ireland. The most dynamic standard-bearer of the renewal was Patrick Dorrian, Bishop of Down and Connor. He paid particular attention to Belfast where by 1834 there were 19,712 Catholics, 32 per cent of the population. For the next thirty years the proportion hovered around the one-third mark, and though the percentage dropped to 24.3 in 1901, the numbers kept rising.

Dorrian launched a general mission in Belfast in 1865, bringing in twelve additional priests to help the

Builders outside the Church of the Immaculate Conception, Tullysarran, County Armagh, which was built between 1920 and 1922 to replace an earlier church.

eight parish clergy of the town. Confraternities of Christian doctrine evangelised children and young adults; adults who had missed confirmation as children were now confirmed in great numbers; and by 1877 the St Vincent de Paul Society alone recorded over 2000 boys attending its Sunday schools. All over Ulster Catholics attended mass more frequently and they also supplemented these with additional services such as novenas, stations of the cross, benediction and retreats. Humble chapels were replaced by larger and more flamboyant structures. The Archbishop of Cashel, ten bishops, fifty priests and 10,000 people attended the laying of the foundation stone for Monaghan Cathedral in 1861 which was to be thirty-one years in the building. St Patrick's Catholic Cathedral in Armagh was even longer in the building: the foundation stone was laid by Archbishop Crolly in 1840; the main fabric was completed in 1873; but the sumptuous interior was not ready until 1904. St Malachy's in Belfast was intended as the town's

procathedral but it was upstaged by St Peter's, dedicated in the presence of Cardinal Cullen in 1866.

The privileged position of the Established Church came under mounting criticism and both Catholic and Presbyterian farmers campaigned – sometimes with force – against the tithe. In the end Gladstone, elected prime minister in 1868, became convinced that disestablishment was the only solution: 'So long as the Establishment lives', he warned, 'painful and bitter memories of Ascendancy can never be effaced'. An important branch of the Union was lopped off with disestablishment in 1869. The Church of Ireland received the generous compensation of £8 million and £764,688 was paid to the Presbyterian Church in lieu of the *regium donum*. The late nineteenth and early twentieth centuries also saw a time of church building in urban centres and in Belfast, included St Patrick's in Ballymacarrett (the country's most populous Church of Ireland parish), numerous neo-gothic Presbyterian churches such as

St Patrick's (C of I) Church, Ballymacarret, east Belfast.

Fisherwick and Cooke Memorial, Clifton Street Methodist Church and the massive Church of Ireland Cathedral of St Anne's in Belfast which replaced the elegant eighteenth-century parish church of the same name.

The Evangelical Revival (also known as the 'Second Reformation') and the Catholic renewal had much in common, yet most Catholics and Protestants were acutely aware of what divided them. Tensions were heightened by street preaching, triumphalist assertion, attempts at proselytising and – above all – by diametrically opposed political aspirations which brought Ulster to the brink of civil war in 1914. The violence, particularly in Belfast and Derry, between 1920 and 1922 was more lethal than all the disturbances of the nineteenth century put together. The island was partitioned and Northern Ireland came to birth in 1921.

During the twentieth century the rapid secularisation of the United Kingdom was only dimly and slowly reflected in Northern Ireland. Among Catholics, church attendance rates were as high as anywhere in the world. The individualism of Ulster protestantism and the strong dissenting tradition there led to the formation of many new sects. Some of these were created because it was felt that the main churches had become too respectable or were losing their former evangelical enthusiasm. The Free Presbyterian Church, founded by the Rev Ian Paisley in 1951, was steadfastly fundamentalist and vociferously opposed the 'ecumenising' tendencies of the Presbyterian Church. Just as in the 1859 revival, the influence of America on fundamentalist churches and groups was very considerable. This influence was most obvious in the Ulster Temple in north Belfast.

Church attendance began a steeper decline as the twentieth century drew to a close, a time when it could be said that relationships between the different churches and their clergy were better than they had ever been. The challenge that churches face at the beginning of the new millennium is that Catholics and Protestants are more separated than they have ever been: more than 90 per cent of those living in 90 per cent of electoral districts in Northern Ireland are of one persuasion or another.

1
The Medieval Period

COMPARED WITH England, or with the other provinces of Ireland for that matter, Ulster has a marked paucity of medieval ecclesiastical buildings still used for their original purpose. In Ulster the only intact churches of medieval stock that remain places of worship are Armagh Church of Ireland Cathedral and St Nicholas' Church in Carrickfergus, while there are fragmentary medieval remains embedded in the walls of Down Cathedral. This compares less than favourably with the estimated 10,000 medieval churches still in use in England. With the exception of John de Courcy's lordship in Down and south Antrim, the English church-building administration did not penetrate Ulster until the seventeenth century and the turbulent history of the province did not allow for the survival of early church buildings.

Irish churches in the period up to the twelfth century were invariably made of wood and cannot be expected to have survived great periods of time, although their existence is proven through archaeological research. Of stone structures, there remain round towers, oratories and monastic enclosures. The major changes in church building came with the intervention of the Cambro-Normans in Ireland in 1171. Whereas native church architecture had only made use of round-headed arches, the Normans introduced the Gothic pointed arch. The main defensive and administrative centre for the Normans was the Pale area with Dublin at its heart and here they built the cathedrals of Christ Church and St Patrick, which represent the nearest equivalents that Ireland has to the early English cathedrals. Church-

West door of Grey Abbey.

building outside the main Norman sphere of influence was more difficult, but was achieved where there was a powerful individual.

One such was John de Courcy, a great church-builder and encourager of the Cistercian and Augustinian orders. His centre of power was Downpatrick, and he developed monastic sites for the Cistercians at Inch, near the town, in 1187 and at Grey Abbey, in the Ards peninsula in 1193. These had cruciform churches which would have derived their influences from the mother church of the order at Furness in the north of England. However, the Cistercian houses throughout England and Ireland all followed the model of the original community in Citeaux in France, and ran on relatively simple lines. St Bernard, the founder, was not in favour of elaborate decoration of a church, and said, 'Leave your body at the door upon entering'.

The cruciform churches which developed under the order had transepts and spacious aisled naves, screens dividing the monks from the lay-brothers and two chapels in each arm of the transept. A feature of Irish Cistercian churches that is unique is the placing of clerestory windows above the pillars of the arch, rather than over the point of the arch. This may have been to keep down the height of the nave walls. An example of this practice can be seen at Armagh Church of Ireland Cathedral, although this was not a Cistercian house.

Although now in ruins, the Cistercian foundations at Inch Abbey and Grey Abbey had substantial churches as well as the ancillary buildings associated with religious houses. De Courcy's wife, Affreca, founded Grey Abbey, and the church consisted of an aisleless nave and transepts and a chancel with tall triple lancet windows; the elaborate west door, which survives, is of particular note. The abbey at Inch was founded by de Courcy as an act of atonement for his destruction of the church at Erenagh and was relatively similar to Grey Abbey, except that the nave had side aisles.

Cathedral Hill at Downpatrick has been a site for worship since the fifth century, with a church built in 1124 by St Malachy, who had introduced the Cistercians to Ireland. However, it was Benedictine rule that John de Courcy established at the centre of his lordship. It was long supposed that the original building was large and cruciform, and that the present cathedral represents only the chancel of that church; there is no archaeological evidence to support this theory. Like all our medieval churches, Down Cathedral suffered repeated attack, both at the hands of man and nature. An earthquake damaged it in 1245 and the Scots burned it in 1315, leaving only the walls standing. It was rebuilt in 1512, but was wrecked twenty-six years later on the orders of the Lord Deputy of Ireland, Leonard Grey, an act that later contributed to his execution. From this time until 1790 the cathedral lay in ruins, used only for the installation of deans and the enthronement of bishops committed enough to stumble through the weeds and fallen stones. It is difficult to ascertain just how much ancient fabric still exists, although engravings of the ruined cathedral accord quite well with the current structure. The architect of the 1790 restoration was Charles Lilly, who took the role of an architectural romantic rather than an antiquarian, giving us a 'Gothick' cathedral. However, he

A thirteenth-century capital in Down Cathedral.

did retain some ancient features, which still survive. The design of the tracery of the large east window was maintained, as was the group of three niches above that once held statues of saints Patrick, Brigid and Columba.

The church probably has a thirteenth-century skeleton at its core, with piers in the nave arcade that are rectangular in plan with attached shafts on the east and west faces. These resemble the nave piers of Inch Abbey which lies about a mile away. Of particular interest at Downpatrick are the capitals in the nave arcade, decorated with foliage, monsters and human heads. These date from the early thirteenth century, but some were heavily restored during and following the 1790 restoration of the building.

The best-known medieval church in Ulster is the parish church of St Nicholas in Carrickfergus which, like the foundations at Inch and Grey Abbey, owes its being to John de Courcy. St Nicholas' was built in 1182 by de Courcy following the founding of the town and its massive castle. He also built houses for the Premonstratensian Order at Woodburn and Whiteabbey. Stones from the Woodburn building are incorporated into the south transept at St Nicholas'. Robert le Mercer extended the church in 1306 by the construction of the chancel, which is longer than the nave. As in the chancel of Armagh Cathedral, built in 1268, there is a deviation from the line of the nave. This deviation is to the south at Armagh and to the north at Carrickfergus, both representing the medieval practice of building cruciform churches with the position of the chancel denoting the inclination of Christ's head when He was on the cross. Ancient features that survive at Carrickfergus include the font and a piscina used to wash the sacred vessels after the administration of the eucharist. Another medieval piscina can be seen at the Church of Ireland cathedral at Raphoe.

St Patrick's Cathedral at Armagh, although to the eye the result of a very thorough 'restoration' of 1834, does have a medieval church at its core. Of its medieval features there remain the crypt, the nave arcade and the low and narrow belfry stair in the south transept.

■ **References**
ASCD, pp 266–72; de Breffny, pp 60–1; HMSO, *Historic Monuments of Northern Ireland* (Belfast, 1987), pp 49–56; Leask, HG, *Irish Churches and Monastic Buildings* Vol 2, p 10.

ST NICHOLAS' PARISH CHURCH, CARRICKFERGUS
Lancasterian Street, Carrickfergus, County Antrim *Church of Ireland*

DOMINATING THIS part of the ancient town of Carrickfergus, St Nicholas' Church dates from 1182, but presents the visitor with a perplexing amalgam of building periods and styles. The church was originally built by John de Courcy and was attached to one of the monasteries that he had also founded, most probably St Mary's Abbey at Woodburn.

As originally built, the church was different from the structure that stands today, although there are substantial medieval remains. The Norman nave had arches that opened out into side aisles and four of the original twelfth-century round pillars with carved capitals can still be seen exposed in the nave walls. The church was extended in 1305–6 by Robert le Mercer who built the chancel that is, uniquely, longer than the nave. The visitor standing in the nave will notice that the chancel inclines to the north, denoting the angle of Christ's head when He was on the cross. The chancel arch of le Mercer's choir sprang from clustered columns, one of which can be seen in the wall behind the pulpit. The windows of the chancel are much as le Mercer built them, with four on the south and two on the north and the great five-light east window. This window retains the ancient banded shafts on the interior jambs.

Just beyond the crossing in the chancel is a narrow window or 'Lepers' Squint', which is said to have served as a means of communication for those afflicted with that dreaded disease. Further east is an alcove containing a blocked pointed doorway that still has its iron door mountings. Apparently this was the 'Priest's Door' and was used by the monks to enter the church for the daily services. The present height of this door and the ancient columns indicate that the floor level has been raised considerably during the course of the centuries, and that the present floor was simply built on top of the rubble of various roof collapses and deliberate destruction. The south transept also bears testimony to the medieval construction of the church in the shape of a fine piscina for the washing of sacred vessels, as well as a blocked

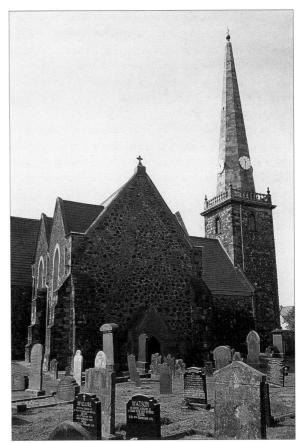

St Nicholas' (C of I) Church, Carrickfergus.

pointed arch indicating the existence of a side aisle or chapel.

By the beginning of the sixteenth century St Nicholas' was 'burned and spoyled by the rebels', and was roofless for forty years. Its fortunes improved with the arrival of Sir Arthur Chichester as Lord Deputy of Ireland and governor of Carrickfergus. In 1614 he set about repairing and extending the church, as a tablet in the nave testifies, stating: 'This worke was begune A 1614 / Mr Cooper then Maior and was wrought by Thomas Paps free /

mason Mr Openshaw being Parson. Vivat Rex Jacobus'. The work entailed building up the arches and sweeping away the aisles, and rebuilding the northern side chapels as a family chapel for the Chichesters. Paps seems also to have been responsible for the south transept or 'Wills' Aisle', and so by this stage the building had gained its cruciform shape. The north transept of 1614 is reached by a flight of seven steps and has beautiful carved Jacobean pew-fronts. This area was the family mausoleum of the Chichesters, and they sleep in a barrel-roofed vault beneath the transept. On the end wall of the transept is the magnificent monument (see p 13) to Sir Arthur Chichester (died 1625) and his wife, Lettice (died 1620). The lord and lady are shown kneeling in prayer with their dead infant between them. Below is the kneeling figure of Sir Arthur's brother, Sir John, who was ambushed and killed by the MacDonnells in 1597. Legend tells that Sir James MacDonnell, on seeing the monument, took out his sword and beheaded the effigy of Sir John, just as he had done in life. This is a grand Renaissance memorial and has no comparison in Ulster, save perhaps the much smaller Hansard monument in Lifford. The roof of the transept is vaulted in plaster, whereas the rest of the church has trussed roofs. The walls of the north transept are covered in cement simulated to look like masonry, and have a quite alarming appearance.

Thomas Paps also added a porch on the south nave wall, but this was converted into a burial vault in 1778. The stone surrounds to the door survive and bear long cuts where soldiers garrisoned at the castle sharpened their halberds. Since 1952 this old porch has served as a baptistry containing a twelfth-century font found at Woodburn. There is a charming stained glass window depicting St Nicholas as Santa Claus riding in his reindeer-drawn sledge.

The elegant west tower and spire were added in 1778 and constitute a fine piece of classical architecture. Like the rest of the church, the tower is constructed of rubble with sandstone dressings. There is a pedimented doorcase, above which is a Venetian window with blind side lights. The top stage of the tower has louvred belfry windows and is surmounted by a balustrade with corner finials which conceals the junction of the tower and the octagonal spire. The old town curfew bell still rings from this tower every evening.

The church contains a number of very interesting fittings, including some extremely rare seventeenth-century Flemish glass. The most impressive example is that on the south side of the nave which depicts Christ being baptised in the Jordan by John the Baptist. Samuel Lewis records that this window was brought to the church in 1800, having come from a private chapel in Dangan House, County Meath. The two 'bull's eye' windows in the gallery contain non-illustrative Flemish seventeenth-century glass. The building abounds with fascinating monuments and floor slabs, the oldest of which is dated 1620. Of particular note is the Gardner monument in the south transept which is adorned with three rather pious-looking cherubs. In the vestry porch there is an iron ball which was fired into the town during the siege by the Duke of Schomberg in 1689. It landed in the churchyard and did not come to light until some time later when a grave was being dug. Also displayed in this porch is a stone gable cross bearing the date 1164. This was discovered under the sanctuary during a search for an underground passage. The stout chairs in the sanctuary are seventeenth-century, and one of them is dated 1685. The chancel area also retains two features of the medieval church, the 'Founder's Tomb' on the north wall, and a carved Norman coffin slab on the south. In medieval times the Founder's Tomb would have been used to represent Christ's sepulchre on Good Friday, and it was decorated and watched from then until Easter Day.

At the Market Place entrance to the churchyard stands the detached war memorial campanile, which was designed by Denis O'D Hanna in 1962, and incorporates an old gateway of 1831. The tower contains a very tuneful ring of eight bells.

As an examination of the fabric of the church, both externally and internally, will indicate, the building has encountered many physical alterations since its construction in 1182. However, the diversity of features from the medieval and Jacobean periods provide an intriguing and fascinating old church, and one which is an ideal starting point for a survey of Ulster's historic churches.

■ **References**

Brett (Antrim), p 29; Drew, T, *The Ancient Church of St Nicholas, Carrickfergus* (Dublin, 1872); Lewis, Vol 1, p 274; Mitchell, GA, *A Guide to St Nicholas' Church, Carrickfergus* (Carrickfergus 1962); UAHS (Carrickfergus), pp 14, 16.

MONUMENTS

FROM EARLIEST times, people have commemorated their dead by the construction of physical reminders. The numerous dolmens, cairns and court graves throughout the Ulster countryside give testimony to this. These earliest funerary monuments were associated with pagan burial rituals, but with the introduction of Christianity, the need to remember loved ones, or local worthies, continued. The study of gravestone inscriptions and church monuments is a useful way of tracing ancestral history and the development of monumental sculpture. Such monuments are a guide to regional masonry skills, family histories, local events of note and architectural taste, or the lack of it.

The majority of our Ulster churches date from the early nineteenth century and after, and therefore many of the monuments on the walls of these churches tend to date from that period. The monuments of the sixteenth and seventeenth centuries are very frequently to be found on the walls of the ruined and roofless churches abandoned in the eighteenth and nineteenth centuries when more convenient and architecturally 'correct' buildings were constructed. However, in the west of Ulster virtually all the seventeenth-century monuments were moved to the replacement churches, and are, therefore, in a good state of preservation. Due to respect for the dead, the Victorians did sometimes incorporate earlier monuments into their churches, even if Georgian architectural and decorative tastes were rather pagan in their righteous eyes. St Macartin's Cathedral in Enniskillen reflects this with its fine collection of monuments, encompassing the seventeenth to nineteenth centuries.

Wall monuments inside churches were mostly the preserve of the wealthy, and indicated the status of those being remembered. An excellent example of this is the very substantial monument to Sir Arthur Chichester in Carrickfergus Parish Church which dates from about 1625. This consists of the figures of Sir Arthur and his wife, as well as other members of the family. Figure sculptures were significant in church monuments right up to the latter part of the nineteenth century. This is evidenced by the very fine collection of monuments in Armagh Church of Ireland cathedral. A large proportion of eighteenth- and nineteenth-century sculptured monuments are to be found in Church of Ireland churches, as other denominations preferred to remember their dead less ostentatiously. However, the Non-Subscribing Presbyterian church in Rosemary Street, Belfast, has a fine array of monuments, while there is a very

The Chichester monument at Carrickfergus.

fine statue of Archbishop McGettigan outside the Catholic cathedral in Armagh.

Seventeenth-century monuments emphasised the transience of life, while the Georgian monuments recalled the exalted station of their subjects. The Victorians were at pains to emphasise the Christian virtues of the departed and reinforced these with biblical quotations. Good seventeenth-century monuments can be found in St Columb's Cathedral, Derry and St Patrick's, Coleraine. Georgian monuments by famous sculptors such as Nollekens, Roubiliac, Rysbrack and Bacon line the aisles of the Church of Ireland cathedral at Armagh, while St Patrick's, Monaghan has a fine array of monuments spanning the entire nineteenth century.

In the first half of the twentieth century Rosamund Praeger (1867–1954) produced a number of monuments for Ulster churches, usually Church of Ireland or Non-Subscribing Presbyterian. Examples of her work can be found at the Non-Subscribing Presbyterian churches at Holywood and Rosemary Street in Belfast, which take the form of wall monuments. Praeger also carved the monument to Sir Hamilton Harty at Hillsborough Parish Church, which is a large limestone birdbath decorated with traditional Irish musicians.

Many Ulster churches will have a war memorial, as many Ulstermen, of all religious denominations, were killed or wounded in the two world wars. By contrast, it is now rare to find people commemorated by lavish monuments, but more common to see memorial windows or some objects of practical use, such as gates, seats or doors.

■ **References**

Potterton, H, *Irish Church Monuments 1570–1880* (Belfast, 1975).

ST PATRICK'S CATHEDRAL, ARMAGH
Vicars' Hill, Armagh, County Armagh   *Church of Ireland*

CHRISTIAN WORSHIP has been conducted on this hilltop site since 445 when, according to tradition, St Patrick built the 'Damhliag Mor' or 'great stone church'. All that may possibly remain of this building are a few fragments embedded in the piers of the current church. The shell of the cathedral dates from the rebuilding of 1268–70 by Archbishop Patrick O'Scannail, who was responsible for the crypt as well as the choir and transepts. A feature of this building that is still very evident today is the southward slant of the choir, a medieval feature of cruciform churches to denote the inclination of Christ's head on the cross. The transept arches erected at this time were probably cut through the walls of the Damhliag Mor.

St Patrick's (C of I) Cathedral, Armagh.

Archbishop Milo Sweteman rebuilt the nave and aisles of the cathedral in 1365, and the existing piers, arches and clerestory date from this time. An unusual feature of the clerestory is that the windows are positioned between the arches rather than directly above them.

A number of despoliations took place in the fifteenth and sixteenth centuries, the most serious being in 1566 when Shane O'Neill burnt the cathedral. Periodic patchings and repairs were carried out during the seventeenth and eighteenth centuries, but the overall appearance of today is the result of a 'restoration' commissioned by Primate Lord John George Beresford in 1834. His architect was Lewis Nockalls Cottingham, a noted medievalist who had been responsible for the restorations at the cathedrals of Rochester, St Albans and Hereford. Indeed, one of the problems with Cottingham's work at Armagh was that he seemed not to grasp that he was dealing with an Irish medieval cathedral, not an English one. George Petrie commented, 'The restorer of the Cathedral should be an Irish historical architect and antiquary. This Mr Cottingham is not.' The red sandstone cladding of the exterior which covers every ancient stone is a result of this 'restoration'.

What we can see today is basically the outline of a medieval church, with the ancient masonry concealed behind mid nineteenth-century stone and plaster. In terms of genuine medieval architecture all that remains visible to the eye is the nave arcade and clerestory; the staircase to the belfry in the thickness of the south transept walls and the aisled crypt which houses fragments of medieval carving hidden here by Cottingham. Some sections of ancient walling have been left exposed in the south transept. The interior of the cathedral is now principally interesting for its fine array of monuments, which include the full-length effigy of Sir Thomas Molyneux (died 1703) by Roubiliac and Rysbrack's recumbent figure of Dean Peter Drelincourt (died 1722). Other sculptors represented here include Nollekens and Chantrey, whose works commemorate primates Robinson (died 1794) and Stuart (died 1822) respectively.

Of the ancient cathedral, more survives perhaps in spirit than in actual physical structure.

■ **References**

Cassidy, H, *St Patrick's Cathedral, Armagh* (Derby, 1991), pp 9–11; Myles, J, *LN Cottingham 1787–1847: Architect of the Gothic Revival* (London, 1996), pp 92–8; Rogers, E, *Memoir of Armagh Cathedral* (Belfast, 1888), pp 112–14.

2

Tudor to Jacobean Churches

FOLLOWING HER accession in 1558 Elizabeth I re-established the crown's supremacy over the church with the Act of Uniformity. Church building could not prosper due to the volatile situation in Ireland, and Ulster, with its hot-headed chiefs plotting English overthrow, was the last section of the country to be brought to heel. The Protestant Reformation, seen as an aid to political supremacy, had made little progress in Ireland due to the lack of preaching in the native tongue, coupled with the reluctance of educated English clergy to take on badly-paid and dangerous Irish benefices.

What little church building did take place in Ulster was in areas where the English felt particularly secure. St Patrick's Parish Church in Newry was built in 1578 by Sir Nicholas Bagnall, and was the first purpose-built Protestant church in Ireland. Although the walls of this church survive embedded in the present nave, the only visible sign of its antiquity is the Bagnall armorial stone in the porch. It is difficult to gauge now what St Patrick's would have looked like originally, but it was probably a simple nave hall, possibly with a west tower. The parish church of All Saints in Antrim, built in 1596, of which substantial portions remain, comprised merely a rectangular nave with an attached chapel for the Massereene family. At Carrickfergus, Sir Arthur Chichester, the Lord Deputy of Ireland, carried out extensive repairs to St Nicholas' Church, constructing a south transept for use as a family mausoleum. The church built at Islandmagee, dated variously as 1596 or 1609, represents the simplicity of Tudor church construction in Ulster. It seems to provide a pattern that was followed for nearly a century, being rectangular with square-headed windows and stout buttresses.

In Ulster there are few churches remaining intact from the seventeenth century or earlier. The seventeenth century was one of continual strife, and many buildings constructed at the beginning of the century barely survived to the middle, let alone the end of the century.

With the accession of James I, the son of a Catholic, there were many Irish who hoped for leniency towards their Catholic faith. However, in 1605 Lord Deputy Chichester issued a proclamation that showed that the king had no intention of allowing religious toleration in Ireland. In fact, all priests were required to leave the country by 10 December 1605. Needless to say, no Catholic places of worship survive from this period. The crown determined to curb Catholic power, and sought to settle large areas of the country with planters, on the forfeited lands of the rebel clans. The settlers were English, Welsh and Scots, and nearly all were Protestant. The Scots brought Presbyterianism with them, but at this stage the ministers practised within the Anglican church. Obviously, these settlers needed places of worship, and many of these were built in a style now referred to as 'Planters' Gothic'. Perhaps the best-known example of this is St Columb's Cathedral in Derry, the building of which commenced in 1628 and was completed in 1633. The contractor for the work was one William Parrott, and the cost was £3000.

At the time of its building, the cathedral consisted of a battlemented five-bay nave with Perpendicular windows, a west tower, and aisles terminating in turrets.

It had a particularly defensive appearance, which was to prove useful, as its roof served as a gun platform during the siege of the city in 1689. While it is the largest of the plantation churches, as a cathedral it bears little comparison to the grandeur of its English counterparts. Writing of it in 1752, Richard Pococke said of St Columb's, that it was 'something like many churches in large English country towns'.

Ireland was still largely devoid of churches and Edmund Spenser commented that even those that had been repaired were 'so unhandsomely patched and thatched that men do even shun the places for the uncomliness thereof'. Progress was attempted during Charles I's reign, with a Commission for the Repair of Churches, while the Irish Convocation of 1634 promoted new church building. Of the churches built at this period (twenty were built in the diocese of Derry and many more were repaired), few survived the civil war in 1641. Indeed, St Columb's Cathedral was preserved only because of its position within the famous walls. Another rather surprising survival is Clonfeacle Parish Church at Benburb: perhaps the destruction of human life here was so great that the destruction of the church building was deemed unnecessary.

By the time of the restoration of the monarchy in 1660 it is said that the majority of Irish churches were in ruinous heaps. Now was the time for a resurgence in the fortunes of the Church of Ireland. In January 1661 the great Jeremy Taylor preached at a service of consecration of two archbishops and ten bishops (one of which was Taylor himself) in St Patrick's Cathedral, Dublin. Many of these prelates set to work providing places of worship for their flocks. Bramhall made extensive progress in his diocese of Derry; at Armagh Primate Vesey had maps drawn up to show areas requiring a church; Taylor, as Bishop of Down, Connor and Dromore, was associated with the building of churches at Dromore, Hillsborough and Ballinderry. Of the surviving churches of this period, the Middle Church at Ballinderry best meets the criteria which Taylor himself expected in a place of worship, criteria framed in *A Form of Consecration or Dedication of Churches and Chappels According to the Use of the Church of Ireland* (1666). This lays down the need for a church building to have a central passage from the west door to the chancel door and steps to 'ascend to the Communion Table'. Aisles to the north and south were also suggested to enable the procession of clergy. In fact, simpler buildings had to suffice: Taylor's churches at Dromore and Ballinderry being merely rectangular structures, as is the church of 1699 at Clonoe, County Tyrone. The

church built by Colonel Arthur Hill at Hillsborough in 1663, and consecrated by Taylor, had at least the refinement of transepts.

The Middle Church at Ballinderry very clearly reflects Taylor's view that a worshipper's progress from the west door was by a series of symbolic 'stations' to get to the holy table, which represented the 'terminus' of reconciliation with Christ. He speaks of the pattern of movement: 'the church porch'; 'by the reading desk'; 'at the chancel door'; 'up to the very rails'. This emphasis on the sacrament of the eucharist is visually projected, as at Ballinderry and Waringstown (built in 1681), by the clear view of the 'fair table' upon entering the church. Of the rails surrounding or enclosing the communion table, the rubrics say nothing. These rails, which still exist at Ballinderry and Waringstown, had the practical purpose of preventing stray animals from profaning this part of the church. There is a rare instance where a church at this time had no rails. In his biography of Bishop Bedell, Alexander Clogie refers to Kilmore Cathedral (which still exists as a church hall) where the table stood in the centre of the choir, 'without steps of gradual ascension or circumvallation by railes, though the custom had prevailed in most churches'. Communion tables from the reign of Charles II can still be seen in Ballinderry, Waringstown and Magheralin, County Down.

The rubrics of the *Form of Consecration* make it clear that the pulpit should stand in the body of the church, yet the canons call for 'a decent pulpit to be set in a convenient place for the preaching of God's Word'. This convenient place was usually on a side wall of the nave.

Baptismal fonts were placed at the west door, a symbolic position to denote the beginning of the Christian journey and from where the new Christian could be welcomed into the body of the church. Few Caroline fonts survive but Ballinderry retains its stone font on an oak plinth. There is a similar one at Dromore Cathedral, along with a contemporary alms box. Other seventeenth-century fonts can be seen at Loughilly, Lurgan and Ballymore, County Armagh and Enniskillen.

Looking particularly at Benburb, Ballinderry and Clonoe churches, a close visual affinity can be seen with the earlier church at Islandmagee – an appearance that the buildings at Waringstown and Castlecaulfield must also have shared. These were all simple rectangular buildings, but it has to be remembered that they were built in troubled times and a long period of survival may not have been anticipated. More importantly, they were constructed to provide, first and foremost, the physical conditions for Anglican worship. As Archbishop William

King of Dublin said, 'We ought to multiply the number of our churches rather than make them magnificent'. Of course, as well as civil unrest and limited resources, there was also dislike of ostentation within the reformed tradition.

Perhaps the last word on the physical appearance of churches in this age should rest with Jeremy Taylor:

'

If we say that God is not the better for a rich house or a costly service, we may remember that neither are we the better for rich clothes; and the sheep will keep us as modest, as warm and as clean as the silk-worm; and a gold chain or a carkernet of pearl does no more contribute to our happiness than it does to the service of religion.

'

The Great Exemplar

■ References

Bolton, FR, *The Caroline Tradition of the Church of Ireland with Particular Reference to Bishop Jeremy Taylor* (London, 1958), pp 204–50; Williamson, HR, *Jeremy Taylor* (London, 1952), p168.

JEREMY TAYLOR (1613–67)
Church of Ireland Bishop of Down, Connor and Dromore

BORN AND educated in Cambridge, Taylor was closely associated with royalism, having served as chaplain to Charles I. These loyalties contributed to his imprisonment during the Commonwealth period and eventual move to Ireland in 1658, where he worked near Lisburn, under the protection of Lord Conway. At the Restoration he was elevated to the bishoprics of Down, Connor and Dromore. While a deeply spiritual man, he was strictly Anglican in his theology and therefore went to great pains to eradicate Presbyterianism within his dioceses. He did much to restore the vibrancy of the Church of Ireland within his dioceses through his devotional writings and church-building activities. He has been described as the 'Shakespeare of divines' and his written works included *Holy Living* and *Holy Dying*. He was responsible for the construction of churches at Ballinderry, Dromore, Aghalee and Hillsborough. He was strongly of the belief that the importance of the sacraments of the church, namely baptism and communion, should be reflected in the physical layout of churches. His churches, largely due to lack of resource, tended to be functional buildings with an internal emphasis on the baptismal font and the communion table. He died at his home in Lisburn on 13 August 1667, having contracted fever from a sick person to whom he was ministering.

Bishop Jeremy Taylor

■ References

Williamson, HR, *Jeremy Taylor* (London, 1952).

ALL SAINTS' PARISH CHURCH, ANTRIM
Church Street, Antrim, County Antrim

Church of Ireland

ANTRIM PARISH Church stands as a rare example of an Elizabethan church which has survived to the present day still being used as a place of worship with its original physical outline existing fairly much as built, although with a few later additions. A perusal of the outside of the building indicates just how much of the Tudor fabric exists; the nave and south transept being constructed of rubble and the tower of black ashlar. A datestone on the north exterior wall states that the church was built in 1596. At this time All Saints had a rectangular nave plus a south transept which served as a vault and pew for the Massereene family. The north and east walls of the church have small holes (three in number) which could have been to facilitate lepers or to serve as musket holes. The north wall of the nave had four bays, as it still does, the second bay from the west being a doorway, traces of which are still detectable. The windows, which remain, were square-headed, of three lights with cusped tracery. The east window, replaced in 1870, was likely to have been very similar to the east window of St John's, Islandmagee. Internally the church would have been filled with box pews surrounding a three-decker pulpit on the north wall. We can glean an idea of this arrangement by looking at the Middle Church at Ballinderry. When All Saints was built a wall divided the Massereene Chapel from the rest of the church to form a separate chapel. This division was removed during subsequent alterations.

Externally, the most outstanding of the later additions are the western tower and spire of 1816. A sum of £1500 was borrowed from the Board of First Fruits, whose architect, John Bowden, probably designed the structure. The tower is of three stages, has sandstone dressings and carries an octagonal spire. Entrance into the church is by the door on the north side, and it can be assumed that the old door on the nave wall was blocked at the time of the construction of the tower. Stepped buttresses run up its three stages and culminate in crocketed pinnacles. Battlements run between these pinnacles and incorporate a clock-face within an ogee-headed arch on each of the cardinal faces of the tower. The western gallery, which is still in use, was added in 1816 at the same time as the tower, which held the vestry accommodation. A new vestry room was provided in 1869 when another south transept was built with the assistance of the Ecclesiastical Commissioners. In 1892, the architect SP Close opened up the wall between the two transepts by providing two

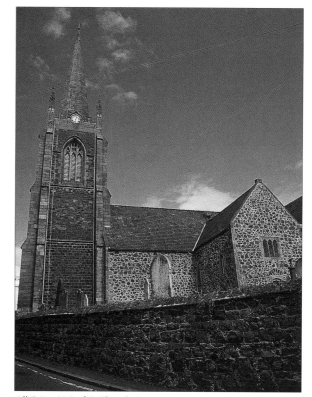

All Saints' (C of I) Church, Antrim.

pointed arches.

During the course of this work the frame of an Elizabethan window was discovered and this is now built into the wall above the arches. Although now laid out as a side chapel, the western section of the south transept served as the Massereene family pew and this is still accessed by steps through a low doorway flanked by panelling which terminates in poppyhead finials. The present appearance of the entire interior of the church dates from 1892, when the trussed roof, bench pews and stone pulpit were all installed. Of the Elizabethan interior, little now survives.

Antrim Parish Church possesses a number of interesting monuments relating to members of the Massereene family. Most prominent is that at the top of the north wall of the nave which commemorates the sixth Earl of Massereene (died 1863), which is the work of JR Kirk of Dublin. The earl is shown reposing in the robes of the Order of St Patrick, and above him rises a Gothic triple canopy capped by the allegorical figures of Faith,

Hope and Charity. Despite the grandeur of his memorial, the earl died in a rather unfortunate manner, from the effects of a fall while pulling up a shrub. Nearby is the fine monument to Chichester Skeffington, fourth Earl of Massereene (died 1816) by John Flaxman. This is crowned by a Greek pediment, beneath which stand two weeping female figures swathed in drapery. In the Massereene Chapel is the richly traceried monument to Clotworthy John Eyre, Viscount of Massereene and Ferrard (died 1905), which is guarded by two angels. At the base of the memorial are items carved in alabaster which reflect the nobleman's interest in freemasonry and music. He was an accomplished musician and the violin carved here has a broken string, signifying that his instrument would not be played following his death, as a mark of respect. This was the work of Harry Hems of Exeter. Next to the monument is a fascinating little window that contains continental glass, said to be fifteenth century in date. The upper panel of the window shows the Virgin and Child flanked by saints Hieronimus and Carolus above a preaching angel. In the lower section is a depiction of the martyrdom of St John the Baptist.

The Decorated east window is filled with glass depicting scenes from the life of Christ, thought to be based on a window in the Lady chapel of Chester Cathedral.

In the graveyard lie the remains of Alexander Irvine, author of *My Lady of the Chimney Corner* and George Victor du Noyer, a noted naturalist and antiquarian. Irvine's ashes rest in his parents' grave beneath a stone bearing the words 'Love is enough', which is a quotation from his work. The burial place of du Noyer is unmarked, but a plaque inside the nave of the church remembers him.

Although retaining its Elizabethan structure, All Saints has had many changes in its physical appearance during the course of its 400-year history. It has the marks of later additions and fittings, many of them aesthetically pleasing in themselves. This process of gradual alteration to accommodate changes in liturgy and architectural taste is common in older churches throughout Ulster.

■ **References**
Potterton, pp 45, 55; UAHS
(Antrim and Ballymena), pp 5–6.

ST JOHN'S PARISH CHURCH, ISLANDMAGEE
Ballycarry, Islandmagee, County Antrim *Church of Ireland*

DESPITE HAVING been built, possibly as early as 1595, St John's has traditionally been known locally as 'New Church'. There is some speculation as to the actual date of construction, with some sources suggesting 1595, while others believe the date to have been 1609. This latter seems the more likely as in that year several parishes were amalgamated to form the parish of Islandmagee. The land in this area was the property of Sir Arthur Chichester, who instigated quite extensive building work on St Nicholas' Church at Carrickfergus in 1614. Similarities that have been noted between the buttresses at Islandmagee and Carrickfergus – which may in fact be the work of the same mason (Thomas Paps) – adding further impetus to the argument that St John's is a building of the early seventeenth century, rather than the late sixteenth century.

St John's, with its time-worn appearance and lonely situation, would give the visitor the impression that it has been little affected by change since its construction. The building as it now stands presents a rectangular structure with two flat-headed three-light lattice windows on the side walls, with a similar east window of five lights. The

windows are fashioned from yellow sandstone, now painted, and have trefoil heads, very like the windows in the south transept of St Nicholas' Church at Carrickfergus, again aiding the process of dating St John's. There are three heavy buttresses on the side walls and two on the east gable wall. Originally, there were also two on the west wall, but these were removed in 1988 when a two-storey porch was added. The bellcote on the western gable of the nave is obviously later than rest of the church, and contains a bell from Ballyclough Church, County Cork, which was made in 1796 by Robert Stottsbury. This end of the church has been altered, as it was shortened by 27 feet in 1827, at the same time as the north aisle was removed. The Ordnance Survey Memoir of 1834 makes mention of this work, and obviously it was necessitated either by a drop in the resident population, or because the church had originally been built on over-ambitious proportions.

When the nave was shortened, one of the original windows was reset in the west wall, while the fragments of the other were taken to a nearby farm to make a boot scraper and a grand entrance to a dog kennel! The west

St John's (C of I), Islandmagee.

wall, as built in 1827, also had a semicircular-headed doorcase incorporating a fanlight. Unfortunately, this was masked by the construction of a porch in 1988 which is rather nondescript in appearance, leaving the building bereft of the slight architectural pretensions that the doorcase and surmounting window gave to this end of the church.

Although now cement-rendered, the church would at one time have been harled, but it seems probable that the

Jacobean builders did not intend the building to have any external coating, given the high quality of the stonework. All of the window surrounds, the string-course and the quoins are of yellow sandstone. As this would have been expensive to quarry and carry, it is unlikely to have been readily covered up. Perhaps after the alterations of 1827 the building looked rather piecemeal, and was harled at this stage to restore some visual uniformity.

The interior of the church is simple, having a stone-flagged floor, lined with bench pews, which are obviously not original. The octagonal wooden pulpit stands to the north of the communion table, while the organ is placed to the south. The communion table itself is placed on a plinth of two semicircular steps. All the walls are plastered and openwork trusses support the roof.

In spite of various alterations made since its construction, St John's still gives us a good impression of how a rural Jacobean church would have looked. Its construction is typical of churches built throughout the remainder of the seventeenth century and can be readily identified in churches such as Benburb and Ballinderry.

■ **References**
Brett (Antrim): p 26; OSM (Vol 10 Antrim III), p 20; unpublished notes held by the DOENI, Environment and Heritage Service (Built Heritage).

ST PATRICK'S PARISH CHURCH, BENBURB - PARISH OF CLONFEACLE
At the entrance to Benburb Priory, Benburb, County Tyrone   *Church of Ireland*

SIR RICHARD Wingfield built this church originally between 1618 and 1622, although it has been subject to alterations, most notably the addition of the tower in 1892.

The nave represents a typical plantation church, being merely a low hall of four bays, with stumpy stepped buttresses. The windows are square with three round-headed lights in each with a single transom. Each has a simple label moulding. The north wall remains much as it was built, but the south wall has been subject to alteration, most notably a rather insensitive slated extension to the third bay from the west. On the south side nearest the tower is a former doorway, now glazed, which has outward-curling label stops. The pointed east window is of four lights and has rather rudimentary tracery, no doubt the work of a local mason. While the body of the church is rendered, the tower shows its stonework construction, which stops it marrying well

with the rest of the building. The tower, possibly the work of WH Lynn, was the gift of the local landowner, James Bruce. All the openings of the tower are round-headed, and it has angled stepped buttresses rising to belfry level and stepped battlements cap the whole structure. The door on the north side was the original entrance, which the architect incorporated into his design. Like the east window and the former doorway on the south wall, this has outward-curling label stops.

As is to be expected of a building of the period, the interior is a plain hall, with a central aisle and a wooden gallery at the west end. The font is seventeenth century in date and is composed of a fluted sandstone bowl resting on a pillar of the same material. A classical pedimented monument on the east wall commemorates Captain James Hamilton (died 1646).

The tower contains two bells, one of which dates from 1948 and is in memory of Corporal Hamilton Wray,

RAF, killed in July 1942. The other smaller bell has a remarkable history, having been cast for the Capuchin order in Limerick. It bears the inscription: 'X IHS MRA FRS LAVDATE IN TYMPANO ET CHORO FR V MATHEW MACMAHON CAPINORVM LOCI: LIMERICENSIS SUPERATOR ME FIERI FECIT DIE 8 IVLY: ANNO DO 1688'. Translated, this means, 'Jesus, Mary, Francis: Praise with the timbrel and in the dance. Brother in Christ Matthew MacMahon, Superior of the Capuchins of the Limerick district, caused me to be made on 8 July AD 1688'. Due to unrest in the country the bell probably never made it as far as Limerick. It may have been brought from Dublin by one of the governors of Charlemont Fort or by Lord Charlemont himself.

The east end of Clonfeacle (C of I) Church, Benburb – built between 1618 and 1622.

■ **References**

Dukes, p 67; Rowan, p 145.

ST COLUMB'S CATHEDRAL, DERRY
Bishop Street, Derry, County Londonderry
Church of Ireland

'

IF STONES COULD SPEAKE
THEN LONDON'S PRAYSE
SHOULD SOUND WHO
BUILT THIS CHURCH AND
CITTIE FROM THE GROUNDE

'

SO PROCLAIMS a stone in the porch of St Columb's Cathedral, reminding us of the construction of the present building in the seventeenth century. St Columba founded a monastery here in 546, which he left in 563 to found Iona. Abbot Flaithbhertagh O'Brolchain and King O'Lochlainn built the great church of Templemore in 1164, and a small inscription stone from this building is preserved in the later foundation stone. It is inscribed: 'In Templo Verus Deus Est Vereque Colendus' ('The true God is in His temple and is to be truly worshipped'). Little is known of the appearance of this church, which was destroyed by the explosion of a powder magazine in 1568.

In 1613, under a charter granted by King James I, the city of London was given responsibility for the settlement of Derry. Defences were constructed between 1614 and 1618 to protect the new houses of the city and their inhabitants. It was not until 1628 that work began on a new cathedral. The cathedral was built under the direction of Sir John Vaughan, Governor of Derry, and the building contractor was William Parrott. The construction lasted for five years and cost £4000.

As completed in 1633, the cathedral had the appearance of a moderately-sized English parish church, comprising an arcaded nave with aisles terminating in eastern turrets, a south porch and a west tower. Old engravings show the interior lined with box pews, galleries in the aisles and a central aisle focused on a pulpit standing in front of a curved communion rail. The style was Elizabethan Gothic, but is now more commonly described in Ulster as 'Planters' Gothic'. The tower originally supported a short spire, but the lead was used to make bullets during the siege in 1689, when the tower roof served as a gun platform. The tower was increased in height and an ashlar spire was added in 1776–78 at the instigation of Frederick Hervey, Bishop of Derry and later Earl of Bristol. Bringing the total height of the steeple to 221 feet, this elegant, if somewhat overpowering adornment, eventually began to give way, and had to be dismantled in 1802. Its builder, the flamboyant absentee Earl-Bishop, survived it by a year, dying in the outhouse of a peasant farm near Rome. A new tower was completed in 1805, and a new spire rising to a height of 191 feet was added in 1823, possibly to designs by John Bowden.

The south porch or Bishop's Court was removed in

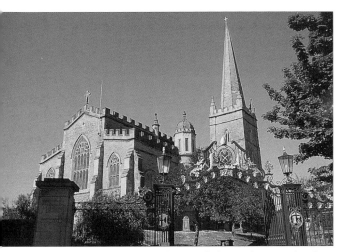

Derry Cathedral – the best known of Ulster's plantation churches.

1825 and the stone commemorating the completion of the cathedral, which was originally above its door, was placed in the tower porch.

Perhaps the largest physical change to the original fabric was carried out in 1887 with the addition of a chancel, designed by the Church of Ireland architect John Guy Ferguson. During construction, seventeenth-century foundations were uncovered, suggesting that a chancel had been part of the original intentions of the planters. Ferguson incorporated the east window of 1859, the work of Joseph Welland, which, judging by early engravings, replicated the foliated tracery of the original window. The chapter house and choir vestry were built on the south side of the cathedral in 1910, to the designs of Sir Thomas Drew. Of all the additions to the building, these are the least sympathetic, being rather harsh in appearance.

A study of the exterior of the cathedral provides ready indications of the various building phases. The cathedral is constructed of rubble schist walls with sandstone trim, and this holds true for all the periods of work. The walls of the nave and aisles from the west tower to the eastern cylindrical turrets are of the seventeenth-century church, with late Gothic windows punctuated by buttresses. The windows of the aisles and clerestory are composed of cusped lancets, set within a shallow segmental arch with a segmental hood moulding. These are three-light windows, except on the south aisle where they are of four lights. The easternmost windows before the turrets were actually added by Ferguson at the time of the addition of the chancel. The half-round turrets at the ends of the aisles mark the termination of the original cathedral, and everything east of these dates from 1887. The turrets

themselves are seventeenth-century work, but the crocketed domes are later additions.

The east wall of the Victorian chancel broadly follows the lines of what went before, except that the Decorated windows of the side chapels are of Ferguson's own design. Formerly there had been two windows on each side, similar to those in the aisles and clerestory. The entire roofline of the body of the cathedral is capped by crenellations, with two octagonal pinnacles at the terminal point of the original clerestory, and a cross on the eastern gable.

The tower is of four stages, with thin clasping buttresses, string-courses and pinnacles similar to those on the roof of the building. The windows are cusped two-lights. The spire is octagonal, with roll mouldings, and terminates in a cross.

Internally, the cathedral is composed of a nave separated from the aisles by seven moulded pointed arches supported on hexagonal columns. The chancel arch and two-bay chancel are the work of Ferguson and adopt round columns. The walls of the aisles have been stripped of plaster, giving a greater air of venerability to the interior. The roof is supported by Perpendicular timber trusses, which are the work of Ferguson, as are the corbel stops fashioned as likenesses of various bishops of the diocese of Derry.

The organ case in the west gallery is particularly fine and is carved in dark mahogany with musical instruments and cherubs' heads. It was the gift of Primate Stone in 1747, and was not made of salvaged timber from the Spanish Armada as folklore would suggest. The pews date from 1861, replacing the original box pews, and are worth noting for their poppyheads, which were the work of father and son woodcarvers. The bishop's throne, rather unusually, sits at the south-eastern end of the nave, and comprises an eighteenth-century Chinese Chippendale chair within a throne surmounted by a wooden spirelet.

The cathedral is rich in monuments, many of which reflect the city's connection with London. In the north aisle can be found the Elvin monument of 1678, commemorating John Elvin, a former mayor of Derry who died at the age of 102. With its spiral columns, garlands and coats-of-arms, this represents a naive attempt at a full-blown classical monument. Every bit as ambitious, and equally primitive, is the memorial to Hugh Edwards, at the east end of the aisle, possibly the work of the same mason as the Elvin monument. The base panel presents a reminder of the mortality of man, with the symbols of death: hourglasses, bells, a book, the gravedigger's tools, skulls and crossbones, and, for good measure, two winged cherub heads. All of the stained glass in the building is post-1860. The most evocative window is that in the choir vestry which depicts the relief of the beleaguered city in 1689.

The tower contains thirteen bells, the tenor bell of the peal weighing 32$^1/_2$ cwt. Bells were given to the cathedral in 1614 and 1630 by the Irish Society and King Charles I presented a peal of five bells in 1638. These were subsequently recast to form the present peal in 1929.

The chapter house has a display of artefacts relating to the history of the church and the city, and the progressive changes to the fabric of the building can be traced through the drawings which hang on the walls. The massive padlocks and keys of the four city gates can be found here, along with fragments of flags captured by the defenders of the city during the siege.

Derry Cathedral has often been likened to an English parish church, and perhaps this comparison is appropriate given the similarity the building bears to some of the older city churches of London. Standing like a great stone sentinel on the highest ground in the city, the cathedral has served the citizens as a place of worship, refuge and defence through some of the most important events in the history of the country.

■ References
Galloway, P, *The Cathedrals of Ireland* (Belfast, 1992), pp 65–9; Rowan, p 376–83; UAHS (Derry), pp 16, 18.

THE MIDDLE CHURCH, BALLINDERRY
Between Upper and Lower Ballinderry, eight miles west of Lisburn, County Antrim   *Church of Ireland*

THE MIDDLE CHURCH stands west of the village of Ballinderry ('the townland of the oak') and is perhaps the most complete example in Ulster of a seventeenth-century 'barn' church.

The church was built for Jeremy Taylor, Bishop of Down, Connor and Dromore, but was not completed until 1668, the year after his death. He had this church built at Ballinderry to replace St Loo's Church on nearby Portmore Lough, which, although it had been the site of some of his most erudite preaching, was considered to be too inaccessible. He had intended to be buried at Ballinderry, but due to the incomplete state of the new church his final resting place was the cathedral that he had constructed at Dromore.

The church at Ballinderry stands much as completed in 1668. It is a simple rectangular building, 71 feet in length and 29 feet in width, surmounted by a bellcote at the west end. At the north-west corner is an external staircase leading up to the gallery. The exterior of the building was originally whitewashed, and its appearance would benefit if this were to be done again. Three windows on the north side and two on the south pierce the walls, which are three feet thick. Each window has three lights with rounded heads, with the exception of the east window, which has five lights. The Middle Church ceased to be the parish church in 1824 when a new church was built closer to Ballinderry. When Francis Joseph Bigger and William Fennell surveyed the church prior to restoration work in 1902 these windows were filled with sheet glass. At the time of restoration they were given bulls-eye panes. These help to add to the quaintness of the church, but are, historically, somewhat out of place. The roof is now slated but would have been covered in oak shingles when first built. In 1791 an applotment or levy was made on the parish of 'one penny per acre for the sake of slating the church'.

The interior reflects the simplicity of the Restoration Church of Ireland with the positioning of communion table and pulpit, each being readily visible to the congregation. This imparts Taylor's emphasis on the sacraments and preaching. Square box pews of Irish oak line both sides of the church, the pulpit being placed about half-way up the north side. The pulpit is a remarkable survival of the 'three-decker' variety, designed to accommodate the clerk, the reader and the preacher. The uppermost tier is topped by a sounding-board to help the preacher's voice to carry. The pulpit retains its candlesticks, the original method for lighting the entire building. There is a pew door inscribed 'AB 1668 AW', which refers to the date of consecration and, presumably, the initials of the churchwardens at the time. Almost opposite the pulpit is a pew known locally as 'Lord

The Middle Church (C of I), Ballinderry.

Conway's Pew'. Taylor must have been canny enough to make such provision for the local landlord, who had given him shelter after he had fled the Cromwellian regime. The church was lengthened to the west by 9 feet and the panelled gallery and external steps were added at the same time. This work may have been carried out, when the church was reroofed in 1791.

At the east end of the church was a timber hanging of the royal arms. This display of loyalty was a common practice in the Church of England, and was no doubt enacted here at the instigation of Taylor. The arms, painted on a heavy oak panel and restored in 1859, can now be seen in Ballinderry's present parish church. Other fittings which are roughly contemporary with the building include the wooden font (not dissimilar to the one Taylor presented to his cathedral in Dromore) and an oak offertory chest dated 1706.

The earliest bell at the Middle Church was inscribed, 'I was cast to the order of Lord Conway 1686 from four Popish bells at the store of the Newrie'. This was then replaced by the bell from the old church at Portmore,

which was inscribed, 'This bell is cast for Portmore by order of Sir George Raidon AN 1681'. Removed in 1869, it was recast for Gilford Parish Church. The present bell dates from 1955, and was the gift of the Higginson family.

Old photographs of the Middle Church, taken before the restoration of 1902, show a ramshackle, ivy-clad old building, and it must be regretted that the over-zealous Edwardian restorers gave it a rather hard appearance. Nonetheless, this is a most evocative church, which makes evident the piety of Jeremy Taylor, a man who had ministered to kings in the splendour of their palaces, and who did the same for men of lesser station in a place such as this.

■ **References**

Brett (Antrim), p 30; Dixon, p 28; Dukes, p 49; *Ulster Journal of Archaeology*, second series, 1897, pp 13–22.

CHURCH BELLS

THE WORD 'bell' is a derivation of the Anglo-Saxon word 'bellan', which means 'to bellow' and from the introduction of Christianity to Ireland bells have been used to signal the hour of religious observance. It is likely that the earliest bells in Ireland were used by the Druids in connection with their pagan rites. Later, Christian missionaries used handbells constructed of sheets of iron wrought into shape, riveted and coated in bronze and number of these may be seen in the Ulster Museum. They would have been rung from the top of a round tower or 'cloigtheach' (Irish for 'house of the bell').

By the end of the fourteenth century, churches were equipped with larger bronze bells which were hung in towers or gable-turrets and swung from side to side by means of a rope connected to a spindle. In England, however, bellringers experimented with ways to improve the manner in which bells were rung, culminating in the reign of Elizabeth I with the use of a complete wooden wheel and rope fixed to the side of the bell. This allowed the bellringer to turn the bell

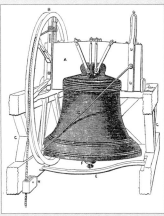

A bell hung for change-ringing.

through 360 degrees, so that its 'tongue' or 'clapper' would strike it at its highest point allowing the sound to reach a greater distance. Three or more such bells constitute a 'ring' or 'peal' of bells and the art of sounding these bells became known as 'change-ringing'. This is a particularly English art and was slow to find its way into Ulster. The earliest ring of bells here was given to the Church of Ireland cathedral in Derry by King Charles I in 1638. Another ring was given to Armagh in 1721 by Primate Thomas Lindsay and the arrival of these bells into the city caused the population to abandon a public execution they had been watching. Today, in Ulster, there are sixteen rings of bells upon which change-ringing is practised. Most of the bellringers belong to the Irish Association of Change Ringers, which was founded in 1898.

The provision and use of bells was not common outside the Church of Ireland during the penal era. However, by the latter part of the nineteenth century most Catholic churches and many Presbyterian churches were provided with one bell and peals were found only where they were the gift of a wealthy donor.

In addition to single bells and peals of bells, some churches were provided with a 'carillon' or a 'chime' where a number of non-swinging bells were installed and chimed by one person pulling at hammers which struck the sides of the bells. Bells rung in this manner can be found in the Catholic cathedral in Armagh and at Sinclair Seamen's Church in Belfast.

The heaviest church bell in Ulster is the 53 cwt bass bell at St Eugene's Catholic cathedral in Derry. Today bells not only announce religious services or observations (such as the angelus), but also ring out for weddings, funerals, New Year and state occasions.

■ **Reference**
Dukes

Bellringers in Hillsborough Parish Church practising in 1950.

HOLY TRINITY PARISH CHURCH, WARINGSTOWN

Banbridge Road, Waringstown, County Down   *Church of Ireland*

UNTIL THE middle of the seventeenth century, the parishes of Donaghcloney and Tullylish, formed a territory called Clanconnell under the lordship of the Maginnes clan. The parish suffered during the 1641 Rebellion, when the church was destroyed and the rector, George Wright, was driven from his house.

Under the Commonwealth much of the land in Ireland was declared forfeit, and a Captain Barrett purchased the lands of Clanconnell before selling them to William Waring in 1658. Waring established the village of Waringstown with a manor house, two streets and a new parish church.

The original church building, which forms the present nave, was completed circa 1681, the work being supervised, it is said, by James Robb, Chief Mason to the King's Works in Ireland. It was consecrated by Dr Essex Digby, Bishop of Dromore, and dedicated to the Holy Trinity.

The new church was a rectangle 52 feet in length with a gable belfry on the west end but without aisles or transepts. The walls were built of boulders with pinnings, with quoins at the angles. Due to later additions to the building very little of the original walling is now visible. The church was lit by three square-headed windows on the north and south walls in addition to windows on the east and west ends. Two of the windows on the north wall seem to be original. The external appearance would have been similar to that of the essentially unaltered Middle Church at Ballinderry, County Antrim.

The most remarkable internal feature was the magnificent oak roof of eight bays which still survives. Each truss has moulded principal rafters, tie beam and a pair of curved braces rising to a pendant with moulded terminal, and projecting sole pieces with moulded side posts, which have terminals moulded similarly to the pendants.

Incised flagstones in the nave floor record the burial place of various members of the Waring family, with the inscription:'Rebecca Pitt, 16___; Jane Waring, 1694; Henry Waring, 1716; Arthur Waring, 1690; William Waring, 1689; and Francis Waring, 1703'.

The first major change to Holy Trinity Church was the construction of the west tower, which commenced in 1745. The impetus for this work is to be found in the will of Archdeacon Henry Jenny, who died in 1742. It states: 'I order that if within six years the parishioners shall think

The interior of Waringstown (C of I) Church, showing the unique seventeenth-century roof structure.

fit to erect a suitable Steeple at Waringstown Church, that one hundred pounds shall be given towards a suitable bell to hang therein.' Work was disrupted when the incomplete structure collapsed in August 1747 but rebuilding soon began and Archdeacon Jenny's bell was hung in the tower in 1750.

The tower is four storeys standing on a plinth, each stage being inset. It rises to a battlemented parapet, surmounted by a low pyramidal shingled spire topped by a gilded finial and weathercock. The west door has a plain semicircular head, as have the upper openings on the tower. Timber stairs rising from the porch give access to the gallery, which may have been built at the same time as the tower. Two bells hang in the tower, the smaller of which is inscribed: 'I BELONG TO DONAGHCLONEY PARISH: SUN PARVA AC SONABILIS CAMPANA'. This bell was fished out of the river Lagan after the rebellion in 1641. The larger bell bears the inscription: 'THE GIFT OF HENRY JENNY, D.D., 1750. CAST AT GLOUCESTER IN ENGLAND BY ABEL RUDHALL'.

The first substantial alterations to the old fabric came in 1829–30 with the construction of a north transept. Increased accommodation was needed at this time due to a rise in the numbers in the congregation, as parish records show there were 121 baptisms in 1824, and a further 704 between 1824 and 1830. This increase in population can no doubt be attributed to the improved prosperity of the village due to linen weaving.

Three bays of the north wall were removed to accommodate the transept, necessitating alternative support for two of the roof trusses. This was achieved by installing two weight-carrying posts. These are panelled with moulded capitals and bases, and are richly carved on each side with fruit and flowers. The roof structure replicates that of the nave. A similar treatment of the roof trusses was adopted in 1859 when the south aisle was added, involving the entire removal of the old south wall. Six posts were erected to carry the roof, but these lack the carving of those on the south.

While the rubble masonry and quoins of these two extensions blends harmoniously with what is visible of the original church, the same cannot be said of the extension to the chancel designed by Sir Thomas Drew and completed in 1888. The harsh appearance of the stonework of the new chancel sits uncomfortably with the speckled rubble masonry of the original walls. However, the work carried out in the interior of the church at this time is highly successful.

The chancel was provided with an oak roof, which is in keeping with the original but not a copy, showing distinctly what is seventeenth century and what is not. Oak panelling rises to a height of 8 feet and carries a frieze carved by Dean Holt Waring (1766–1850). The east window was built to a design found among the dean's papers. During the reconstruction the pulpit was moved to its present site at the junction of the chancel and the north transept. Although later in date, its design is typical of a seventeenth-century pulpit, with a sumptuously decorated sounding board and flanking scroll-work enrichments. When the church was first built the pulpit would have been situated on the south wall and would have had a three-decker arrangement (as at Ballinderry).

Despite the number of alterations to the church since its construction in 1681, the building gives a strong visual and atmospheric impression of a parish church of the Caroline period.

■ **References**
ASCD, pp 336–8.

ST MICHAEL'S PARISH CHURCH, CASTLECAULFIELD
Castlecaulfield village near Dungannon, County Tyrone   *Church of Ireland*

THE TOWN of Castlecaulfield was founded by Sir Toby Caulfield, later Lord Charlemont, following a grant of the townland of Ballydonnell to him by James 1 in 1610. The parish church has the appearance of a building of great age, but is, in fact, a rather confusing collection of fragments of different ages welded together.

It is claimed that the original church was built by Rev George Walker, the governor of Derry during the siege, as a replacement for the old church at Donaghmore which was destroyed in 1641: this church consisted simply of a tower attached to a nave. The present tower is of three stages with quoins at the angles and capped by stepped battlements. On the south face is a sundial dated 1685. The columned west door at the foot of the tower and the belfry openings on the upper stage are all round-headed. The tower originally had a squat pyramidal roof, as indicated in a mid nineteenth-century engraving.

The most interesting of all the church's seventeenth-century remnants is the gabled south porch of 1685, which represents a rural attempt at architectural sophistication. It is composed of two rather crude Tuscan columns resting on high plinths flanking the round-headed door. These columns support an entablature upon which stand two strategically swathed cherubs who thoughtfully hold open the Bible (at Psalm 24, vs 7–10) for the benefit of parishioners. The westernmost nave windows must be contemporary with the original construction of the church and are Perpendicular in style with cusped lights surmounted by a wheel. The hood mouldings terminate in curious carved heads which were probably brought here from the old church at Donaghmore. With their curly moustaches and pointed beards they have variously been described as looking like King Charles I and even Sir Toby Caulfield

The south porch of Castlecaulfield (C of I) Church.

himself. Other carvings include the Charlemont arms over the tower door, and, at the south-west eave, an angel clutching a key and a serpent.

St Michael's obtained its present appearance some time after 1860, as unsigned drawings remain which show the extension of transepts and chancel. It is thought that these drawings came from the offices of the architects Welland and Gillespie. Before this extension the church was so crowded that boys sitting in the chancel had to stand up to allow the preacher to get into the pulpit. The Victorian work is quite sensitive to the antiquity of the remainder of the building, and incorporates a number of carvings from the earlier structure. The windows of the nave are reflected in the end windows of each transept, and it is reasonable to assume that the carved heads on these windows are seventeenth-century. However, the western window of each transept is the creation of the Victorian architect, being in the Decorated style. The old east window was copied for the chancel; at the apex of the

window is a carved seventeenth-century angel holding open the Bible at a text which is now illegible from ground level. According to local historian, Major YA Burges, the texts quoted are Genesis Ch 28, v 7, and Leviticus Ch 19, v 30.

Internally, there is a gallery at the west end, with a Gothic frontal carried on two Doric fluted columns. There is a coved plaster ceiling in the nave, while the ceilings of the transepts and chancel are of timber. The original nave windows at the west end have clear glazing set in very solid lattice-work, with painted glass in the uppermost wheel sections. In the south, the symbol of Alpha appears, with Omega in the north, the first and last letters of the Greek alphabet symbolising the fact that God encompasses everything. The east window has the dove, representing the Holy Spirit, in the top section, beneath which is a row of shields, and the lower four lights depict the four evangelists, Matthew, Mark, Luke and John.

On the north nave wall are matching classical monuments to Rev George Evans (died 1801) and his wife Priscilla (died 1792) and to Sarah Maria Evans (died 1844). There is also a classical monument to Rev George Walker (killed at the Battle of the Boyne) and his wife, Isabella (died 1703), who are buried in the chancel. There is a rather pretty one commemorating Edith Burges (died 1894), which is decorated with two very colourful angels.

The church stands on a rising ground in an extensive graveyard, which is entered through very fine eighteenth-century gate piers with spherical finials. The large Burges family mausoleum takes the form of a classical temple with four Doric columns. A plaque at the church gate commemorates the poet, Rev Charles Wolfe (1791–1829), curate of Donaghmore.

■ References

Burges, YA, *History of St Michael's Church, Castlecaulfield* (Dungannon, 1966), pp 6–9; Rowan, pp 174–5; UAHS (Dungannon and Cookstown), pp 51–2.

ST MICHAEL'S PARISH CHURCH, CLONOE
Killary, near Coalisland, County Tyrone *Church of Ireland*

St Michael's (C of I) Church, Clonoe.

ALTHOUGH THERE has been a church on this site since 1431, it was ruined and disused by 1622. Church building had to be put in hand in Ulster following much of the destruction during the unrest of the last decade of the seventeenth century. King James' army had managed to wreck most of the churches in the diocese of Derry, while the garrison at Charlemont Fort had a similar effect in that part of the country. St Michael's was rebuilt in 1699, as a stone in the church porch relates: 'This church / was repaired ye / Rd Wil Delgarn / Rector Thos / Morris Esq Church / Warden An Dom 1699 / One Lord One Fa / ith One Baptism'. It can be assumed from the existence of this stone that fragments of the fifteenth-century church remain incorporated in the present structure, although it has essentially the appearance of a plantation church.

The church is basically a rectangular rubble-built hall with a west porch and bellcote. The nave is of three bays of paired round-headed lancet windows, with a pointed east window with tracery similar to that in the east end of Clonfeacle church. Although the church was re-ordered in the last century, losing its original pews and pulpit, it retains the simple air of a seventeenth-century church, open truss-work roof and a central aisle leading to the communion table. The windows of the side walls are filled with lattice glazing, while the east window has stained glass, which dates from 1940 and is not too overpowering.

The mason responsible for the inscription stone in the porch appears to have carried out work for the nave. At the north end of the nave is a stone containing instructional information for parishioners. It is inscribed: 'Laud Deo Adi / Soli Deo Gloria / Fear God / Honour The / King / Love Your Neighbour / Pray Alwyes / The Gift of / Thos Morris / Esq 1700 / God is Our Portion / and Inheritance'. This stone is also decorated with a crude and intimidating angel's head. On the opposite wall is another example of the work of this local master mason, Thomas Morris's own memorial, which is decorated with the family coat of arms. It reads: 'Laud Deo Soli Deo Glori / Here Lyeth / The Body of Thos / Morris of Mount / Joy Esq Who Depar / This Life The 4 day / of Setembr Anno / 1712 Aged 62 years'.

Although the fittings have been altered, this little church, set somewhat off the beaten track, is a late example of a plantation church, but resembles those built perhaps eighty years earlier.

■ **References**
Rowan, pp 199–200

ST ANDREW'S PARISH CHURCH, BALLIGAN
Balligan (signposted off the road between Greyabbey and Kircubbin), County Down · *Church of Ireland*

HISTORICAL INFORMATION regarding this church can be found in the 'Third Report of His Majesty's Commissioners on Ecclesiastical Revenue and Patronage in Ireland' of 1836. This tells us of Balligan Church 'situate in Inishargie Parish … built in 1704, since when it has been repaired and improved at different times at the expense of the parish'. The parish of Inishargie ceased to exist in 1849, and the church is now administered by Ballywalter parish. This is a simple building, painted white, with a distinctly rural appearance. The church is a small rectangular building lighted by lattice windows on the north and south walls, with a large

St Andrew's (C of I) Church, Balligan.

semicircular-headed window on the east gable. There is a bellcote on the west gable, which is presumably later than the original construction of 1704.

Writing about the church in 1966, Denis O'D Hanna, who had been responsible for its restoration, gave an account of the interior of the building, as well as information on fittings commonly found in Jacobean churches. The stone inner-porch doorcase, which is dated 1704, could stylistically be fifty years older. This time lag, as Hanna points out, was not uncommon in the country districts of Ulster, due to poor roads and civil unrest. The nave, which also accommodates the communion table, has a single aisle and is flagged with Scrabo stone. The roof is entirely of wood and is held together with wooden pegs or 'tree nails'.

Of the internal woodwork, the two Gothic reading desks, pupit and choir stalls seem to be later than the construction of the church and are probably Victorian. The font is of uncertain date, but Hanna assures us that it is 'very ancient'. The Gray organ, which stands at the south-east wall, was built between 1770 and 1780 and came from Kircubbin Parish Church, having previously been in Kegworth, Leicestershire. Many Ulster churches of the seventeenth and early eighteenth centuries appear to have been without an organ. In some cases music may have been provided by a parish 'band' who employed string and woodwind instruments.

During the time of the restoration work in 1966, Denis O'D Hanna presented the Jacobean-style chandeliers, the two reading desks and the chest which sits in the porch. He explained that many churches of this period would have had such a chest for the collection of tithes. Often, a chest was provided for holding vegetables, game, fruit, fish and meat, which were then distributed to the poor of the parish. Hanna also speculated that the church porch would have had a cat whip to keep 'satanic' strays off holy property! Balligan Church stands as a simple, but striking, example of the basic functional requirements of the Church of Ireland after the Restoration.

■ **References**
Beckett, JC, *Inishargy Through the Ages* (Belfast, 1966), pp 7–11; Hanna, D O'D, article in the *Church of Ireland Gazette*, 19 August, 1966.

3
Vernacular Architecture:
Penal Chapels and Eighteenth-Century Meeting Houses

WRITING OF Irish churches in 1867, James Godkin considered the positions of the established and non-conformist churches during the penal era, and noted the 'well-endowed rector, ministering to a congregation of twenty or thirty people, while a thousand members of the disinherited Church kneel upon an earthen floor in a rudely constructed chapel'.

The eighteenth century has been described as something of a golden age for the established church, turning up men of the calibre of Dean Swift and Bishop Berkeley, but it was a time of degradation and difficulty for those who were not members of the Church of Ireland. The piety of the priests who walked the country lanes and hedgerows to minister to their flocks contrasted with the privilege of many of the Anglican clergy who owed their positions to high estate or influence at court. Jonathan Swift, who went to considerable trouble to conceal his own piety, claimed that the English administration sent only the finest and most devout clergy to Ireland. The problem was, he felt, that they got as far as Chester, and were then ambushed by villains who brought their letters of appointment on to Ireland in their places!

Following the Williamite Wars there were high hopes of religious toleration in Ireland, as framed in the articles of the Treaty of Limerick. However, the Irish parliament was not prepared to countenance leniency towards Roman Catholics. For about twenty years from 1695 various acts of parliament denied Catholics the right to higher education, to hold arms, and all bishops were to leave the country by 1 May 1698, with moves being made

to prevent them from returning. Restrictions placed on church buildings stipulated that they should be placed three miles outside a town, and should not have a tower or bells. There was no law preventing the construction of Catholic places of worship, but they did have to be discreet, and many congregations were simply too poor to build themselves a church. It was felt that Catholics supported the deposed King James II and his heirs, and this fear made the English administration disinclined to prevent these harsh measures.

While the penal laws were harshest on the Catholics, the Sacramental Test Act of 1703 (demanding the taking of 'the Lord's Supper according to the usage of the Church of Ireland') effectively discriminated against Presbyterians and other dissenters such as Quakers and Moravians, by preventing them from taking public office. The restrictions on Presbyterians reached their height in 1714, the year of Queen Anne's death, when the doors of their meeting houses were actually boarded up. However, after the passing of the Jacobite threat in the mid eighteenth century, official suspicion of Catholicism receded, and the repressive laws were not rigidly adhered to.

Such buildings as were erected by Catholics and Presbyterians at this time have, in the past, been categorised as 'penal chapels' and 'meeting houses'. However, both can be brought under the umbrella of vernacular church architecture which is essentially functional and the churches which the Catholics and Presbyterians built reflect this in their appearance, just as much as a barn or a domestic dwelling would. Indeed, in viewing an eighteenth-century church of these denominations, it is rather difficult, externally, to tell the difference. This relationship is due to the circumstances under which both denominations operated in Georgian Ireland. Unlike the Church of Ireland, neither had the benefit of wealthy patrons, and both suffered poverty, their wealthiest members being middle class at best. However, unlike their privileged Anglican countrymen, both denominations had strength of numbers, and so the need arose to provide the most extensive church accommodation on the most slender of resources.

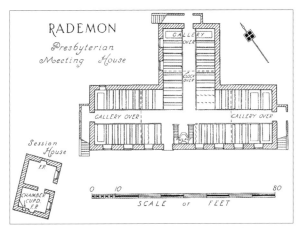

The floor plan of the T-shaped meeting house at Rademon, County Down.

Virtually all the pre-Reformation churches in the land were in the hands of the Anglican church, and therefore the Gothic style of architecture was broadly associated with that branch of Christianity. So at this stage, for ideological and pecuniary reasons, the Catholics and Presbyterians turned their backs on this idiom, moving rather towards a functional austerity in their buildings. Writing on the origins of 'barn' churches in 1952, Denis O'D Hanna said that the simple vernacular Presbyterian church building of the eighteenth century can be seen as a built expression of the Reformation. Having shunned the Gothic style of the Church of Ireland, the Presbyterians had to establish a tradition of their own, and so they looked to Scotland, the bastion of Presbyterianism. The meeting house built at Downpatrick in 1711 borrowed from Scotland the classic T-shaped layout, and this functional and economic plan was also to be adopted for Catholic churches. In the case of the Presbyterian churches each arm of the 'T' was filled with pews or benches, with a gallery above providing maximum accommodation in a restricted space. In fact, access to the galleries was often by external staircases, so

that there was no wastage of internal seating space. The other important aspect of these T-shaped buildings was that the entire congregation faced the focal point of the liturgy or service of their denomination, having dispensed with the Anglican longitudinal aisle arrangement. In the case of the Presbyterians, the focal point was the lofty pulpit placed at the centre of the long wall – the physical positioning reflecting the centrality of the word of God.

Catholic churches had crosses positioned on the gables but apart from these it would have been difficult to discern whether the building was Catholic or Presbyterian, as both had a similar shape and both were built of stone with slated or even thatched roofs. A good example of a T-plan Catholic church which survives is St James', Aldergrove, County Antrim. Catholics were poorer than Presbyterians, and their resources rarely stretched beyond floors of packed earth. There were often no pews or benches, as at this time the congregations traditionally stood during the mass. Whereas the Presbyterians gave the prominent long wall position to the pulpit, the Catholics placed the altar here. This was their physical expression of communication with God and its central and readily accessible position increased the visibility of liturgy of the mass in a way which was eventually lost until after the Second Vatican Council in the 1960s. The only marked difference from the austerity of the nonconformist meeting houses could be seen in the painted stations of the cross or an altar-piece, which might have been brought with some difficulty from the Continent.

A simpler layout was found in the rectangular church structures which were also built in the eighteenth and early nineteenth centuries. These had a door on the end and one on a side wall, as at St John the Baptist, Drumcree, or two doors on one side as at Kildoagh, County Cavan or Poyntzpass, County Armagh. At Ardtanagh, near Dromara, County Down, we even find three doors. An aisle ran from gable to gable in front of the pulpit or altar, while another aisle joined it from the door on one of the longer walls. On either side of the altar or pulpit would have been a door leading to the sacristy or minister's room.

To increase the seating accommodation there was a gallery around three sides of the interior. In some churches there was simply a gallery at each end which would have been accessed by the terminal doors of the building. Quite often in rural areas these separate doors and galleries served as independent entrances and seating areas for men and women. This was certainly the case in Moravian worship, where men and women sat apart, as at

Gracehill, County Antrim, just as they were laid to rest at either side of their graveyards. This segregation was taken a step further by the Quakers at Moyallon, County Down, who provided themselves with a separate room for women in their meeting house.

There are two separate doors on the fine facade of Dunmurry Non-Subscribing Presbyterian Church, which, with its rubble walls and hipped roof can be easily labelled as a 'barn' church. Perhaps this term is over-used and it is better to refer to this genre of buildings as vernacular churches, but there is no denying that substantial churches such as those at Ardtanagh, Dunmurry and Coagh do have the physical characteristics of barns. Indeed, the main elevation of the church at Rademon has something of the appearance of the house of a well-to-do farmer. As the century progressed, concessions were made to architectural elegance, such as the use of Gibbsian door surrounds. Later again, the facade of Ardtanagh Church had false windows installed to avoid the embarrassment of wide expanses of blank wall.

Most curious and inventive of the meeting houses are those of Rosemary Street First Congregation, Belfast, and Randalstown, both of which are elliptical. The inspiration for these may, possibly, have come from St Andrew's 'Round Church' in Dublin. Internally, Rosemary Street is entered on the narrow section of the oval, whereas Randalstown is an oval entered on the long side, just as St Andrew's was. This can be seen as a curved adaptation of the layout of rectangular meeting houses, with the pews and galleries huddling around the pulpit.

In his book, *A Boy in the Country*, John Stevenson gave his impression of the 'Old Meeting House', and it may prove useful to include it here, not so much for the architectural description it provides, as to gauge the impression which such buildings had on the worshipper. Stevenson recalls:

'

Its walls exhibited no subtle harmonies of form or colour or space; they knew no grace of carven stone. Bare and projectionless, whitewashed inside and out, they rose high to a roof of simplest form a roof can take. The regularly-spaced, square-headed windows filled with cold clear glass, lit an assemblage of high-backed unpainted pews, dominated by an ungainly square pulpit reached by straight steep steps, an interior as unbeautiful as presaged by the outer form.

'

It should be borne in mind that this was written in 1912 when there was not quite the same appreciation of vernacular architecture as exists today.

The church buildings which survive from the penal era serve to show the ingenuity and resourcefulness of the congregations in harnessing their small assets. They also demonstrate the tenacity of the Catholics and Dissenters in providing themselves with places of worship in the face of considerable difficulties.

■ References
ASCD, pp 313–4; Craig, p 224; Hanna, D O'D, *Ulster Barn Churches: Their Origin and Development* (Belfast,1952); McCullough, pp 81–3; Stevenson, J, *A Boy in the Country* (London, 1912), Ch 26.

STREAM STREET NON-SUBSCRIBING PRESBYTERIAN CHURCH, DOWNPATRICK
Stream Street, Downpatrick, County Down   *Non-Subscribing Presbyterian*

THIS IS one of the earliest of the surviving T-shaped Presbyterian meeting houses, having been built, according to the Archaeological Survey of County Down, before 1729. The sign at the church gate indicates that it was built in 1711. The variety of dates suggests either a long period of building or that the 1711 structure may have had to be replaced in 1729.

The T-building was rendered a cruciform later in the eighteenth century by the addition of a session house on the south side. This is certainly a building in the vernacular idiom, for it has no composed facade as we see at Rademon, but is strictly functional in its design and appearance. Its chief interest lies in its largely original state. It is rendered and slated with round-headed windows, some of which have regular Georgian glazing and some of which have Georgian Gothic glazing. Clear-glazed windows gave the congregation a view of God's creation, as well as glimpses of the tombstones, a reminder of the transitory nature of life. The eastern and western arms have external gallery stairs enclosed in

Stream Street Non-Subscribing Presbyterian Church, Downpatrick.

The pulpit in Stream Street church. Note the position of the gallery.

porches, whereas the stair enclosure on the north is the full width of the arm.

When the church was built, there were two tall round-headed windows on either side of the pulpit, but the western one was removed late in the eighteenth century to allow for the new session house. The space formerly occupied by this window now has a 'squire's pew' high up on the wall, and this can be seen as a reminder of the 'laird's loft', recalling the Scottish foundations of Presbyterianism. This gallery-cum-pew is composed of a shallow arch set on two pilasters with moulded capitals and bases. The front of the gallery is balustraded. Galleries were also provided in each arm of the church and these are supported on timber columns which rest on pedestals. The fronts of the galleries are panelled with balustrades above, but have no panelling on the sections corresponding with the aisles below. This would have helped to give a clear view of the pulpit. At the end of each arm the ground-floor pews are raised for the same reason. The ceiling is barrel-vaulted above a cornice, and its proximity to the galleries creates a rather cavernous effect.

The octagonal pulpit is particularly fine and is placed at the centre of the long wall, at the apex of the aisles. It is known as the 'Thomas Nevin Pulpit' after the minister who served here between 1710 and 1744. The preaching stage is panelled and rests on four struts with cusped spandrels. Entrance into the pulpit is by a door from the session house incorporated into the woodwork supporting the sounding board. There was originally a clerk's seat directly beneath the pulpit. The aisles are lined with fine box pews and are flagged. David Caddell presented four copper collecting shovels in 1754 and another was given in 1767 by John Graham. A further shovel is unmarked but appears to be of a similar vintage.

The church is set in a pleasant graveyard entered through stout gate-piers topped with garlanded urns. Some of the family burial vaults are unusual with high concave pyramidal roofs.

■ References
ASCD, pp 314, 343–4; UAHS (Downpatrick), p19.

ABBEY STREET PRESBYTERIAN CHURCH, ARMAGH
St Patrick's Trian, Abbey Street, Armagh, County Armagh   *Presbyterian*

ALTHOUGH THIS building has not been used as a church since the early twentieth century, and is now part of the St Patrick's Trian, it represents a very early survival of Presbyterian church architecture.

Writing in 1703, Thomas Ashe noted that Armagh had 'one of the greatest meeting houses in ye north'. It is fair to assume that this church dated from the seventeenth century as Lewis makes mention of the foundation of the congregation in 1670. It is to be regretted that this building was demolished as recently as 1970.

In 1722 the congregation provided itself with a new place of worship, 'The New Meeting House', in Abbey Street. The datestone, which still exists beneath the main window reads: 'Anno Domini 1722'. Jonathan Swift felt that the title 'new' was ironic, given that the Presbyterians used stone from the ruined abbey of saints Peter and Paul in the building. While some of the carved stones of the abbey can still be detected on the church, two fourteenth-century capitals have been removed to the Armagh County Museum.

As built in 1722, the church was basically a T-plan structure, but the addition of a session and minister's room in 1880 rendered it an asymmetrical cruciform. The church was built of pink rubble sandstone with limestone quoins, with external staircases on the arms of the 'T' to allow access to the galleries. The windows were square-headed on the ground floor and round-headed at gallery level. In 1880 the fenestration was changed, most notably by the insertion of a large mullioned and

The former Abbey Street Presbyterian Church, Armagh.

transomed window on the gable of each arm of the 'T'. The old windows were blocked, as were the gallery doors, following the removal of the external staircases. Looking at the stonework, it would appear that the arm nearest the street was widened. Finally, the building was rendered and a now illegible inscription stone placed beneath the original datestone to commemorate these changes. When the building ceased to be used as a church it served for a time as a church hall, and, hardly surprisingly, the interior was altered. However, in recent years the render has been removed, allowing the observant eye to note the constructional changes which have been effected over time, such as the old gallery windows discernible on the gable walls. The church has been restored and, externally, provides a solid example of an early eighteenth-century meeting house.

■ **References**
UAHS (Armagh), p 43; unpublished notes held by the DOENI, Environment and Heritage Service (Built Heritage).

MAGHERALLY PRESBYTERIAN CHURCH
Magherally, near Banbridge (off the A1 dual carriageway), County Down   *Presbyterian*

THE CONGREGATION of Magherally dates from 1656, although the present building, then known locally as The Meetin' was not constructed until 1734 as a T-plan church. In 1791 it was described as being divided into a 'long house and isle [sic]'.

This fine church is a large T-shaped building approached through grand entrance gates and set next to a sympathetically designed church hall, which sadly hides the church from the approach road. The long wall of the building is of six bays, the central two being round-headed, while the rest are segmental-headed, as are all the other windows in the church. All are Georgian glazed. There is a door at the gable wall of each arm of the 'T', with a window above which would previously have been a door into the gallery. The gallery which faces the pulpit was installed in 1791 along with external access stairs. These stairs have now gone, as have the galleries which existed in the other arms. Curiously, the existing gallery does not appear to have any means of access. It is panelled and rests on two timber columns painted to resemble marble.

Magherally Presbyterian Church.

As at Rademon and Downpatrick, there is a long aisle running from door to door, with a shorter aisle joining it at the central point. The bench pews are very obviously not original, although it seems that the church did not have fixed pews until 1808, when the old moveable benches were replaced. The Georgian pulpit has also gone, and been replaced by a semicircular Victorian preaching stage which is fronted with ornate metal scrollwork. However, despite these changes, the church retains the air of a Georgian preaching house, both in structure and atmosphere. The interior is bright and spacious with a coved ceiling enriched by gilded roses. Behind the pulpit is a bronze tablet to the memory of Rev John Dunwoodie Martin (died 1946), the brother-in-law

of the author and scholar Helen Waddell. On one of the gable walls are two similar plaques commemorating two of Rev Martin's sons who were killed in the Second World War. Outside is a war memorial obelisk which incorporates fine bronze reliefs of scenes of war on land and sea.

■ **References**
OSM (Vol 12, Down III), p 115.

MOYALLON FRIENDS MEETING HOUSE
Stramore Road, Moyallon, County Down

Religious Society of Friends (Quakers)

MOYALLON FRIENDS Meeting House stands in pleasant wooded countryside, a fitting place for a building where worship is centred upon peace and the influence of the Holy Spirit.

Meetings have been held by the Society of Friends at Moyallon since 1692 when worship began in a private house. In 1736 the present meeting house was constructed and the graveyard laid out on land provided by John Christy. The Christy property in the district passed on through the female line to the Wakefields and later to the Richardsons, by whom it is still held. The meeting house is a rectangular-gabled building, once harled but now cement rendered, with a caretaker's house of two storeys at right angles. Access to this house and the range of stables is through a coach arch at the southern end of the building. In association with these stables is a flight of stone steps to help people to mount their horses.

The northern half of the main building is occupied by a large meeting room which retains its original oak fittings. The room is lit by two round-headed Georgian glazed windows in the west wall. There is a wainscoted dado with moulded capitals, while the south wall is occupied by a two-tiered elders' desk, the upper tier of which is reached by stairs at each end. The west gallery, although now enclosed to provide alternative accommodation, retains its panelled front with moulded capping and is supported on two columns with half-round columns against the walls. These columns are on pedestals, with moulded bases at the seat level of the pews, and have capitals supporting an entablature. The bays beneath the gallery are enclosed by panelled screens, ingeniously hinged at the top so that they can be lifted and fixed to the underside of the gallery, to increase the

Moyallon Friends meeting house.

size of the meeting room if required. This space beneath the gallery and the gallery itself are each lit by a pair of windows in the north wall and a round-headed window running through both levels on the west wall. Access to the gallery is by a staircase rising from the west porch.

At the south-west corner of the meeting room is a door leading to a half-landing which gives access to an external door below, and to what was once the women's meeting room above the coach arch. This room reminds us that it was formerly the custom of Quaker men and women to worship separately. The women's meeting room is lighted by five windows and the furnishings date from the nineteenth century, as does, presumably, the verandah which extends along the west side of the meeting house.

■ **References**
Chapman, GR, *Historical Sketch of Moyallon Meeting* (nd), pp 2–3.

GRACEHILL MORAVIAN CHURCH
Cennick Square, Gracehill, County Antrim   *Moravian*

TAKING THE road into the square at Gracehill is rather like taking a step back in time, for this Moravian settlement remains largely unspoiled in appearance. The village was founded in 1746 by John Cennick and consisted of a self-sufficient community of thirty-nine residences. Visiting the place in 1837, Samuel Lewis noted that 'the sisters support themselves by various kinds of needlework'. They also ran a school for young ladies, while there was a boys' boarding school in the brethren's house next to the church. The village was laid out around a square which housed the brothers and sisters, but the most important building

Gracehill Moravian Church.

in the settlement was the church, the foundation stone of which was laid on 12 March 1765. It was opened for worship on 6 November of the same year, having been built by the community's own tradesmen. The building overseer was John Reinhard Schloezer, his presence reflecting the fact that the 'mother' community for the Moravians was at Hermhut in Saxony.

The church has a relatively simple external appearance, reflecting the lives of the brethren who worshipped there. It is five bays in width, with three large round-headed windows flanked by doors with smaller windows above. These windows have architraves and are filled with sashed Georgian Gothic glazing. The timber doorcases have dentilled entablatures supported on fluted pilasters and are decorated with carved leaves tied with ribbons. This work has been attributed to Rev Jons Fredlizius, a Swedish brother of the community. The existence of the two doors indicates the segregation of the sexes during worship, and a visit to the peaceful graveyard behind the church shows that this segregation extended into death; male burials on one side, females on the other.

Originally, the church did not have a clock turret, and the first one was built as late as 1880. However, this had to be taken down and replaced in the 1920s by the present turret and slated spirelet that would not look out of place on a New England church. The building is quoined and was harled originally, but is now cement rendered and lined to simulate masonry. It is flanked by the manse and warden's house, both of which have hipped roofs.

As completed, the interior of the church was much simpler than it is now, having an openwork roof (as opposed to a ceiling) and a packed clay floor. Work carried out in 1842 and 1866 left the interior much as it is now. The beautiful 'tulip' pulpit dates from 1842 and has a preaching stage which is reached on each side by sweeping balustraded staircases. It occupies a prominent position on the long wall, a typically nonconformist characteristic. Propriety is maintained in the seating arrangements with separate doors leading to the end galleries, as well as individual doors leading to the adjoining buildings. The galleries are carried on cast iron columns and there are brass chandeliers.

This is indeed a 'neat and commodious building', as Lewis described it, and it makes a positive contribution to the conservation area in which it stands.

■ **References**
Brett (Antrim), pp 36–7; Lewis, Vol 1, p 140.

AGNUS DEI

Agnus Dei

IN CHRISTIAN symbolism Jesus is often represented as the Lamb of God. Christ, the victim of human sin has been equated with the paschal lamb (1 Corinthians, Ch 5, v 7; Revelations Ch 5, v 6) and this can be found in the buildings of many denominations. It is the particular symbol of the Moravian church, where it is always accompanied by the banner of victory.

Moravians originated in the fifteenth century as the followers of the Czech reformer John Hus. Following a period of persecution they had a renaissance in Saxony in the early eighteenth century and came to Britain in the 1730s, later becoming involved in the evangelical revival heralded by John and Charles Wesley. Rev John Cennick came to Ireland in 1746 and three years later founded Ireland's first Moravian congregation in Dublin. Today there are five Moravian congregations in Ulster, the most notable being in the Moravian settlement of Gracehill, County Antrim. The Moravian church is quite unencumbered by written doctrine and the central belief in the need for salvation through Jesus Christ is expressed in a simple statement known as 'the ground of the Unity'.

■ **References**
Foy, JH, *Moravians in Ireland* (Belfast,1986).

ARDKEEN CATHOLIC CHURCH
Saltwater Bridge, between Kirkubbin and Portaferry, County Down

Catholic

HARDLY TOUCHED by the hand of time, this quaint little building stands much as it was when it was built in 1777 by Father Daniel Doran. The church is a simple rectangular structure with white roughcast walls and a slated roof. The door is placed on the gable, has a fanlight and is opened by a latch. There are four Georgian Gothic sashed round-headed windows on the wall facing the road, while there are two on the back. On the opposite gable to the door are three small round-headed windows filled with lattice glazing.

The simple white interior gives a very strong impression of the conditions of pre-emancipation Catholic worship. Low box pews, minus their doors, line the stone-flagged aisle and lead the worshipper to the altar behind its balustraded rail. The altar itself is of wood and represents a naive attempt at the Gothic style, having probably been made by a local carpenter. Its detailing is picked out in light blue, which contrasts with the white which covers virtually every other surface. To the right of the altar, and within the rail, stands the confessional, which is little more than a castellated booth. The circular, basin-like font sits by a window just outside the rail. Hanging from the exposed rafters of the roof is an iron light pendant, which is obviously of great age. This is a spartan church, containing the bare necessities for worship, which were all that could be acquired under the

Ardkeen Catholic Church.

austerities imposed by the penal code.

The churchyard is full of old and very interesting tombstones, but of particular note is the sandstone copy of an Irish high cross. This marks the burial place of fathers Maguire, Kehoe and Linney, at the spot where they had celebrated mass, presumably in the open air as was often the case in the eighteenth century. Access to the churchyard is by a set of iron gates, or by a stile for the more energetic.

It is extremely fortunate that this important little church has survived in such original condition.

DUNMURRY NON-SUBSCRIBING PRESBYTERIAN CHURCH
Glebe Road, Dunmurry, County Antrim   *Non-Subscribing Presbyterian*

THIS HANDSOME building is an excellent example of the demand for simplicity in church buildings made by the preaching denominations during the eighteenth and early nineteenth centuries. The congregation at Dunmurry was established in 1676, although no traces remain of their early meeting house. At the rear of the present church is a stone inscribed: 'Anno Christi 1714. Georgii R.J.', which indicates that at least the lower section of the session room is older than the rest of the current building which was completed in 1779.

The interior of Dunmurry Non-Subscribing Church.

Inscription stones set over the entrance doors on the main facade reveal more about the erection of the church. 'This house was rebuilt at the expense of the congregation of Dunmurry, 1779', proclaims the left-hand stone, while that on the right says, 'Rev James Stouppe, AM, Minister'. Looking at a church such as this it is easy to appreciate how the term 'barn church' evolved, for here is essentially a sturdy stone building with a hipped roof, which in structure is close to many of the farm buildings which could once be seen in rural Ulster. However, the church is endowed with many rather sophisticated elements in its structure. The Gibbsian surrounds to the windows and doors contrast smartly with the random stone of the walls. Further refinement is to be found in the sandstone plinth, eaves-course and tablet surrounds. The windows are Georgian-glazed with the exception of the central window on the main facade, which is filled with Victorian stained glass. This church is said to be the work of the Belfast architect, Roger Mulholland, who was much influenced by the pattern-books of Gibbs.

The church is filled with panelled box pews arranged along two short aisles and a longer aisle running in front of the pulpit, which is placed centrally on the long wall. The galleries on either side of the interior are approached by balustraded staircases rising from the sides of the internal porches. The pulpit is entered by a stair with curved flanking bannisters and is placed against the front of the organ gallery. At the foot of the pulpit is an upholstered seat, designed for the use of the clerk. The organ pipes are contained within a small traceried case and, like the rest of the church, this is painted a pale grey. The two internal porches are later, with pediments enriched by more recent gilt cherubs, the work of a gifted member of the congregation. Four classical marble monuments of the nineteenth century are arranged two on each side of the pulpit, and commemorate the Reverends TH Scott and Henry Montgomery, Mary Hyndman and Lieutenant Henry Montgomery. The only stained glass window in the building depicts the nearby Collin Glen and was erected to the memory of John Wellington Stouppe McCance (died 1863) and Henry Jones McCance (died 1900).

Dunmurry Non-Subscribing Presbyterian Church stands in pleasant grounds, which contain a number of finely-lettered tombstones.

■ References
Brett (Antrim), p 39; Brett (Mulholland), p 12; Curl, p 13; Dixon, p 49.

CATHOLIC CHURCH OF ST JOHN THE BAPTIST, FORMERLY AT DRUMCREE

The Ulster Folk and Transport Museum, Cultra, Holywood, County Down   *Catholic*

THIS EVOCATIVE church building, used until the 1970s, was originally at Drumcree, County Armagh, but is now reconstructed at the Folk and Transport Museum at Cultra. It gives a good impression of the physical circumstances under which Catholics worshipped during the penal era. The church was built in 1783, and was three miles from the nearest town, as the law required. It would originally have had whitewashed walls, a thatched roof and a packed mud floor. The church as it now stands had evolved to this state by about 1900, although it retains its essentially penal appearance.

Externally, it is a simple rendered rectangular structure with a small extension to house the sacristy. All the windows are Georgian Gothic glazed and there is a door on one of the short walls, and another, which may have been added later, on the long wall opposite the altar. As with all eighteenth-century Catholic churches, there is a cross on each gable.

Inside, there is an aisle with a mosaic-tiled floor running the length of the building from the door and terminating at the traditional curtained confessional. The aisle is intersected at about the half-way point by a shorter aisle from the other door opposite the altar. The altar is placed on one of the long walls and is completely white, with the wooden reredos being a naive mixture of classical and Gothic elements. The altar is flanked by the two doors to the sacristy and is enclosed by a timber railing which also accommodates a smaller, though similar, altar dedicated to the Blessed Virgin Mary. The arrangement of the altar as the focal point of the building is accentuated by the panelled timber gallery on three of the walls. The

gallery contains an organ with a fine traceried case. This was built in 1846 by Lawless of Dublin and was presented to the museum by the late Lord Dunleath.

The former Drumcree Catholic Church.

The roof is of timber trusses, which presumably once supported the thatch, but these are now in-filled with plaster ceilings, decorated with five ornate rosettes. The stations of the cross are replicas of religious paintings and are entirely appropriate in their setting.

St John the Baptist's Church stands as a very valuable reminder of the austerity which was placed on Catholic and dissenting worship in the eighteenth century, but proves that simple faith still managed to exist. This is reflected in the church's only monument, which commemorates Rev John Coyle (died 1803), erected by his brother, Rev Michael Coyle (died 1815). According to the memorial, Fr John was 'Constant in prayer in meditation high /Removed from Earth and tending to the sky /Wise gentle humble modest and kind /Grace in his speech and virtue in his mind'.

■ **References**
OSM (Vol 1, Armagh), p 29.

STATIONS OF THE CROSS

THE STATIONS found on the walls of Catholic churches are designed to help people to meditate on the sufferings of Jesus from the time of His judgement to His crucifixion. Traditionally there were fourteen stations, which probably originate in the practice of pilgrims at Jerusalem following the route of the Via Dolorosa and their desire to re-experience this method of prayer in their own churches.

Examples of the stations can be found in Ulster Catholic churches, expressed in a broad range of artistic styles. The old Drumcree Catholic church, now in the Ulster Folk and Transport Museum has copies of eighteenth-century stations

which were oil paintings on canvas. Paintings such as these may have been brought to Ulster from the Continent. In the nineteenth century, stations were carved from wood and stone, and numerous examples of this work exist in churches of this period. In modern church buildings the stations are also

A station from St Patrick's Catholic Church, Clogher.

very much works of art in their own right, and good examples can be found at St Theresa's, Sion Mills and at the convent chapel at Cookstown. These are the work of Ray Carroll and Benedict Tutty respectively.

ST COLUMBA'S CHURCH, LONG TOWER
Long Tower Street, Derry, County Londonderry

Catholic

LONG CONSIDERED the cradle of Christianity in the city of Derry, there has been a church on this site since Columba founded his monastery here in 546. This church became known as the 'Dubh Regles' – the Black Church. In the twelfth century, Flaithbhertagh O'Brolchain erected the Templemore church which survived, with subsequent alterations, until 1558. Sampson, in his 1802 survey of the county, mentions the fact that the stump of the Columban round tower still survived and was being used as an icehouse. It was this round tower which lent its name to the church.

The present church owes its origins to Bishop McDevitt (bishop 1766–97) who instigated building work in 1784. This was completed in 1786 at a cost of £2800. It was a hall-type building, capable of holding 2000 worshippers, with an earthen floor and the high altar placed at the eastern end. As far as decoration was concerned, the altar was embellished with marble Corinthian capitals from Naples, which were presented by the Earl-Bishop of Derry. This eighteenth-century building provided the bones of the present chancel of the church.

The first of many extensive alterations to the fabric of the building occurred in 1810 when Bishop Charles O'Donnell (bishop, 1798–1819) extended the nave and added the galleries, and the altar was moved to the transept on the main axis of the nave. A stone set into the current central aisle records: 'Site of High Altar in Long Tower Church 1812–1908'. The church finally took on its present appearance in 1908 when extensive work was carried out under the direction of EJ Toye. He extended the church, most notably by the construction of a further transept to produce a double-gabled transept. The result of this work is that the church is an elongated T-shape, with the altar on what is effectively the long wall. At the same time as these enlargements, Toye added the copper-covered cupola to the roof. The church is constructed of local whinstone, with sandstone surrounds to the windows. Such random rubble stone as is used came from the demolished gaol at Lifford. The tympana of the doors are filled with representations of ancient Irish saints. The exception is the tympanum of the main west door, which shows the Virgin and Child.

Internally, the integrated sanctuary/transept area has almost overpowering decoration, which contrasts with the austerity of the long nave. The church proliferates

The altar of Derry's Long Tower church, which incorporates capitals given by the Earl-Bishop of Derry.

with stations and other religious paintings in oil. The high altar has a very fine baldachino composed of four fluted columns with gilded Corinthian capitals supporting a dentilled entablature. These are the capitals which were the gift of the Church of Ireland Earl-Bishop of Derry. The baldachino is flanked on each side by three unfluted marble columns. The altarpiece, and its attendant paintings were the work of McEvoy of Dublin, and are of oils painted on copper. Above the baldachino is a representation of the Last Supper, also by McEvoy. The altar frontal, carved by Edmund Sharpe of Dublin, depicts the death of St Columba. The ceiling of the church is coved and is richly decorated with an ornate cornice. Two Corinthian columns support the ceiling at the valleys between the double transepts. At the south-east corner is a charming apsidal chapel. Judging by the subject of the windows here, this must have served originally as a baptistry, although it now houses a fine copy of the Book of Kells.

Much of the rich stained glass in the church is the work of Earley of Dublin, although the gallery windows are by Meyer of Munich. By contrast the tall sashed round-headed windows in the nave are clear.

St Columba's contains a number of items of statuary presented by past parishioners, but two monuments are particularly worthy of note. That commemorating Rev Hugh Monaghan (died 1838) shows a female figure holding a cross and chalice, while the monument to Rev William McDonagh (died 1839) has a woman praying by an urn. Both monuments employ the allegorical device of upturned torches.

This church is not, and in appearance probably never was, a typical 'penal chapel'. This was dictated by the circumstances under which it was built. In the latter years of the eighteenth century there seems to have been a large degree of religious harmony in the city. The Church of Ireland bishop had an enlightened view as regards religious toleration, and in 1789 the entire citizenry and their clergy were able to gather as one and celebrate the centenary of the raising of the siege. St Columba's cost £2800 to build, which was a hefty amount in the 1780s, so obviously money was available to enable the building of a more substantial and ornate church than its simple rural contemporaries.

■ **References**
Rowan, pp 385–6; UAHS (Derry), pp 31–2.

RADEMON NON-SUBSCRIBING PRESBYTERIAN CHURCH
Rademon, Listooder, near Crossgar, County Down   *Non-Subscribing Presbyterian*

FROM THE outside, this robust church building could easily be mistaken for a very substantial farmhouse, presenting, as it does, a long facade two storeys high and eight windows in width. Originally a Presbyterian meeting house, the architecture reflects that denomination's emphasis on preaching rather than visual ostentation. Indeed, the centrality of preaching is very obvious here, as this is a T-shaped meeting house, with all the seating in the building facing the very tall pulpit. The T-plan was a feature of Scottish Presbyterian meeting houses, and the origin of the influx of settlers into County Down is echoed in the places of worship which they built.

An examination of the stonework of the northern arm of the T-plan reveals that the present building had a predecessor on the same site. An inscription stone placed over the main entrance tells the tale of the current structure: 'This House was Built in the Year of Our Lord 1787 which was the 21st year of the Revd Moses Nelson's [sic] Ministry in this Place'.

The church is built of rubble with pinnings and has sandstone dressings. The main facade is eight bays wide, with semicircular-headed windows. These all have Georgian Gothic glazing, sashed on the ground floor, but shorter and unsashed on the upper level. The arched doorcase contains a spider-web fanlight and is surmounted by the inscription stone, which is decorated by crossed branches tied with ribbons. Each arm of the T-plan has an external flight of steps leading to a gallery.

Rademon Non-Subscribing Presbyterian Church.

The northern and eastern arms also have doors at ground level to give access to the aisles. A similar door existed on the western arm, but this was subsequently built up.

Internally, the church is well maintained and retains the air and appearance of an eighteenth-century meeting house. As was the norm in T-shaped meeting houses, the pulpit prominently occupies the centre of the long wall. It is of semi-octagonal plan, with stairs flanked by moulded balusters and has a panelled back-board enriched with fluted Ionic pilasters. Above this is the sounding board decorated with a dentilled cornice. On the gallery front immediately opposite is a splendid clock inscribed: 'Ann 23 Ministerii Mos Neilson AD 1789'. Apparently, even after two centuries this clock still keeps remarkably good time. There are box pews throughout, those in the extremes of the aisles being raised, one of which has been cleverly and sensitively converted into a small minister's room. The galleries are carried on slender timber columns with moulded capitals, while the actual gallery fronts are decorated with criss-cross railings. The ceiling is flat and is decorated by a large central boss with acanthus leaves enclosed in a key-patterned border. The congregation retains its collecting shovels and extensive set of communion pewter.

In the graveyard stands a separate session house and minister's room, and nearby is the sunken entrance to the family vault of the Rev Moses Neilson. Attractively situated along a wall-lined lane, Rademon Non-Subscribing Presbyterian Church really does merit a visit to gain a glimpse of what a rural Ulster preaching house would have been like in the late eighteenth century.

■ **References**
ASCD, pp 348–9; UAHS (East Down), p 51.

THE NEILSONS OF RADEMON

THE PRESBYTERIAN Nelson family included many scholars and educationalists, the most famous of which were Moses and his son William who chose to be known as Neilson. As well as founding the church at Rademon, near Crossgar in County Down, Rev Moses Neilson established a teaching academy there, where local people of all denominations could be educated. He was chosen as Moderator in 1797–98. His son William wrote *An Introduction to the Irish Language* (Dublin, 1808) while helping his father with the teaching at Rademon. A minister in Dundalk, William Neilson became the youngest Moderator of the Presbyterian church, in 1806, at the age of thirty-one. He used to preach sometimes for his father at Rademon and was accustomed to doing so in Irish. In the unsettled year of 1798, he was arrested while preaching

in Irish, but was released after confirming his loyalty to the crown. A classical scholar, he took up a senior post briefly in the Belfast Academical Institution before dying, aged forty-seven, in 1821. His father Moses, at the age of eighty-two, took over his classes until a replacement could be found.

■ **References**
Blaney, R, *Presbyterians and the Irish Language* (Belfast, 1996), pp 56–65; Ó Saothraí, Séamus, *An Ministir Gaelach Uilliam Mac Néill (1774–1821)* (Belfast, 1992).

William Neilson

RANDALSTOWN 'OLD CONGREGATION' PRESBYTERIAN CHURCH
Portglenone Road, Randalstown, County Antrim
Presbyterian

THIS ELLIPTICAL church is highly individualistic and thoroughly charming, and is the meeting place for Randalstown's 'Old Congregation', a body which dates back to 1655. A plaque over the entrance door indicates that the church was 'Built in 1790, Thomas Henry, Minister'. According to the Ordnance Survey Memoir the construction cost £600 and the foundation stone was laid on 12 July 1790.

The appearance of the church has been subject to change since its construction, so it is useful to describe it first in its present state. The body of the church is an oval, built of brown basalt rubble with a slated roof. On the longer front section of the oval is a hexagonal porch, also of basalt, which is crowned by a pleasant hexagonal cupola. The sides of the cupola are pierced by louvred sound openings for the bell and Georgian Gothic glazed

windows. The main windows in both church and porch are pointed and have Y-tracery, while there is a row of oculus windows lighting the internal gallery. Particularly pretty is the oval window with interlacing glazing bars placed over the front door. Although the most substantial part of the building dates from 1790, the porch is an addition of 1830, while the upper sections of wall and the oculus windows were successfully and discreetly added in 1929, matching stone being brought from ruined cottages near Lough Neagh. Before this time, the church had a steeper roof and a lower cupola, and old photographs show a building with a rather hunch-backed appearance.

Inside the porch rises a steep double staircase giving access to the gallery, winding its way around the bell-rope which hangs down the centre of the porch. The body of

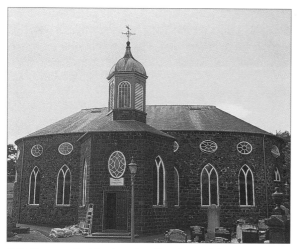

'Old Congregation' Presbyterian Church, Randalstown.

position on the 'long wall', surrounded by a gallery, which in this case stops two windows short of either side of the pulpit, and which has an undulating panelled front and is carried on cast iron fluted columns with bell capitals. The pews are arranged to focus on the pulpit and there is a long aisle running between the side doors. The vast flat expanse of ceiling is relieved only by a central plaster rose. At the rear is the pretty session house, which is also the result of the 1929 alterations. It is two storeys in height, with a curved roof and square-headed windows filled with Georgian Gothic sashed glazing.

Although it can be categorised as a vernacular church, this building is of significance principally for the ingenuity of its design, and the manner in which the familiar elements of a meeting house have been touched by inventiveness.

the church is entered through a set of doors which incorporate Gothic glazing. The internal arrangements are very much as would be found in a rectangular Presbyterian church of this date, with the pulpit in a focal

■ References

Brett (Antrim), pp 40–1; Killen, p 221; OSM (Vol 19, Antrim VI), p 42; UAHS (Antrim and Ballymena), p 25.

ST JOSEPH'S CHURCH, POYNTZPASS
Chapel Street, Poyntzpass, County Down

Catholic

ALTHOUGH THE physical appearance of this church has changed since its construction in 1794, it remains a building of the penal era and retains a number of features of interest. A lease was signed on 9 June 1792 for a 'Piece of ground designed for a Chapel and Chapel Yard'. Among the signatories were Fr John Maguire and the local landlord Alexander Thomas Stewart. He had been out on a walk one day and was touched to see the devotion of his Catholic tenants worshipping in the open air.

It is related locally that, during construction of the church, the masons were also working their way through a bottle of whiskey. To their horror, the priest paid them a visit, and the bottle had to be hidden in the wall. As it became clear that he was in no hurry to leave the site, they had no choice but to build the bottle into the wall!

When first constructed, the church was a fairly typical 'penal chapel', with the altar on a side wall, two doors on the facing wall and a gallery at each end. The south wall still retains two pointed windows, the spacing of which suggests that the altar stood between them. Photographs taken at the begining of the twentieth century show St Joseph's as it was until 1907. It was harled and

St Joseph's Catholic Church, Poyntzpass.

whitewashed, with a hipped roof with stepped gables on the projecting porches, which were surmounted by a cross. In these photographs a sundial is evident on the north wall. This still exists and was made in 1817 by one Thomas McCreash, dated and bearing the name of Father Henry Campbell. It reminds us of the passage of time and our mortality with the words, 'Memento Mori'. McCreash also made sundials for the local Anglican church and the chapel at Mullaghglass. The windows of the church were originally filled with Georgian Gothic sashed glazing.

The alteration of these features presumably took place in 1907 as a window over the altar reads: 'Pray / for the intention of Ann Theresa Murray / Girvan Scotland / Benefactor to this church 1907'. The work involved removing the stepped gables and making the easternmost door into a window. The end walls were provided with gables, with three small lancet windows in the eastern end

and an oculus window on the west. Internally, the eastern gallery was removed and the church given a longitudinal layout. However, it would appear that the western gallery, approached by a balustraded staircase, is original.

The church possesses a ciborium, dated 1807 and 1808.

■ References

Anderson, M, *St Joseph's, Poyntzpass* (Newry, 1996), pp 9, 38, 39.

TYRONE'S DITCHES PRESBYTERIAN CHURCH

Tyrone's Ditches Road, Drumbanagher, about three miles off the A1 dual carriageway, County Armagh   *Presbyterian*

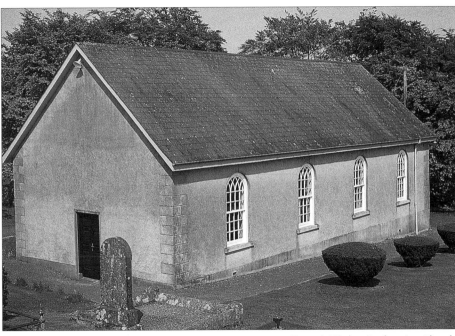

THE CONGREGATION which meets in this venerable building was originally known as Drumbanagher, and first acquired the name Tyrone's Ditches at the time of the ordination of Rev Samuel King in 1765. The present church was built in 1797 and hides itself from the country road in the protection of a large hollow. It is yet another example of the T-shaped meeting house, but it is a low structure without provision for galleries. The only alteration that seems to have taken place since its con-struction is the removal of the box pews and their replacement with bench pews. However, these follow traditional lines and are arranged to focus on the pulpit.

The church is roughcast with quoins at the corners, and has a slated roof. The long wall is of four bays facing the undulating graveyard, and all the windows are round-headed with Georgian Gothic sashed glazing. Internally, the church is very simple, having no porches or attached minister's room, although there is one nearby. The only noteworthy features are the ornate ceiling rosettes.

This is a little-known church, and difficult to find, with architectural features that take little time to describe.

Tyrone's Ditches Presbyterian Church.

However, as with so many churches in this book, it is not the appearance alone which strikes the visitor, but the atmosphere. An old building such as this, by its very survival, bears silent testimony to the past generations of worshippers who cared for it and who now lie at rest in its peaceful burial ground.

■ References

Killen, p 125.

COAGH PRESBYTERIAN CHURCH
Coagh, County Tyrone

Presbyterian

Coagh Presbyterian Church.

THE CONGREGATION at Coagh dates from 1708, although the present church building is probably of the late eighteenth century. The church sits at the head of a drive surrounded by beech trees, and has the simplicity of a New England preaching house. Its high half-hipped roof gives it very much the label of a 'barn' church. Although the walls are now painted, it was most likely to have been harled and whitewashed originally, which would have emphasised its rural appearance.

The church is basically a large hall, 54 feet by 56 feet. The facade is framed by quoins, and is five bays wide with two round-headed windows on either side of the central door, the fanlight of which is filled with ornate scroll-work. There are four windows on the side walls, which unfortunately have been glazed with uPVC imitation Georgian windows.

Box pews line the two aisles of the simple, but light, interior. There is no gallery: a rural church of this size would have no need for one. The only concession to ornamentation is the shallow arch behind the pulpit, which is supported on unfluted pilasters. The pulpit itself is obviously not original, but harmonises well with its surroundings. As with so many Presbyterian churches of this era, there is an extensive collection of communion pewter.

■ **References**
Killen, p 94; McCullough, pp 80–1, 85; Rowan, p 198.

ST TIERNEY'S CHURCH, ROSSLEA
Monaghan Road, Rosslea, County Fermanagh

Catholic

St Tierney's Catholic Church, Rosslea.

THIS IS a perfect pre-emancipation church, set in a lovely old graveyard shaded by mature trees. There are two very fine cut-stone gate piers, with a quaint stone stile to one side, giving access to the graveyard, which has an abundance of individualistic and finely-lettered old tombstones.

Lewis says of the church: 'The Roman Catholic Chapel is a very handsome edifice of stone, with a campanile turret: the interior is highly embellished; the windows are enriched with stained glass, and over the altar-piece is a fine painting'. St Tierney's Church was built in 1819, and was given its tower in 1834. This tower gives the visual impression that the interior of the church should be arranged longitudinally, but this is not the case. The church is rectangular, with four bays of pointed windows with Y-tracery. The window surrounds are quite elaborate, with fluted sandstone columns, as well as capitals and hood mouldings. The gable windows have Georgian Gothic sashed glazing. At one end is a two-storey porch with an oculus window and a castellated parapet. Presumably when the church was built there was a similar porch at the other end, but this has been replaced by the pinnacled tower. Over the tower door is a plaque which reads: 'Deo Optimo Maximo Dedicatum MDCCCXXXIV [1834]'. With the exception of the tower, the exterior of the church is roughcast.

The interior is a delight and, when full of worshippers, it still gives a feeling of what Catholic worship at the beginning of the nineteenth century must have been like, in spite of the use of modern liturgy. The altar is placed on the long east wall, the most prominent feature of the altar-piece being the dark and intriguing oil painting of the Crucifixion. This painting is mounted within two fluted Doric columns which support a broken pediment. On either side are two fluted pilasters which carry a dentilled entablature, all painted white with the panelling picked out in beige, as is the gallery front. The actual altar, ambo and seat are modern, but being of white marble they are unobtrusive in their surroundings. A raked gallery runs around the other three walls of the interior and is carried on seven quatrefoil columns. The open king-post roof appears to be original, but the internal slope has been panelled at some stage.

Next to the church is the old schoolhouse which has been converted for use as a local heritage centre.

■ References
Lewis, Vol 2, p 538; McCullough, p 81; Rowan, p 479.

ST JAMES' CHURCH, ALDERGROVE
Aldergrove near Glenavy, County Antrim

Catholic

THERE IS some confusion as to the actual date of construction of this unspoilt penal chapel. The Ordnance Survey Memoir claims that the church was built in 1802 on the site of one burnt in 1798. However, O'Laverty in his history, *Diocese of Down and Connor*, says that the first church at Aldergrove was erected by a Fr Crangle who died in 1814. O'Laverty goes on to speak of 'the present church, erected by Father McMullan in 1824'. Whatever the precise date, this is certainly a building of the early nineteenth century, erected before the Catholic Emancipation Act.

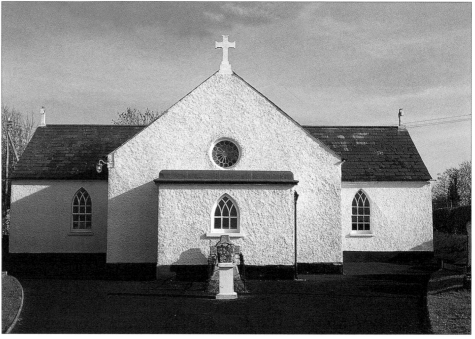

St James' Catholic Church, Aldergrove. This photograph was taken in 1996, before an arson attack seriously damaged this beautiful little building. It has now been reconstructed.

St James' is a cruciform church, with the internal appearance of a T-plan chapel, as the arm behind the altar serves as a sacristy. Just as it was at the time of the Ordnance Survey Memoir, the church is 'roughcast and neatly whitened', with very pretty Georgian Gothic sashed windows with clear glass. The only hint of any architectural adventure is the oculus window above the porch. Each gable is surmounted by a simple white cross.

White is the predominant colour of the interior, the exception being the wall behind the altar, which is maroon. This shows the pristine white reredos off to advantage. The pews are of light oak and sit on a red tiled floor. At the top of the main aisle are two memorial slabs let into the floor. One marks the burial place of Rev James McMullan, who died in 1841. The other slab marks the resting place of someone named Kerr, but the inscription is virtually indecipherable. The low gallery is later than the rest of the church, but fits in quite nicely, being fronted with elegant balusters, all painted white. The rail enclosing the altar displays carving similar to that in the

gallery, but it is stained rather than painted. The altar is made of timber with exquisite Gothic tracery. On either side of the sanctuary is a gilded column flanking the altar and the doors to the sacristy. The stations (which are presumably not original) have also been painted white. Quite intriguing is the holy water stoup in the aisle wall, which incorporates a piece of roughly-hewn stone. This was brought here, according to O'Laverty, by Rev James McMullan, it having originated in the old church at Templepatrick. At the back of the aisle, near the door, is a simple white oval font resting on a pedestal, which was brought here in 1933 and is believed to have originated at the old church at Gartree, County Antrim.

This beautiful little church was seriously damaged by fire in 1997 and has since been the subject of restoration when alterations were made to the altar and the entrance porch.

■ References
Brett (Antrim), p 42; OSM (Vol 21, Antrim VII), p 82; O'Laverty, pp 329, 333; UAHS (West Antrim), pp 10, 27.

4

Eighteenth-Century Classical Churches

THE EIGHTEENTH century was the age of enlightenment, and there was an increased focus upon the civilisations of ancient Rome and Greece. It was felt that 'reason', a guiding principle in those civilisations, could once more prevail. This interest in the classical period extended beyond political theory to literature, art and architecture, both domestic and ecclesiastical. In Dublin a programme of church building commenced, with input from architects such as Thomas Burgh, Isaac Wills and Edward Lovett Pearce, who is said to have supervised the building of Downpatrick Parish Church in 1735. The use of Gibbsian surrounds to the windows here suggests the influence of James Gibbs' *Book of Architecture.* In the eighteenth century we do not see the widespread use of Roman or Greek porticoes which would mark Presbyterian church architecture a century later, but rather there was an application of sophisticated classical elements to the traditional rectangular form. Throughout the century, architects such as Cassels, Cooley, Mulholland and Johnston designed churches, but frequently it is not possible to name the architect, and it is apparent that many churches were the result of a builder making use of a pattern book. Gibbsian surrounds were prominently used by Michael Priestley at St John's, Ballymore, and to the English traveller of the mid eighteenth century these would have seemed rather archaic. Neo-classicism advanced more slowly in Ireland than in England. Here the restraint of the classical Ulster church is encountered more often than the self-assurance of a Wren church.

Among the earliest excursions into classicism is the

St John's (C of I) Church, Moira.

Church of Ireland church of St John, Moira, County Down. As with the majority of Church of Ireland classical and 'Gothick' churches of the period, this is simply a

49

rectangular hall. Its rectangular parameters are so rigid that the tower is virtually flush with the facade, projecting from it only slightly. The architect is not known, and it appears that the front of the church may have been pieced together from pattern books. Perhaps the best feature is the doorcase, which is segmental-arched with moulded architrave and key-block, framed with pilasters. These support an entablature with triglyphed frieze and dentilled cornice; the key-block and spandrels have acanthus carvings. For its rural setting and date, this is a very commendable piece of neo-classicism and would have competed favourably with many a Dublin doorcase of the time. The remainder of the facade is enriched with cut-stone window surrounds, string-course and quoins, but is not well articulated. It may be useful at this point to allow Moira Parish Church to give us an insight as to the internal arrangements of a classical eighteenth-century Anglican Ulster church.

The churches were invariably rectangular, being comprised of a tower, in the foot of which was a vestibule, flanked by vestries or by gallery access; the church proper was a nave with an integral chancel. In some cases, such as Knockbreda and Hilltown, there was a chancel appended to the nave. The liturgical arrangements of the interior differed little from the plantation churches; a central aisle led the worshippers' attention to the holy table behind its rails; the three-decker pulpit occupied one of the long walls. The difference between a plantation church and a classical church was in the decoration. The west gallery, which held the organ, would have been carried on fluted or unfluted columns, the capitals of which would have been of the Doric, Ionic or Corinthian orders. Rather than exposing the basic roof structure to the genteel parishioners, the ceiling would have been barrel-vaulted in plaster, its edge daintily trimmed with a delicate plasterwork cornice, and enriched at its highest point with radiating rosettes. A feature almost universally found in the chancel was the articles of faith, as at Moira. It was essential for an Anglican to know and embrace the Lord's Prayer, the Ten Commandments and the Apostles' Creed. The ideal place to exhibit these was on the reredos behind the holy table, making the area enclosed within the rails the focal point of worship. The display of these articles was not, of course, confined to classical buildings, for they still survive, for example, at the 'Gothick' church of Lisnadill, County Armagh.

Given that Moira represents an early attempt at a hall and tower classical church, it is fair to see it as a prototype for the progressively more architecturally correct churches at Knockbreda and Ballycastle. At Knockbreda, Richard

Cassels uses classical elements quite sparingly, but the chief success of his composition lies in his massing and the confidence with which he constructs his facade. Of interest too is the use of a broach spire. The prominent positioning of these classical churches – on a hill at Moira, in the market square at Hilltown and Ballycastle – reflects the visual importance of public buildings in Irish towns, which were also moulded in the classical idiom at this time.

Moira, Knockbreda and Ballycastle churches are progressively more successful in their use of classical elements and in their sense of adventure. Holy Trinity Church in Ballycastle has a fine cut-stone facade which is a compendium of classical architecture. It is all here: pediment, columns, quoins, architraves, Venetian window, balustrade and spire. Indeed, the tower of St Nicholas', Carrickfergus, has many common features with that at Ballycastle, suggesting a growing appreciation of the application of classical traits to the extent that they could even be used to adorn a medieval church.

As well as providing a prominent building, which reflected the church's position in society, a well-conceived structure reflected the importance and standing of the landlord who was instrumental in having it built. The wealthier the patron, the grander the church. It was Viscountess Middleton who built the church at Knockbreda, and the use of Richard Cassels, architect to the nobility, would have demonstrated how well connected she was. The pretensions of Hugh Boyd and Wills Hill, Earl of Hillsborough, can be seen in the churches they built in Ballycastle and Hilltown respectively. The Primate's Chapel at Armagh, completed in 1786, has been described as one of Ireland's finest classical ecclesiastical buildings. With its exquisite Ionic facade, it almost represents a prototype for the sort of neo-classical churches which would be built, mainly for the nonconformist denominations, in the seventy years which followed. The Primate's Chapel was designed by Thomas Cooley and completed by Francis Johnston for Archbishop Richard Robinson, a cultured Englishman. The primate had peppered his archdiocese with 'Gothick' churches designed, or even mass-produced, by Cooley. It is interesting, therefore, that he should have chosen the classical style for his own place of worship. This is possibly explained by the fact that classical architecture reflected the ideals upon which the archbishop had improved the city. He rebuilt the Royal School, constructed the observatory and the public library, and planned a university. The city was to represent culture and learning, and a chapel built as a Roman temple fitted perfectly into this setting. Besides this, country churches built in a 'Gothick' style and a private chapel in the classical manner served also to reflect the diversity of Robinson's taste and breadth of knowledge.

Roger Mulholland's Rosemary Street First Presbyterian Church (Belfast, 1783), is an important building, not only for its fine physical appearance, but because it stands as an introduction to the neo-classicism which was to become associated with the architecture of nonconformist churches in the first half of the nineteenth century. Mulholland endowed Belfast with an elegant building, which has been slightly disimproved by later hands. His facade, replaced in 1833, was a well-behaved lesson in classicism, employing rustication, pilasters and pediment, all arranged with symmetrical precision. JS Curl describes the building as 'perhaps the most distinguished of the Presbyterian churches built in the eighteenth century'. With its elliptical plan, curves and undulating balcony front, there can be few other Presbyterian churches of the period to equal it, especially as Curl says that its sophistication suggests Bavarian Rococo.

Applied to traditional church structures, the classical architectural vocabulary enriched the appearance of ecclesiastical buildings in a period of relative peace in the country. The idiom allowed churches to make a positive and graceful contribution to the physical landscape. Whereas they had formerly been rather gloomy functional buildings which seemed to cower in an apprehensive and defensive fashion, they now exhibited the confidence of the church and its adherents.

■ **References**
Curl, p 13; Loane, pp 4–5; McCullough, p 77.

ST JOHN'S PARISH CHURCH, MOIRA
Main Street, Moira, County Down

Church of Ireland

A DEED dated 16 November 1722 marks the foundation of the parish of Moira, and it was in the following year that the parish church of St John was built. Since that time the facade of the church has suffered only minor changes. The church is well sited at the head of a long expanse of grass, with an avenue to one side that forms a visual link with the grounds of Moira Demesne across the road. Although this is still a fine setting, regrettably a number of intrusive developments in recent years have tended to hem in the church. The structure of the building is simple enough, a rectangular hall with a square tower and spire at the west end. It is the main facade which renders the building so interesting, as it presents an early attempt at true architectural elegance, even if the various elements are not well articulated. The facade is three bays wide and two storeys high, with a pediment breaking against the sides of the tower. The central doorway is particularly striking, being composed of unfluted pilasters supporting a triglyphed frieze, dentilled cornice and segmental pediment. The key-block and the spandrels have acanthus decoration. On the ground storey, segmental-arched windows with key-blocks flank this door, and these are similar to the windows above.

A frequent criticism of the design of the church is that the central window on the upper storey is awkwardly dissected by the top of the doorcase, but it would appear that this window was not part of the original plan. Writing in 1957, the then rector of the parish, Rev H Hughes, states that this window was added in 1877 to provide additional internal light after the gallery was in-

The west door of Moira (C of I) Parish Church.

stalled. Indeed, this is verified by a glance at a mid nineteenth-century engraving of the church, which shows the facade without the offending window. The engraving also shows the original slate-hung spire, which was destroyed in a gale in 1884. This was replaced by the present copper-clad spire, which is lower than the original. The reduction in the height of the spire, and the choice of covering, serve to emphasise the somewhat graceless quality of the tower.

The facade is enriched with stone dressings, and the wall areas are roughcast. Despite the shortcomings of the overall design, this has to be admired as a serious early attempt to create a classical facade, and given that the name of the architect involved is not known, it may be reasonable to assume that this is the work of a skilled local mason acting as amateur architect. The remainder of the exterior is undistinguished, the side walls each containing three segmental-headed windows with key-blocks, and the east window being semicircular-headed, again with a key-block.

The nave of the church has a central aisle, leading the eye directly to the beautiful reredos, enclosed within a semicircular railing. The railing and the nave doors are said to have come from the long-demolished Moira Castle. The exquisitely carved reredos is composed of three bays, the central bay being bounded by two fluted Corinthian columns and the outer ones enclosed by terminal fluted Corinthian pilasters. These carry a richly-carved frieze, festooned with swirls of foliage, at the centre of which is a vase flanked by cherubs. Above this is a dentilled and modillioned cornice. Each bay of the reredos serves as a written reminder of the articles of the Church of Ireland faith, as it is inscribed with the Lord's Prayer, the Ten Commandments and the Creed. Many Georgian churches would have had such a reredos, often in place of a window on the east wall, but at Moira there are both.

■ **References**
ASCD, p 330; Curl, p 8; Dixon, p 35.

HOLY TRINITY PARISH CHURCH, DOWNPATRICK
Church Street, Downpatrick, County Down *Church of Ireland*

THE STOUT tower of this church is said to have been one of the towers of John de Courcy's castle. This is fanciful, and it is more likely that the structure dates from 1560 when the first parish church, dedicated to St Margaret, was built. As indicated on the gate pier at the entrance to the churchyard, the edifice of 1560 was rebuilt (except for the tower), in 1735, when work is said to have been supervised by Sir Edward Lovett Pearce.

The exterior has an austere classical appearance, being a large rectangular hall of slightly coursed rubble, with a three-stage battlemented western tower, which is inset at each storey. The windows have Gibbsian surrounds, the eastern gable has a fine Venetian window and the corners of the walls have quoins; all are of sandstone. High up on the western nave wall are indications of two blocked-up windows, suggesting that the church may at one time have had a gallery. In the foot of the tower on the west side is the original broad pointed doorway, now Georgian-glazed, as is the present entrance, on the south side.

Inside, the church is a vast hall, rather clinical in appearance. There are three segmental-headed windows on the north side of the nave with Georgian glazing, while the four windows on the south side have Victorian diamond-shaped panes. When rebuilt in 1735, the

Downpatrick (C of I) Parish Church.

church had a tall pulpit placed on the south wall, surrounded by box pews. According to the Ordnance Survey Memoir there were fifty pews of 'irregular sizes', and these may have been dependent on family sizes and pew rents. Although work was carried out in 1834, when the present flat plaster ceiling was installed, the bench pews appear to be later Victorian. The ceiling has a very plain cornice and five plaster rosettes; all very seemly except that there is a break at the eastern end to prevent the ceiling from truncating the east window. Notable among the furnishings is the charming traceried organ case standing to the right of the communion table. Nearby on the north wall is a monument to George Scott Tate who was killed at the Punjab in 1889; this is decorated with two military helmets. Opposite is a large and well-painted memorial to Dean John McNeal (died 1709), which has a large scallop shell rising from a pediment carried on Tuscan columns.

During the course of its history, this parish church has had to facilitate some of the functions of the cathedral, which was in ruins until 1790.

■ **References**
ASCD, pp 324–5; OSM (Vol 17, Down IV), pp 40–1; UAHS (Downpatrick), pp 28–9.

KNOCKBREDA PARISH CHURCH
Church Road, Knockbreda, Belfast   *Church of Ireland*

KNOCKBREDA PARISH Church was built in 1737 by Anne, Viscountess Middleton, on a site presented by her son, Arthur Hill, Viscount Dungannon. With a wealthy patron it is no surprise that a renowned architect was employed. He was Richard Cassels, a native of Hesse-Cassel and a prolific architect in Dublin, responsible for a number of great country houses, such as Carton, near Maynooth. Although obviously a talented architect, he rarely allowed his buildings to display much more than an air of competence.

The facade of Knockbreda Church is of two storeys and three bays and gains a progressive vertical thrust from the triangular pediment of the doorcase, reflected by the pediment at eaves level and crowned by a broach spire. The entrance doorcase has a Gibbsian surround. As completed, Cassel's design had a square chancel and apsidal transepts. The first post-Reformation church in Ireland to have an apse was St Ann's Church in Dawson Street in Dublin, completed in 1720, and it is tempting to speculate that this influenced Cassel's plans. The original layout of the church was altered, quite sensitively, in 1883 by Sir Thomas Drew. His work involved the construction of an apsidal chancel and a west gallery.

On entering the building the visitor is struck by the darkness of the interior, and this is entirely due to the Victorian stained glass. The nave and transepts are barrel-vaulted in plaster and groined at the intersections, while the chancel has a similar ceiling, but at a slightly lower level. A dentilled cornice runs around the entire circuit of the building, while the chancel also has a modillioned entablature, supported on six pairs of Ionic pilasters. The church interior is further enhanced by the dramatic changes in level, both the transepts and chancel being raised above the nave. The west gallery, added in 1883, is panelled and behind it rise two slightly over-sized

Knockbreda (C of I) Church, designed by Cassels.

Ionic columns. It could be that they are original and lost their bottom halves when the gallery was installed.

All the monuments in the south transept, which are in a simple classical style, commemorate the Kinahan family, while those in the north transept are to members of the Bateson family of Belvoir, nearby. However, the most interesting memorial is that on the south wall of the chancel which perpetuates the memory of Arthur, first Viscount Dungannon, whose grandson was the illustrious Duke of Wellington.

The churchyard surrounding the church is notable for its wealth of funerary monuments, particularly the late eighteenth-century mausoleums. The recent over-zealous tidying of the churchyard has regrettably robbed it of much of its character.

■ **References**
ASCD, pp 333–4; Carmody, WP, *History of the Parish of Knockbreda* (Belfast, 1929), pp 13–15; Curl, p 8; Dixon, p 35; Harris, pp 72–3; Larmour, p 105.

ST JOHN'S PARISH CHURCH, BALLYMORE
Ballymore, off N6 south of Dunfanaghy, County Donegal *Church of Ireland*

THIS RATHER lonely church serves the parish of Clondehorky and was built in 1752 to replace an older place of worship at Dunfanaghy, the ruins of which can still be seen. The Board of First Fruits gave the parish £300 towards the cost of building some time prior to 1766, and possibly even before 1745, when plans were being made to construct the present church.

As it stands, St John's was designed by Michael Priestley of Derry. Like the other remaining examples of his work (Lifford Court House and Port Hall House), this church borrows its key architectural elements from James Gibbs' Book of Architecture, 1728. Given that the exterior of the church is simply a rendered hall, it is the detail that lifts the building. The four segmental-headed sashed windows on the south wall and the massive Venetian east window (also sashed) are all graced with heavy Gibbsian surrounds. This form of external ornament would have appeared rather tired had this church been built in England, but in the remoteness of mid eighteenth-century Donegal it must have seemed quite sophisticated. On the west gable is a stone bellcote which has rather an Italianate air about it. Below this is a later porch with another Venetian window. Attached to the north side of the church is a single-storey vestry room, added by Joseph Welland in 1853.

The visitor is struck by the bright, spacious quality of the interior, helped by the very generous proportions of the windows, especially the east window, which dominates not only the east wall, but the whole interior. The woodwork throughout is of very high quality, and it is likely that the pews were once of the box variety, and have simply had their doors removed. The gallery at the

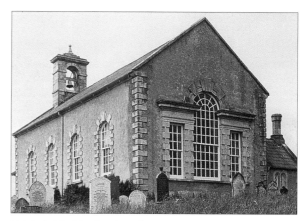

St John's (C of I) Church, Ballymore.

west end is carried on fluted columns which are capped by bell capitals. Panelled wainscoting covers the walls to a height of about 6 feet. On the north wall are four segmental-headed recesses to balance the appearance of the windows on the south wall. Of course, the architect could just as easily have provided four windows here, but it was quite often the practice in Georgian church-building to have a solid north wall to spare the parishioners the fury of the north wind. The communion table is placed within a wooden rail and backed by a pedimented reredos.

St John's is a fine example of a rural Ulster Georgian Church of Ireland church.

■ **References**
de Breffny p 118; Rowan, pp 123–4.

HOLY TRINITY CHURCH, BALLYCASTLE
The Diamond, Ballycastle, County Antrim *Church of Ireland*

BEGINNING LIFE as a chapel to the parish of Ramoan, the classical church of the Holy Trinity was built in 1756 by the local landlord, Hugh Boyd, son of the Rev William Boyd, rector of Ramoan, 1679–81. It has been described as 'probably the best church, architecturally, in the county'; indeed, the elements composing the facade read like an inventory of classical features.

The church is entered through an elegant pedimented

doorcase carried on fluted Doric half-columns. While the pediment is dated 1756, the entablature is inscribed: 'Fear God / Honour the King'. Stone plaques above the flanking square-headed doors also carry biblical quotations. That on the north reads: 'Keep thy foot when thou / goest to the House of God and / be more ready to hear than / to give the sacrifice of fools'. And on the south: 'Not forsaking the / assembling of our / selves together'. The tower projects forward from these flanking walls and the gable is cut by the tower. Above the central door is a Venetian window with blind side lights. This in turn is surmounted by a large clock-face, oversized so as to be seen from a distance. On the south face of the tower is a sun-dial. The tower is capped by a balustrade which encloses the foot of the octagonal spire. The whole facade, while not on a large scale, is a lesson in the articulation of classical elements. In 1761 the tower was provided with a ring of five bells cast by Lester and Pack of London, only one of which still survives, along with two later bells. It is inscribed: 'LESTER AND PACK LONDON FECIT 1761'.

The fine west door is reflected by a matching doorcase inside the church at the west end of the nave. This door is flanked by two arches. The church was repewed and the east end rearranged in 1875, but the original wainscoting seems to survive on the nave walls. The four round-headed windows on the nave walls each have architraves and keystones and are connected by a dado. The ceiling is a barrel-vault rising from the plain cornice and is decorated with a radiating rosette which incorporates a Greek key pattern. At the east end is a shallow apse with a semi-domed ceiling which is painted in a deep blue with gold stars. The soffit of the chancel arch is enriched with plaster rosettes and the keystone has the Chi Rho. The keystone of the central of the three east windows has the

symbols of Alpha and Omega, as does the pilastered reredos. The chancel fittings are all Victorian, but the octagonal carved wooden pulpit (presented in 1875) is a rather good example of its type and is in memory of Rev Hugh McNeile, Dean of Ripon.

The monuments on the nave walls all commemorate members of the Boyd family, whose connection with the church has held since its construction to the present day.

Ballycastle Parish Church – a well-executed classical front.

■ **References**
Brett (Antrim), p 31; de Breffny, p 127; Dukes, p 50; UAHS (North Antrim), p 46.

SYMBOLS

The **CHI RHO** is a symbol particularly found in the sanctuary areas of Church of Ireland and Catholic churches. It is a combination of two Greek letters, X (Chi) and P (Rho), representing the first two letters of Christ's name.

ALPHA and **OMEGA**, the first and last letters of the Greek alphabet represent God, almighty and eternal (Revelations Ch 21 v 6), as the beginning and end of everything. Alpha and Omega can be seen on the altars and communion tables and in the stained glass in churches of most of the major denominations.

The **BURNING BUSH** is the symbol of the Presbyterian Church in Ireland and also of those churches of Presbyterian theology. The account of the burning bush is found in the book Exodus when God spoke to Moses. The inscription under the bush, 'Ardens Sed Virens', 'burning but living', refers to the ongoing life of the church, even during times of persecution. This symbol can often be seen on pulpits or in stained-glass windows.

The **SACRED MONOGRAM** (IHS), usually found in Catholic or Church of Ireland churches represents the first three capitals of the Greek version of the name Jesus, and also of the phrase, 'Jesus our Saviour'.

In many churches, the symbol of the fish may be found, and this is a very ancient Christian symbol. The fish is known as **ICTHUS**, the letters denoting the Greek initials for 'Jesus Christ God's Son Saviour' and was used by the early Christians as a secret code to enable them to identify their co-religionists at times of persecution.

■ **References**
Ellwood Post, W, *Saints, Signs and Symbols* (London, 1964).

Icthus

Chi Rho and Alpha and Omega

Burning bush

The Sacred Monogram

ST RONAN'S PARISH CHURCH, COLEBROOKE

Colebrooke, Aghalurcher off the A4 to Enniskillen, County Fermanagh *Church of Ireland*

VISIBLE FOR miles around due to its crowning position on a hilltop, this church is of interest for its fine eighteenth-century classical appearance, as well as its associations with the Brooke family.

St Ronan's was built in 1762 with the help of £200 from the Board of First Fruits. Given its rather remote setting, the church is incredibly large and is composed of a four-bay nave, with a tower and spire, a north transept and a projecting chancel, all with very fine cut-stone detail. The tower is of three stages, of rubble construction with quoins, string-courses, Gibbsian window surrounds and a parapet with blind arcading and pinnacles. On the ground floor is a pleasant little Diocletian window. The whole structure is topped by an octagonal spire. There are Gibbsian surrounds to the nave windows, and the similarities in style and date would lead one to speculate that the same hand was at work here as at Lisbellaw Church. The nave is of coursed rubble and has pedimented gables, the southern one being broken by the off-centre tower. At the other end, the pediment holds an oculus window, and is reflected by the smaller pedimented gable of the chancel.

The interior of the church has been subject to alteration, most notably in 1873, and it can be assumed that the shallow vaulted timber roof and trusses date from this time, as do the bench pews. The chancel is set behind a broad round-headed arch and has a barrel-vaulted ceiling.

The church's connection with the Brooke family is reflected by the raised family pew which occupies the

north transept. Above this, on the nave wall, hang banners relating to notable members of the family, including banners of the Order of the Garter and the Order of the Bath, which were held by Field Marshal Viscount Alanbrooke and the banner of the Order of the Garter, held by Basil, first Viscount Brookeborough, Prime Minister of Northern Ireland,

St Ronan's (C of I) Church, Colebrooke.

1943–63. Other members of the family are recalled by wall monuments: that to Lieutenant Francis Brooke, who fell at Waterloo, shows a horse without its rider. Sir Henry Brooke (died 1834) and his wife Harriot (died 1836) are commemorated by a sarcophagus holding two draped urns, flanked by the allegorical figures of Hope and Charity, who has two infants. The monument includes a badger, which can be found elsewhere in the church, as it is the emblem of the Brooke family.

■ **References**
Lewis, Vol 1, p 16; Rowan, p 201.

LISBELLAW PARISH CHURCH

Lisbellaw, County Fermanagh *Church of Ireland*

ACCORDING TO Lewis, this church was built in 1764 by the first Earl of Ross, who is buried in the vault below. The three-bay roughcast nave must date from this time, and it has segmental-headed windows with Gibbsian surrounds, quoins and eaves cornice, while the contemporary chancel has a Venetian window. The Gibbsian treatment to the windows is rather similar to those at Colebrooke Parish Church, which is of roughly the same date. This suggests that the same local craftsman

carried out the work.

The building, which sits on top of a hill, was rendered L-shaped in 1793 by the addition of a north transept, with eaves cornice and windows similar to those on the nave. While this extension blends in well with the earlier work, the same cannot be said of the west tower which was built in 1894. Apparently there had always been a tower, but the present three-stage rubble structure does tend to detract from the classical grace of the rest of the

The interior of Lisbellaw (C of I) Church.

building, especially with its gaunt belfry windows.

Internally, the church is bright and, although remodelled in 1853, does retain its classical air. The visitor enters under the neo-Gothic wall-mounted organ case, and is immediately struck by the Venetian east window, with its Doric columns. It contains a depiction of the Ascension of Christ which was placed here in memory of the men of the parish killed in the First World War. The chancel itself is set apart from the nave by an arch, and its barrel-vaulted ceiling has a pleasant plaster vine and grape motif tied by a ribbon. The central nave window shows Christ as the Good Shepherd, and is in memory of Rev RJ St Leger, rector 1958–93.

The external appearance of the nave of Lisbellaw Church has some parallels with that at Ballymore, County Donegal, and shows the simple application of classical elements to churches in a rural setting.

■ **References**
Lewis, Vol 2, p 277; Rowan, p 356.

ST JOHN'S PARISH CHURCH, HILLTOWN
The Square, Hilltown, County Down

Church of Ireland

THIS PLAIN, yet handsome, small village church, sited in the market square, was built in 1766 by Wills Hill, Earl of Hillsborough, later the first Marquis of Downshire. This was a busy period of church-building for the earl, as he was also building the church at Hillsborough at the same time. As completed, St John's consisted of a four-bay nave with a small chancel and a square west tower. A small vestry was added to the south-east during the Victorian period. The exterior is now cement rendered and lined to simulate masonry, but would originally have been of stone. The pinnacles of the tower, the quoins, the dressings and the plinth upon which the building rests are all of granite.

The quoined tower is of three stages. The entrance is now by a semicircular-headed doorway on the north side, which is mirrored by a similar recess on the south. However, the original entrance was a square-headed doorway on the west face, which now presents only a recess. Each stage of the tower is marked by a string-course and is slightly offset. The second stage has circular openings on the north, south and west sides; that on the south is blocked and that on the north is now concealed by a clock face. The top stage has a semicircular-headed sound window with keystones on each face. Above is the parapet capped by a granite pinnacle at each corner. The

The sanctuary of St John's (C of I) Church, Hilltown.

nave is lighted by four semicircular-headed windows on each side.

Inside, the church is simple, but has an air of elegance. The nave is virtually a hall with a shallow barrel-vaulted ceiling, which rises above a dentilled cornice. Each window in the nave has moulded plaster surrounds, probably similar in date to the cornice. At the west end is an elegant pedimented doorcase supported on fluted pilasters with moulded capitals and bases. The chancel arch has fluted Doric pilasters supporting a fluted arch and what appears to be a later hood-mould proclaiming

'Holy, Holy, Holy, Lord God Almighty', and terminating in round bosses. The side walls of the chancel have panels which once bore the Lord's Prayer, the Ten Commandments and the Creed, as were often found in Georgian churches, serving as visual reminders of the Anglican articles of faith. The actual worded panels are now in Rathfriland Parish Church. The pews are of Victorian pine and no doubt replaced earlier box pews which, along with the octagonal pulpit, must have been installed about the same time as the construction of the vestry room. The font is also octagonal and is made from white marble on a round red granite shaft. Around the top of the font is the inscription, 'Suffer the little children to come unto me and forbid them not'. At this end of the church there are pews set in collegiate fashion for the choir, with a harmonium on the south side.

The single bell hanging in the tower was the gift of the Earl of Hillsborough and is inscribed 'Thomas Rudhall Glocester Founder 1772'. It was made at the same time as the peal of bells for Hillsborough Parish Church; the *Belfast News-letter* of 10 November 1772 records the arrival in Belfast of eight bells for Hillsborough and a bell for 'the church lately built by his lordship for the parish of Clonduff'.

At the time of writing, Hilltown Parish Church is no longer being used for services due to the decline of the congregation, but a local group has plans to convert the building for community use. It is to be hoped that this will come about, and that this fine old church may serve once more as a focal point in the area.

■ **References**
ASCD, pp 328–9; Barry, p 68; Curl, p 8;
UAHS (Rathfriland and Hilltown), p 20.

FIRST PRESBYTERIAN CHURCH, ROSEMARY STREET, BELFAST
Rosemary Street, Belfast   *Non-Subscribing Presbyterian*

OPENED ON 1 June 1783, and replacing an earlier meeting house, Rosemary Street church is the oldest place of worship in the city. The congregation had decided to build a new meeting house in 1781, and the architect appointed was Roger Mulholland, who was responsible for the imaginative elliptical plan. He had shown the church committee a model of how an elliptical rafter system could be built, and accordingly, on 12 May 1781, he was requested 'to alter the design of the new meeting house to be a perfect ellipsis'. Francis Hiorne of Warwick, engaged in the building of St Anne's Church, was thanked by the committee for submitting plans for their meeting house, and was asked 'to favour us with a plan of the seats in the manner he would think best to have them laid out'. Since plans came from a number of other sources, it is uncertain who was ultimately responsible for the seating arrangements.

Although the building has been subject to a number of changes since its completion, it is worth describing it in its original shape. It was admired by John Wesley, who preached in it in 1789, and also by the Earl-Bishop of Derry, who delighted in circular structures to the extent that he donated fifty guineas to the building work. The plan was an oval constructed in red brick, with a classical frontispiece accommodating a porch and session room. This facade comprised a rusticated ground floor surmounted by four Ionic pilasters carrying a pediment.

The interior was completely elliptical with a gracious canopied pulpit and a gallery carried on fourteen Corinthian columns and two terminal pilasters. Above, the ceiling had plaster panels and was supported on plaster vaults. Opposite the pulpit the gallery was swept forward and enriched with carved rosettes and urns. The entire building was seated with box pews and it was possible to circumnavigate the central oval of pews. The gallery windows were filled with semicircular-headed Georgian glazed windows, which have long since been replaced with frosted and patterned glass, much to the detriment of the interior.

It is assumed that the gallery was once accessed by a spiral staircase, and this situation was improved in 1833 by the erection of a new deeper portico, with stairs to the gallery and session room. This change necessitated the destruction of the original facade and the erection of the present stuccoed front with coupled Ionic pilasters and a balustraded parapet. While this is all quite seemly in itself, a perusal of old engravings indicates how graceful the facade once was.

The sounding board was removed from the pulpit in 1862 to allow a better view of the new Venetian window marking the fiftieth anniversary of the ordination of Rev William Bruce. However, the sounding board was retained and put to use as a sturdy table in the session room, where it can still be seen. In 1906–7 the most extensive and regrettable alteration took place with the provision of an extension behind the pulpit to hold a new organ. This involved breaking the ellipse, and although the line of display pipes of the organ cushion the effect slightly, this extension is rather awkward and necessitated the removal of the plaster vaults above the section of wall which was removed. The case of the Lewis organ sits within a panelled arch carried on unfluted pilasters, while the Venetian window behind peers timidly over the tops of the pipes.

The walls beneath the gallery have a very fine collection of neo-classical monuments, all of which are elegant, although some are of particular note. The monument to John Holmes Houston (died 1843) takes the form of a sarcophagus supporting a draped urn, protected by a pediment carried by four Corinthian columns. The Rev William Bruce (died 1841) is commemorated by a memorial designed by Sir Charles Lanyon. Again this has a pediment, but this time supported by two pilasters decorated with upturned torches, allegorical symbols of death. Patrick MacDowell was responsible for the fine memorial to William Tennent (died 1832), which shows the deceased sitting beneath the branch of a tree engrossed in a book. Mr Tennent was, according to the inscription, 'firm when exposed to the reactions of power'. This is a veiled reference to his radicalism in the 1798 period and it is said that meetings of the United Irishmen took place in the church. In the porch is the First World War Memorial, the work of Rosamund Praeger, depicting a heroic youth.

There are six stained glass windows within the body of the church, believed to have been designed by Meyer of Munich. The window in memory of Samuel Martin (died

The elliptical interior of Rosemary Street Non-Subscribing Presbyterian Church before the addition of the organ chamber.

1872), founder of the Sick Children's Hospital, fittingly depicts Jesus Christ surrounded by children. The Bruce window behind the organ was destroyed by a nearby bomb in 1972 and replaced by modern glass decorated with rosemary and ivy motifs, although it is difficult to see due to its position.

Despite the alterations made since 1783, 'First House' remains one of the most interesting churches in Belfast and stands as a good example of the work of Roger Mulholland.

■ **References**

Brett (Belfast), pp 5, 14; Curl, p 13; Larmour, p 3; Moore, T, *First Presbyterian Church, Belfast, 1644–1994* (Belfast, 1994), pp 17, 18, 33.

FORMER CHAPEL OF THE CHURCH OF IRELAND ARCHBISHOPS OF ARMAGH
Within the grounds of the offices of Armagh City Council, Palace Demesne, Armagh City
Church of Ireland

SITUATED AT the side of the former palace of the Archbishop of Armagh, this elegant private chapel reflects both the confidence of the established church in the eighteenth century and the exquisite taste of its creator Archbishop Richard Robinson.

Robinson, later Baron Rokeby, was an English cleric who became Archbishop of Armagh in 1765, a position which he held until his death in 1794. It was his wish that Armagh should become a dignified university city worthy of being a primatial see. He constructed a public library, an observatory and many of the other substantial

Georgian buildings which line the city streets. Unlike his predecessors, Robinson chose to reside in Armagh, and so needed a fitting residence and private chapel. Like the palace, the chapel is the work of Thomas Cooley, but was completed by Francis Johnston after Cooley's death in 1784. Considered to be 'one of the most superb examples of Georgian neo-classical architecture in Ireland', the chapel was completed in 1786.

The exterior is of dressed ashlar limestone, just like its palatial neighbour. The facade, which is on the east, to avoid turning its back on the palace, is composed of a flight of five steps, on the uppermost of which stand four columns with Ionic capitals supporting the pediment. The tall panelled entrance door is recessed behind the columns. The north and south walls each have four semicircular-headed windows, although an inspection of the interior shows that two of the windows on the north wall are false. The sanctuary is also lighted by a semicircular-headed window.

A vestibule leads straight into the chapel proper, and also to a staircase to the gallery on the left, or into what was probably a vestry room on the right. The chapel presents a delicate and airy combination of woodwork and plasterwork. The walls are divided by Corinthian pilasters resting on a podium of panelled waxed oak which rises to a height of about 1.5 metres. The stalls line the north and south sides of the interior, facing each other in collegiate fashion. On the south side there is a break in the stalls to accommodate a marble chimneypiece, while the same position on the north is occupied by the archbishop's throne. During worship the primate would have sat here like a spiritual squire, surrounded by his

The former Church of Ireland Archbishops' Chapel, Armagh.

household and lesser clerics. The throne consists of two fluted Corinthian columns surmounted by a broken pediment which bears a carved mitre. Like all the other woodwork, the throne is of waxed English oak, and of exceptional quality. The sanctuary area is closed by wrought iron communion rails with an oak top. The actual communion table and fittings are not original to the chapel, but are appropriate nonetheless. Like the two westernmost windows of the nave, the sanctuary window is filled with stained glass, installed in 1895 as a memorial to Primate Lord John George Beresford. The window was formerly filled with glass painted by Francis Egington of Birmingham, no doubt similar to his existing east window at Hillsborough.

At the opposite end of the chapel is a musicians' gallery, flanked by two Corinthian pilasters, bow-fronted and swathed with crimson drapes. The pair of carved Corinthian columns at the back of the gallery originated elsewhere, but are very fine and worthy of the building in which they stand. Above the gallery are two sets of plasterwork arms, one of Robinson as archbishop, the other of him as Baron Rokeby.

The chapel is paved with local limestone, chequered with smaller settings of black Kilkenny marble. The ceiling is a shallow coffered barrel vault, each coffer decorated with a plaster rosette.

Following the sale of the palace demesne to Armagh District Council in 1975, it is no longer permissible to use the chapel for religious purposes and it is now, quite fittingly, used for concerts and civic functions.

■ References
Curl, p 13; Stuart, p 446; UAHS (Armagh), pp 173–5.

The Archbishop's throne.

5
Eighteenth-Century Gothic Churches

ACCORDING TO DS Richardson, the troubles of the seventeenth century in Ireland brought to an end the age of Gothic architecture, which had been heralded by the Normans five centuries before and was characterised by the use of pointed windows. However, aspects of 'Planters' Gothic' suggest that there was an element of 'Gothic Survival', making the notion of a 'Gothic Revival' less clear cut. A look at what is known of the use of Gothic in Ulster in the eighteenth century gives a glimpse of the situation as it really was.

The same intellectual investigation which had brought the neo-classical movement into being also spawned interest in Gothic. This was inevitable, given the intensive study that was being carried out on the art, architecture and literature of antiquity. Gothic was rediscovered along the way, and this would account for the fact that such Gothic (or 'Gothick' as it was referred to in the eighteenth century) churches as there are, date from the second half of the eighteenth century. An age of romanticism was dawning, and this was fired by 'Gothic' novels such as Horace Walpole's *Castle of Otranto.* For his own house, Walpole chose the 'Gothick' style of architecture, and this was very much with a 'k'. This house, Strawberry Hill, gave its name to the genre of 'Gothic' which we see in the eighteenth-century house or church. This was not a constructional Gothic, but rather a spiky, decorative pasteboard type of architecture. A good domestic example of Strawberry Hill Gothic in Ulster can be seen at Castleward, County Down. The fact that one facade of the house is Gothic and the other classical reflects the intellectual search into antiquity and the diversity found at this time, as well as the differing preferences of two marriage partners.

Allied to this intellectual interest in the past, there was still a perception in the popular imagination that Gothic was a most Christian of styles. Witness the number of humble penal churches which had pointed windows filled with sashed glazing, as at Drumcree, County Armagh, serving as pale reminders of the ecclesiastical nature of the building. Such Gothic churches as were built in Ulster, and in Ireland as a whole, made little particular reference to Perpendicular or Decorated Gothic, but by the use of simple pointed windows filled with Y-tracery or sashed glazing merely suggested that they graced a Gothic building. Pinnacles placed on a tower or at the top of flimsy buttresses served to underline this impression. The structural and liturgical arrangement of these 'Gothic' churches differed little from their neo-classical counterparts.

A very striking example of this is the old parish church of Kilmore, County Down, built in 1792 and now at the Ulster Folk and Transport Museum. Compare this building with the neo-classical church at Ballymore, County Donegal, and we see the very obvious physical common denominators. Both have a solid north wall, a feature quite common in the eighteenth century to retain heat. In the internal arrangements it can be seen that both churches are quite simply rectangular halls endowed with differing architectural genres. There is an element of confusion at Kilmore, for along with the Gothic features, it boasts a front door with a Gibbsian surround. The average Anglican church of the eighteenth century,

'Strawberry Hill Gothick' – the Bishop's throne at Hillsborough.

whether in town or country, was constructed as an auditorium, and the application of Gothic elements demonstrated that the architects involved had little true understanding of Gothic architecture, but were certain of the impression they sought to create.

The Gothic churches which the Earl-Bishop of Derry and Archbishop Richard Robinson built for their flocks still followed the simple tower and hall pattern of earlier neo-classical parish churches, a design which would prevail for the first thirty years of the nineteenth century. At least we know that these prelates actually employed architects, for example Michael Shanahan, Thomas Cooley and Francis Johnston. Whereas pattern books had been used to piece together classical church facades, Cooley seems to have developed a pattern book of how to piece together an entire church. His plans, held at the Armagh Public Library, have detailed instructions for tradesmen, relegating the building of a church almost to the realms of the construction kit. The idea of a set pattern for a Gothic church can be seen in the strong similarities between Cooley's church at Grange, County

Armagh, and the slightly earlier church at Mountjoy Forest, County Tyrone. There is certainly no doubt that Grange Church is the 'parent' of the church which Cooley's pupil, Francis Johnston, built at Ballymakenny, County Louth, between 1785 and 1793. Given that Primate Robinson could see Grange spire from his palace, and the Earl-Bishop liked his church spires to adorn the countryside, we can strongly suspect that it did not matter that the churches were of a sham Gothic, as long as they 'did the trick' visually! The Earl-Bishop even had a spire built on a ruined church at Lough Beg in his Ballyscullion demesne, simply to act as an eye-catcher.

The parish church at Hillsborough, County Down, and Down Cathedral, are more sophisticated examples of their genre. At Hillsborough there is a departure from the rectangular structure, and the component parts of a Gothic church are present; nave, transepts, chancel and even a separate sanctuary. Here there is originality of design, as opposed to the simple hall and tower church. The tracery in the sanctuary and the decoration of the bishop's throne are very much in the genre of Strawberry Hill. Having failed to secure Hillsborough church as the cathedral for the diocese of Down, the Earl of Hillsborough helped to instigate the restoration of the ruined cathedral at Downpatrick. The architect employed for this venture was Charles Lilly, and once again we are presented with a rather romanticised image of a church of the middle ages. Lilly did follow structurally what he found on the site, as pre-restoration engravings show, but the interior owes much to Hillsborough Church, especially in the plasterwork and the organ case. However, the treatment of the nave as a collegiate church, with the box pews facing each other across the aisle, does strongly represent the revival of a medieval feature. This is an early example of the revival of a cathedral choir based on monastic precedent.

In Ulster, and Ireland as a whole, there are not many examples of Georgian Gothic church architecture, but those there are demonstrate an intellectual yearning for the distant past. The structural and liturgical similarities between neo-classical and 'Gothick' churches prove that these genres are but two sides of the same coin.

■ **References**
Loane, pp 30–3; Richardson, pp 14–15.

ST MALACHI'S PARISH CHURCH, HILLSBOROUGH
Main Street, Hillsborough, County Down
Church of Ireland

OFTEN DESCRIBED as one of the finest eighteenth-century churches in Ireland, Hillsborough Parish Church is certainly outstanding in terms of its architecture and landscaped situation. However, nearby development has had a detrimental impact on this once gracious sylvan setting and. A church was built on this site by Colonel Arthur Hill in 1663, replacing one of 1636, which was destroyed in the rebellion five years later. Walter Harris, writing in 1744, speaks of a 'spacious, well-contrived building erected on a rising ground, in the form of a cross, and dedicated to St Malachias; at the west entrance whereof is a handsome Gothick portal'. This building had become derelict by 1750, and so work of restoration, which virtually amounted to a rebuilding, was begun in 1760 at the expense of Wills Hill, Earl of Hillsborough and later first Marquis of Downshire. The new church took thirteen years to complete and cost around £20,000.

In 1819 Andrew Jamison, a glazier who had worked on the church, recorded the names of those involved in the construction of the building. Unfortunately, the name he could not remember was that of the architect. It has been suggested that it was Sanderson Miller, who had designed Strawberry Hill for Horace Walpole, although this seems unlikely as Wills Hill was not introduced to this architect until three years after work had started at Hillsborough. Other architects whose names have been suggested are George Stapleton and Francis Hiorne. Jamison mentions William Gardiner and his sons, John and Charles, both of whom worked on Hillsborough Church. 'Charles was a very clever man, little more than twenty, who drew beautifully, and he and his brother John had the entire direction in building the church and made many alterations to the drawings and plans'. Evidently these two young men, especially Charles, played a large role in the design of the church. Many years later Wills Hill became involved in the restoration of the cathedral at Downpatrick, and the architect employed there was Charles Lilly of Dublin. The church at Hillsborough has many architectural features in common with the cathedral, and it may not be unreasonable to attribute its design to Lilly. Whoever the architect may have been, it is obvious that Wills Hill had a considerable influence on the design. 'Is it not time to fix upon the shape, height, etc. of the pinnacles of the Great Tower?', he asked his agent in June 1772. The position of the

organ, the shape of the communion rails and even the thickness of the lead flashings on the roof are all of his doing. It seems reasonable to assume that the church is, in fact, the result of an amalgamation of talents.

The church grounds are entered through a symmetrical entrance screen of ornamental railings, gates and pinnacled Gothic gatelodges, which were built in 1772 as schoolhouses, but now accommodate the sexton and a parish room. The church is approached from the gates by two parallel drives which are bounded by rows of mature lime trees. As seen from these avenues, the church presents a graceful tower surmounted by an octagonal spire, framed by two transepts, each with its own terminal tower. The building is cruciform, composed of nave, transepts and chancel, with the added embellishments of a west tower, transeptal towers and a sanctuary. The exterior is rubble masonry, and traces of the earlier church can be detected by examining the walls below sill level. Indeed, the delightfully grotesque dripstones beneath the windows date from the 1663 building. The most imposing feature of the exterior of the church is the west tower, with its spire which rises to a height of 210 feet. The tower is divided into three stages and has angled weathered buttresses which culminate in tall pinnacles. All the external dressings are of sandstone. On the west face of the tower are two armorial plaques, bearing the dates 1774 and 1636 (which recalls the date of the first and short-lived parish church). The windows in the tower are all of three trefoil-pointed lights. The transeptal towers are of three stages divided by sandstone sills and crowned by parapets pierced by trefoil-headed openings and surmounted by pinnacles. The windows of the nave, transepts and chancel have sandstone mullions and are of three lights with a two-centred head above. The largest and most imposing window in the building is the tall east window of four pointed and transomed lights with vertical tracery in a two-centred head. The chief interest of this window is the painted glass in the upper sections, the work of Francis Egington of Birmingham, and made from drawings by Sir Joshua Reynolds, first president of the Royal Academy. The window depicts a group of chubby cherubs hovering in the presence of a dove, representing the Holy Spirit, and establishes the colours for the other windows in the church, being blue, green, red and gold.

Entering the church through the west door, the visitor

finds himself in an octagonal room giving access into the baptistry and nave. There is a niche set into the wall of this porch containing a fine marble bust of Wills Hill (1718–93). A man of considerable artistic taste, he was responsible for the construction of the church and surrounding town, as well as serving as the secretary of state for the American colonies and inventing the screw-on top for lemonade bottles. Although the bust is unsigned, it is considered to be the work of Joseph Nollekens.

Internally, the nave, transepts and chancel walls are plastered and painted a suitable cream colour with shafts and ribbing picked out in white. The ceilings are semicircular barrel vaults with moulded cross ribs. These ribs are supported on moulded shafts with capitals and bases. The plaster rosettes at each bay and the central plaster boss are also in white and are composed of acanthus leaves. In the sanctuary, the east wall has an arcade of pointed arches with quatrefoils below. Something of a curiosity is the way in which the floor levels of the transepts are elevated and approached by flights of steps. The fine oak transept screens were designed by Denis O'D Hanna.

At the west end is a choir gallery with a front of three bays carried on four moulded columns. The organ contained here was built in 1773 and was the work of John Snetzler, a native of Bavaria. We are told that on many occasions he determined to return home, but in the end his liking for English beer proved too much to leave behind! St Peter's Church in Drogheda has the only other remaining example of Snetzler's work in Ireland, but it is not nearly so complete as the Hillsborough organ.

The woodwork throughout the church is of extremely high quality, and the high oak box pews remain intact. In the south transept stands the very fine bishop's throne, a reminder of Wills Hill's frustrated hope that his parish church would become the cathedral of the diocese of Down. The throne is of oak, carved with a mitre on the back and is surmounted by an ornate traceried canopy. Similar craftsmanship can be seen in the tall hexagonal pulpit, complete with pedestal support and sounding board enriched with delicate parapet tracery. Although oak was used throughout most of the church, the sanctuary was lined with Lebanese cedar, topped by tracery of satinwood. The inspiration for this supposedly came from the biblical description of Solomon's Temple.

The chamber organ in a classical case sitting in the chancel was built by George Pike England in 1794. It is interesting to note that England learnt his trade under the auspices of John Snetzler, and it is good to

St Malachi's (C of I) Church, Hillsborough.

have the work of each under the one roof. The England organ was presented to the church by the seventh Marquis of Downshire in 1924.

On the north nave wall is a beautiful monument of 1774 to the memory of the reverends Henry and Peter Leslie. With its sorrowing cherub leaning against an urn, this monument is known locally as 'the naked baby', and is signed 'Nollekens fecit'. The other really noteworthy memorial is that to Arthur, fifth Marquis of Downshire (died 1874) by J Forsyth. Surrounded by allegorical emblems, the widowed Marchioness and her infant son are shown gazing at a portrait of the deceased. Ironically, during the tolling of the church bells for the fifth Marquis' funeral, the fifth bell of the peal became cracked.

Other fittings of interest in the church include the very substantial chair in the north transept. This was originally placed in the Chapel Royal in Dublin and was used by the Lord Lieutenant of Ireland when he worshipped there. Three Gothic chairs in the sanctuary are said to be the work of Thomas Chippendale, while there is a small and naively carved chair made from timbers removed from the roof-timbers of Hillsborough Fort in the nineteenth century. During service in the church the Corporation Pew in the south transept is graced with the 48-inch-long silver mace of the defunct town corporation. Made by Charles Aldridge of London in 1786, the mace bears the arms of the royal family, the town, Ireland and the Downshire family.

The west tower houses a peal of ten bells, the original eight having been cast by Rudhall of Gloucester in 1772, and presented by Wills Hill, whose cypher appears on the tenor bell. Two more bells were added in 1972, and named John and Jonathan after the rector, Canon John Barry, and his son Jonathan, both of whom were members of the bellringing team.

In writing an appreciation of the church building, Canon Barry, author of the definitive history of Hillsborough, notes the number of idiosyncratic elements brought into play in the construction of this remarkable edifice. This, he feels, reflects the imagination and taste of Wills Hill and the many facets of his personality are mirrored in the building which he brought about.

■ References
ASCD, pp 327–8; Barry, pp 46–51; Harris, pp 96–7; UAHS (Mid Down), pp 9–11.

CHURCH ORGANS

MUSIC HAS long been a part of worship in Ulster; used to varying degrees depending on denomination, liturgy and local taste. The instrument most commonly associated with church music is the pipe organ. The earliest surviving instruments in Ulster seem to date from the eighteenth century and these are few in number. It would seem that up to this time churches in Ulster simply did not have the need for a musical instrument. Hymn singing did not gain prominence until the Victorian period and only the psalms were sung or recited without accompaniment. In the eighteenth century only the larger Church of Ireland churches had an organ and elsewhere there either was no music or a parish band may have played at services. Presbyterians and Catholics had little or no use for music at all.

The interior of Hillsborough Parish Church, showing the organ built by John Snetzler in 1773 and the light fittings designed by Sir Albert Richardson, installed in 1956.

The grander Church of Ireland cathedrals and churches did have organs, which were situated in a west gallery surrounded by seating for a choir. The notion of a processing choir is a Victorian one. Where an organ was provided it was usually paid for by a wealthy patron who could afford an organ builder. At Armagh and Hillsborough the generosity of an archbishop and an earl paid for the services of the eccentric and expensive John Snetzler. At Down Cathedral the organ was reputed to have been the gift of King George III and to have come from Windsor Castle, although it is now thought to have been built either by Samuel Green in 1802 or by Hull of Dublin in 1819. Having an organ also brought with it the expense of employing an organist and someone to pump air into the instrument.

By the early to mid nineteenth century the organ had found its way into an increasing number of Anglican churches, and those that could not afford one, or find a donor, usually purchased a harmonium. The need for music increased during the nineteenth century due to the development of hymn-singing. This had been used as an evangelising tool by Wesley during the eighteenth century and was to be harnessed by Mrs CF Alexander (the wife of the bishop of Derry), as a means of instructing children in the ways of the Christian faith in the nineteenth century. While the Church of Ireland and Methodist churches embraced music, Presbyterians were not so enthusiastic and largely maintained their tradition of chanting the psalms, led by a precentor, who employed his voice, a pipe or a tuning fork. Only in the latter part of the nineteenth century did the organ become fully utilised within the Presbyterian church. The new Catholic churches built after the middle of the nineteenth century were provided with organs, and these were usually placed in a west gallery, as at Cookstown and Omagh.

These developments meant greater demands on the organ builders who now made a good living from their trade. Telford of Dublin and Conacher of Huddersfield were the two most likely sources of an organ for an Irish church. Some smaller church organs may have come from large private houses.

Recognition of the value of the church organ has been underscored by the creation of Historic Organ Certificates by the British Institute of Organists and seven Ulster organs have gained this certification. The five church organs are:

Glenarm Church of Ireland Church, County Antrim, built in 1871 by JW Walker.
Kilmore Church of Ireland Church, County Down, built by Hill in 1865.
Kilmore Presbyterian Church, County Down, built in 1925 by Evans and Barr.
Our Lady of Lourdes Catholic Church, Moneyglass, County Antrim, built c 1925 by Evans and Barr.
Templepatrick Church of Ireland Church, County Antrim, built by Holdich.

The largest church organ in Ulster is that in St Anne's Cathedral, Belfast, built by Harrison and Harrison.

ST AIDAN'S PARISH CHURCH, GRANGE
Salter's Grange Road, Grange, County Armagh
Church of Ireland

ARTHUR YOUNG, in his 1775 *Tour of Ireland*, comments that the church at Grange '… is erected of white stone and having a tall spire makes a very agreeable object in a country where churches and spires do not abound, at least such as are worth looking at'. The church was built at the expense of Archbishop Richard Robinson, and was one of a series of churches designed by his architect, Thomas Cooley. The church at Grange was built in 1773 as a chapel-of-ease to Armagh, and its spire provides an eye-catching view from the primate's demesne. The need to meet both spiritual and aesthetic needs is reflected in the church-building activities of the Earl-Bishop of Derry in the same period. The hill-top site was presented by Sir Capel Molyneux, whose family had a connection with the parish until the early years of the twentieth century. The church was not actually consecrated until 1782.

The 'white stone' from which the church is built is limestone, taken from a quarry about half a mile from the building. The west tower is the most striking external feature, and it rises in three stages with corner buttresses with arrow slits, and culminates in an octagonal spire. Around the base of the spire is a band of blank arches, which are repeated on the four pinnacles. The sound windows on the uppermost stage of the tower are pointed with hood mouldings, while below is a narrow light filled with latticed glass. Above the pointed west door are two stone shields: that on the left displays Robinson's arms impaled on those of the archdiocese of Armagh, while that on the right bears the arms of Dean Hugh Hamilton. Flanking the foot of the tower are two rooms with blank window recesses, all capped by straight castellations. The later transepts of 1843, added at the same time as the chancel, detract slightly from the facade as they project two blank walls out at the sides of the church. At the entrance gates are lodges for the school teacher and the school itself. These serve nicely to frame the view of the church from the Salters Grange Road.

The addition of transepts and chancel involved alterations which robbed the interior of the character Cooley had given it. Indeed, Lisnadill Parish Church gives some idea of what Grange probably looked like prior to 1843. Of the pre-1843 internal appearance the gallery remains, but it was only added in 1823, although Cooley's designs had called for a gallery. The original box pews have given way to the present bench pews which line the aisle. The Georgian glazing has also been removed and

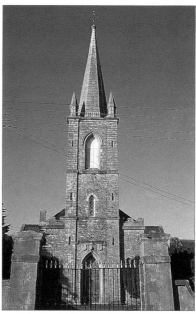

St Aidan's (C of I) Church, Grange.

replaced by traceried windows. There is a plaster cornice, which is composed of a series of arches, while the nave and chancel ceilings are flat. The four-light east window is by Beatrice Elvery.

There are a number of monuments in the nave commemorating the Molyneux family of Castle Dillon. The memorial to Sir Capel Molyneux Junior (died 1832) and his wife Margaret (died 1831) states: 'To those that knew them any detail of their many virtues would be unnecessary. But let this tablet record for the information of strangers and posterity'. Above it is a draped bust of Sir Capel. A monument to General Sir Thomas Molyneux (died 1841) has the allegorical emblem of two upturned torches, while the general's military career is recalled by a furled flag.

The facade of Grange church shows the almost 'pattern book' design which Cooley applied to the churches for his primatial patron. He obviously influenced his apprentice, Francis Johnston, who went on to design a very similar church for Robinson at Ballymakenny, County Louth, between 1785 and 1793.

■ References
Loane, pp 38–41; Young, A, *A Tour Through Ireland in 1776, 1777 and 1778*, Vol 1, p 139.

RICHARD ROBINSON (1709–94)

**Church of Ireland Archbishop of Armagh
and first Baron Rokeby**

BORN AND ordained in England, Robinson came to Ireland as chaplain to the Duke of Dorset, the Lord Lieutenant of Ireland. Rising through the Irish House of Bishops, he became the Primate of Ireland in 1765 and held this position until his death. He was created Baron Rokeby in 1785. Robinson was a devoted clergyman who endeavoured to prevent absenteeism among the clergy and he worked hard to improve the condition of the church in his archdiocese. Little is known of his abilities as a preacher or theologian, but he has left a wealth of architectural reminders of his archiepiscopate. He employed the architect Thomas Cooley, who provided the plans for the County Armagh churches of Grange and Lisnadill. The city of Armagh itself bears testimony to Robinson's guiding hand, as he provided the primatial palace and chapel, the public library, the observatory and also the street layout. According to a later biographer, he converted Armagh, 'Not from brick, but from mud, to marble'. It was his intention to provide the city with a university, although this did not happen in his lifetime. The archbishop is buried in the crypt beneath Armagh's Church of Ireland cathedral and is commemorated by a monument by Nollekens in the south aisle.

Archbishop Richard Robinson

■ **References**
Rogers, E, *Memoir of Armagh Cathedral* (Belfast, 1888).

ST CADAN'S PARISH CHURCH, TAMLAGHTARD

Tamlaghtard, County Londonderry   *Church of Ireland*

THERE IS some confusion as to when this church was built, the dates being given variously as 1778, 1784 and 1787, but Lewis describes it as a large and handsome edifice in the early English style of architecture, built in 1777. The church owes its existence to the zeal of its parishioners, who donated £150 towards its construction, while the remainder of the £700 cost was raised by subscription. It is strongly suspected that the Earl-Bishop of Derry may have had a hand in the construction of St Cadan's, for he gave the old church to the local Roman Catholics for use as a place of worship.

This is a simple, but good, example of an eighteenth-century Gothic church. Built of rubblestone with ashlar dressings, it is a hall and tower church with three bays of pointed windows, filled with Y-tracery and clear glazing. There are no windows on the north wall – a common enough feature of churches at the time, but very practical here on such an exposed site. The west tower is of three stages, all the openings being pointed. The parapet has crenellations, as have the wings to the left and right of the foot of the tower. It is suspected that these wings were a later addition to the church, but drawings signed by Joseph Welland and dated 15 March 1854, put this supposition in some doubt. If these plans are to be believed, the wings were original and Welland and Gillespie's work on them merely extended to opening the

St Cadan's (C of I) Church, Tamlaghtard.

formerly blind side windows. The drawings also show how the interior of the church was until 1854, when the chancel was added. There had been a pulpit set behind a reading desk on the blank north wall surrounded by box pews. Under the new arrangements, an octagonal pulpit of Bath stone was placed at the south-east and a desk at the north-east. The king-post trussed roof probably dates from this time, as does the gallery. The east window in the chancel is of three lights and has cusped tracery with latticework glazing.

Externally, the church provides an unassuming example of the hall and tower type of Gothic church which was to be widely used a quarter of a century later by the Board of First Fruits.

■ **References**
Lewis, Vol 2, p 591; RCB, drawings by Joseph Welland; Rankin, p 43; Rowan, p 121; UAHS (North Derry), pp 46–8.

ST JOHN'S PARISH CHURCH, LISNADILL

Lisnadill, on the Newtownhamilton Road from Armagh, County Armagh

Church of Ireland

THE CHURCH at Lisnadill retains many of the internal features which the architect Thomas Cooley gave it, and demonstrates how the needs of eighteenth-century Anglican worship were visually enhanced when a wealthy patron was involved. Like the church at Grange, this building was erected by Archbishop Richard Robinson. Lisnadill Church was consecrated in 1782, having been completed along with a glebe house, 'in a style truly

The interior of St John's (C of I) Church, Lisnadill, showing the reredos. In the Georgian period a reredos such as this would have been quite common.

characteristic of their noble founder'. The church is a three-bay hall with hipped roof at the east end and a four-storey west tower. While the body of the church is rendered, the tower displays its rubble construction with ashlar dressings. On either side of the circular window on the west face of the tower are the coats of arms of Primate Robinson and Dean Hugh Hamilton, as at Grange. The uppermost stage of the tower has pointed louvred openings with Y-tracery; crowning this stage are battlements and four corner pinnacles. The nave windows are attractively glazed in the 'Strawberry Hill' manner, while there is no east window. On the west wall on each side of the tower is a small lattice window, while the south wall is dissected awkwardly by a lean-to shed.

By the west door there are rooms to the left and right that support half the gallery, with the gallery stairs on the right. The central aisle is lined with box pews, with later pews in the chancel arranged in collegiate fashion. At the west end the gallery is carried on quatrefoil columns, and is fronted with hexafoil motifs in the panelling. The pulpit and desk have been altered since the construction of the church, although the pulpit looks as though it may be a re-working of the original one. It is made of wood, is octagonal and rests on a concave pedestal with moulded top and bottom. Each panel is filled with Gothic motifs.

At the opposite side of the church is a small organ in a traceried and castellated case. Where the east window would commonly be found in many churches, here there is a fine reredos, which is scripted with the Creed, the Ten Commandments and the Lord's Prayer. These articles of faith are framed by two half-columns supporting an ogee arch, within which is painted the dove of the Holy Spirit. This is a rare survival of an instructional reredos, and it was copied by Cooley's pupil, Francis Johnston, for his church at Ballymakenny, County Louth. An iron rail encloses the communion table and the reredos. Cooley's hand is evident in the elegant Armagh marble font on its thin column, which is very similar to the one found at his church at Tamlaght. The generosity of Primate Robinson is underlined by his donation of the silver chalice and paten which are still used in the church.

■ References

Loane, pp 44–6; Stuart, J, *Historical Memoirs of the City of Armagh* (Newry, 1819), p 448.

TAMLAGHTFINLAGAN PARISH CHURCH, BALLYKELLY
Ballykelly village, County Londonderry

Church of Ireland

AS WITH the churches at Ballyscullion, Tyanee, Banagher and Tamlaghtard, the parish church of Tamlaghtfinlagan owes its origins to the church-building zeal of Frederick Hervey, the Earl-Bishop of Derry. Although it is more sophisticated than the noble prelate's earlier churches, it was built with only his written supervision, as he had left his diocese in 1791, never to return. The church was completed in 1795.

Sitting on a little knoll among the trees, the church has been described as the most handsome of the Earl-Bishop's sacred buildings. With his usual canniness, the bishop managed to augment his own subscriptions towards the church with donations from another source – in this case the local landlord, John Beresford. There is a certain amount of speculation as to the architect of the building. For the building of his palace at Downhill, the Earl-Bishop had employed the architect/mason Michael Shanahan, who was responsible for the churches at Banagher and Tyanee. At Tamlaghtfinlagan it seems that Shanahan may have designed the church, but not supervised its actual construction, as the contractor was one John Mitchell. According to the Ordnance Survey Memoir, the church was 'an exact imitation of a church on his [the Earl- Bishop's] estate in England'. Lewis in his *Topographical Dictionary of Ireland* of 1837 describes the church as 'a small but handsome edifice, in the early English style, with a large square tower and lofty octagonal spire'.

The church is built of rubble stone with freestone dressings and consists of a tower and spire, nave and later north aisle and chancel. Commenting on the building, without its chancel, in 1806, Sir Richard Colt Hoare said it looked as though 'the head was too large for the body'. Old engravings show that it did look as if it was about to topple over. Given the Earl-Bishop's love of spires, this overbearing vertical emphasis was perhaps the desired effect. The tower is of three stages with the entrance door on the south face. On the western face there was originally a blind pointed recess, but this has now been filled, quite sympathetically, with a Y-traceried window holding glass which commemorates the connection of the Fishmongers' Company (one of the London companies) with the church. Above are pointed louvred openings and then an arcade of blind pointed recesses which divides the second and third stages. Circular louvred openings pierce the third stage. Above the castellations and corner

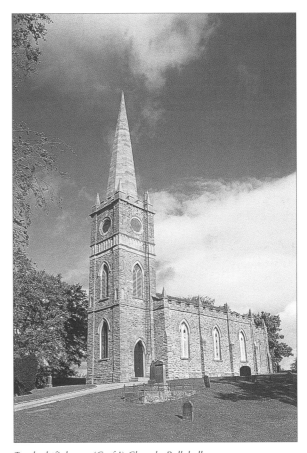

Tamlaghtfinlagan (C of I) Church, Ballykelly.

pinnacles rises the graceful octagonal spire. The nave is of three bays of Y-traceried windows. The bays are divided by buttresses capped by pyramidal finials and the parapet is castellated. The chancel of 1851 was added by the Fishmongers' Company at the same time as the vestry and gallery and blends harmoniously with the nave, particularly with the replication of castellated parapets and finials. There appears to be no record as to who designed these additions. In 1859 a north aisle was added to the design of Joseph Welland, and it has three bays of two-light lancet windows.

The Georgian simplicity of the interior has been somewhat lost with the addition of the north aisle, which has a lean-to roof and sits behind three arches resting on sandstone columns. The nave ceiling is coved, while the western gallery of 1851 has a Gothic panelled front. The east window is of three lights and was reconstructed during the restoration of the church in 1934. The windows in the nave are of latticework and incorporate the arms of the Irish Society, the Fishmongers and the Beresford family.

The most outstanding monument in the church is that on the east wall to Mrs Jane Hamilton (died 1716). The deceased is shown kneeling in classical attire, resigning herself to her eternal destiny as two hovering cherubs hold a crown of glory above her head. Beneath, mournful putti weep and wring their hands. This monument is copied from Grinling Gibbons' monument to Mrs Mary Beaufoy (died 1705) in Westminster Abbey. On the south wall are monuments to Rev George Vaughan Sampson (died 1828), the first agent of the Fishmongers' Company. Next to this is the memorial to

his son Arthur (died 1859), who was the agent for thirty-four years, and in whose honour Sampson's Tower near Limavady was built. James David Beresford, who died at sea in a storm in 1807, is remembered by a memorial depicting a phoenix and an anchor and rope.

This fine church with its 'strutting steeple and spire' (as the Earl-Bishop wrote of it) is a pleasant example of eighteenth-century Gothic and stands, as was intended in 1795, as 'an example to posterity how well the squire and the Bishop could draw together'.

■ **References**
Rankin, pp 40, 42; Rowan, p 121; UAHS (North Derry), pp 27, 30; OSM, Vol 25, Londonderry VII, 1834–5, pp 68–9.

FREDERICK HERVEY (1730–1803)
Church of Ireland Bishop of Derry and fourth Earl of Bristol

DESPITE ACQUIRING the wealthy bishopric of Derry through the patronage of his brother, the third Earl of Bristol, who was Lord Lieutenant of Ireland, Hervey proved himself to be an ardent church-builder who had a genuine concern for the condition of the clergy and people of all denominations. At a time when the Church of Ireland enjoyed a privileged position in Irish society, Hervey extended a hand of friendship to Catholics, providing them with places to say mass and contributing to the construction of chapels. He was actively involved in the Volunteer movement and openly supported the notion of Catholic Emancipation. The Earl-Bishop was also well known as an eccentric and on one occasion organised a horse-race between the clergy of the different religious denominations. He was an enthusiastic traveller who gathered art treasures from around Europe to embellish his great palace at Downhill, County Londonderry.

The Earl-Bishop died in the outhouse of a peasant dwelling near Rome. Apparently the Catholic owner of the house was unwilling to allow a non-Catholic clergyman to die in his home. The Earl-Bishop's body was shipped back to England in a casket disguised as a packing case, as the sailors would have refused to sail had they known a corpse was on board!

Frederick Hervey, Earl of Bristol and Bishop of Derry.

■ **References**
Fothergill, AB, *The Mitred Earl: An Eighteenth Century Eccentric* (London, 1974); Rankin, P, *Irish Building Ventures of the Earl Bishop of Derry* (Belfast, 1972).

6
Nineteenth-Century Meeting Houses and Neo-Classical Churches

AFTER THE Act of Union of 1801 the religious situation in Ireland began to change. Presbyterians were first given royal grants, and later annual stipends for their clergy. The Catholic Emancipation Act of 1829 removed the restrictions from the practice of that faith. Given a freer rein there was a tendency towards the building of more handsome places of worship, particularly on the part of the Presbyterians. The style chosen for the building of the new 'preaching houses' was to be neo-classical. This may seem a little anachronistic given that the Church of Ireland had employed this style over fifty years previously, but there was little desire to emulate the Gothic traits now being seen in contemporary Anglican churches, and Presbyterians were not shy about constructing grand, full-blown classical porticoes.

A number of churches were built which were unashamedly old-fashioned; the Non-Subscribing Presbyterian Church at Crumlin looks for all the world like a solid eighteenth-century meeting house, and it is with some surprise that we find it is dated as having been built in 1835. It is, however, a neo-classical building, but stylistically in the eighteenth-century mould. It has a gabled facade which struggles to form a pediment, but which remains a gable. It is, however, a thoroughly charming building. Another lovely, but sadly derelict, building is the former Methodist church at Donaghmore, County Down. This does not appear on the 1833 Ordnance Survey map, but cannot have been built very much after this date. It has a simple symmetrical gabled facade of three bays; central door and margin-paned windows on the lower level and three round-headed

The former Methodist Church at Donaghmore, County Down.

windows above. The interior is lined with box pews and the sanctuary area has a rather Anglican arrangement, with the pulpit to one side and a pinnacled Gothic reredos on the end wall flanked by two curious round-headed windows filled with mullions and a quatrefoil motif. It is obvious that less sophisticated churches had to be built where resources were limited, and this is evident in the Moravian churches at Ballinderry and Kilwarlin. These churches fall very much into the category of vernacular church architecture, and have the cosy arrangement of a manse joined onto the church, and at Kilwarlin the former schoolhouse is included as part of the structure. The Presbyterian church at Inch, County Donegal, had also used this arrangement of church and manse combined.

It is perhaps ironic that any religious denomination should choose to build in the classical idiom, the architectural style of the pagan ancient world. It could be said that neo-classical architecture was austere, chaste and ordered, and therefore reflected the image of Presbyterianism, while allowing the buildings to make an impact on the local scene without being mistaken for another denomination. They might have found a new means of presenting a church facade, but Presbyterians did not change their primary function of the preaching of the word of God, and the churches built at this time are very much auditoriums. They are rectangular buildings with the pulpit now placed on the focal end wall, with the aisles leading towards it and a U-shaped gallery which effectively placed the preacher at the centre of the congregation's vision (and hearing). This auditorium form was also employed by the Methodists, the best example being in Portadown. It should also be mentioned that it was more practical to have a classical frontage on a rectangular building than it would have been on a T-shaped one.

In many instances the churches were very plain halls with a temple-like front applied so as to show their best side to the entering worshippers. There was often a marked contrast between the facade and the sides; startlingly so at Kilmore Presbyterian Church, County Down, of 1832, where the solid Ionic pilastered facade gives way to bleak rendered side walls. Similarly, the fine front of Clough Non-Subscribing Presbyterian Church is set onto a long and plain hall. The very elegantly correct, columned and pedimented front of Holy Trinity Church of Ireland Church in Kircubbin, County Down, by John Millar, uses classical sophistication to divert attention from its rather lowly side elevation. Even John Bowden was guilty of this at St George's, Belfast, by tacking the grand second-hand entrance front from Ballyscullion Palace onto a completely nondescript box. He could be pardoned, as the church was then hemmed in by houses.

In 1833 William Farrell gave Christ Church, Belfast, a good cut-stone Ionic columned facade, but was happy enough for it to expose its red-brick flank to Durham Street. In its present dangerous and burnt-out state this is a sad building. Both St George's and Christ Church prove that, with galleries, it was just as important to the Church of Ireland as it was to the Presbyterians to accommodate as many worshippers as possible in the smallest space possible.

Not all the neo-classical churches were of this Hollywood-set type, and some had sides as elegant as their fronts. Richard Suter's Presbyterian churches at Ballykelly and Banagher, built for the Fishmongers' Company of London, have sophisticated facades, united to the sides by a continuation of string-courses, eaves and window surrounds. The greatest accolade of all for these two churches is the comparison drawn between them and Inigo Jones' St Paul's in Covent Garden. If the Fishmongers were happy to pay, then Suter was quite right to design with flair. The Non-Subscribing Presbyterian Church at Banbridge, County Down, is another church with a handsome facade echoed in the treatment of its side and rear walls.

A lesson in strict classical simplicity can be seen in WJ Booth's chaste Presbyterian church of 1843 at Draperstown, County Londonderry, which demonstrates classicism in its most elemental form. It is a severe building, of ashlar with a pedimented gable supported on plain pilasters flanking windowless recesses. The six-bay depth of the hall-church has very plain square-headed windows.

The Presbyterian church utilised a particularly talented architect in John Millar, 'to whom the lovers of classical architecture owe a debt of gratitude' (the *Northern Whig*, 16 August 1835). He designed the unusual and muscular church at Portaferry, County Down, which takes the form of a Greek temple sitting on a high podium. Millar's greatest contribution to neo-classical church architecture has to be his use of a cupola on the Presbyterian Church at Castlereagh, County Down, and, as the *Northern Whig* pointed out, this must have been the first use of a belfry on a Presbyterian church in Ireland. This graceful building reminded JS Curl of the work of Sir John Soane. Especially pleasing are the circular fluted gate piers adorned with Greek key patterns and topped by garlanded urns. The entire church has, decoratively, something of the crispness of a freshly-iced wedding cake.

Something has already been said of the interiors of neo-classical Presbyterian and Methodist churches, but a number of these have, by necessity, been altered due to developments in forms of worship. The first Presbyterian hymnal was not introduced until 1898, and up until that time it had been the practice only to sing the psalms. There was no musical accompaniment or choir, and the congregation took their note from a precentor, who sat at the foot of the pulpit. He would have given the first note using his own voice, or with a tuning-fork or a single-noted pipe. One of these pipes is preserved in the museum of the Presbyterian Historical Society in Church House, Belfast. The enthusiasm, or resistance, with which organs and hymns were received varied from congregation to congregation, but their introduction meant changes in the layout of churches. Pews had to be removed from around the foot of the pulpit to provide space for the choir, and the organ was placed in an ante-chamber behind the preacher. This arrangement still allowed the pulpit and its occupant to be the focal point of the church. With the move away from communion with a common cup, administered from tables in the aisles, a single table now sufficed, and this was placed below the pulpit. The Non-Subscribing Presbyterian Church at Banbridge is one of the best examples of how a Presbyterian church looked before such innovations. The Methodist church also has many examples of this neat and ordered arrangement of table, pulpit and organ on the focal wall. By the middle of the nineteenth century there was a serious move towards Gothic architecture, but the Methodists clung onto the neo-classical style a little

longer. Their best architect of the time was Isaac Farrell, who designed the churches at Belfast's Donegall Square and Coleraine. The latest of this genre is that built in 1865 at Enniskillen. It is a somewhat sombre creation by WJ Barre, who was at the same time working on the Lombardic-style University Road Methodist Church in Belfast. It is unfair to dismiss these churches as representing the tail-end of a genre, for the Methodists had always been a modest body of Christians who sought to create the best conditions for preaching, and were therefore slow to embrace the idea of even restrained and dignified adornment in their buildings. An architect is bound by the tastes and desires of those employing him, and the use of neo-classical architecture did continue, albeit to a lesser extent, until late into the century, one example being the Catholic Oratory at Buncrana, County Donegal, which was built in the 1890s. The vast number of very fine neo-classical churches in Ulster suggests that the nineteenth century saw a growing confidence in all the major denominations, and no doubt this confidence percolated into the broad acceptance of Gothic which we can see in the churches of the second half of the nineteenth century.

■ **References**

Curl, p 14; de Breffny, p 142; Holmes, F, *Our Presbyterian Heritage* (Belfast, 1985), pp 132–3; UAHS (North Derry), pp 27–30.

ST GEORGE'S PARISH CHURCH, BELFAST
High Street, Belfast   *Church of Ireland*

THE PRESENT St George's Church of 1811–16 replaced the old corporation church, attended by the town sovereign and burgesses. This building had been pulled down in 1774, when the first St Anne's was constructed as the parish church for Belfast. When the present St George's was built on the old site, it was designed to serve as a chapel-of-ease to the parish church. The Board of First Fruits made a gift of £4500 and a loan of £1000. The board was not usually so generous, but the fact that the church was to bear the name of the King may have loosened the purse-strings: a similar situation prevailed when St George's Church was built in Dublin.

The church was designed by John Bowden, who provided a plain preaching box elevated by its elegant

facade. The church's portico originally graced the oval palace of the Earl-Bishop of Derry at Ballyscullion, County Londonderry, which was the work of either Francis Sandys or Michael Shanahan. After the Earl-Bishop's death the palace was dismantled and the portico purchased by the Bishop of Down and Connor, Dr Nathaniel Alexander, who presented it to the parish and had it transported via the Lagan Canal. The portico consists of four unfluted Corinthian columns which support a pediment bearing the arms of Belfast and the diocese of Down and Connor. Behind the portico the wall is slightly convex, and has semicircular-headed niches flanking the entrance door and the window above. Two outer doors give access to the gallery lobbies and the facade terminates with fluted pilasters.

Bowden's original plans show that the church was originally a four-bay hall with an apsidal chancel, pierced by three niches. Judging by the spacing of the mullions of the east window on these plans, it must have been a Venetian window. The plans also feature sketched indications of a central aisle as well as two outer ones, and indeed this is how the seating was arranged. The pulpit was a three-decker affair and stood in front of the chancel. Fourteen columns with Corinthian capitals support the gallery, and this work appears to be original.

Due to alterations carried out by WJ Barre and subsequent architects, St George's now sits awkwardly between being a Georgian church and a High Victorian one. Barre decried the Georgian architecture as 'debased Grecian' and removed the old flat ceiling and exposed the timber truss roof (plans for this work by Welland and Gillespie also exist), as well as designing a new pulpit. The chancel was rebuilt in 1882 to the designs of Edward Braddell to serve as a memorial to Rev WM McIlwaine. The chancel walls are decorated darkly with murals by Alexander Gibbs (who helped to decorate Keble College Chapel) and depict the life of Christ, as well as showing saints Michael, Gabriel, Raphael and Uriel. The reredos displays Matthew, Mark, Luke and John with a central Agnus Dei. The chancel arch is carried on Corinthian pillars, which were part of Bowden's design. Above are paintings of Mary and Joseph.

The screen was also designed by Braddell in 1885, but was not erected until 1928. It is a memorial to Rev Hugh Davis Murphy and is composed of four fluted Corinthian

St George's (C of I) Church, Belfast. The very grand portico came from Ballyscullion Palace.

columns, above which is a tympanum carrying an image of the Agnus Dei. On the north-east wall are two identical monuments to Mary Frances Preston (died 1865) and Arthur Francis Preston (died 1867), while to the right of the chancel is a memorial to Sir Henry Pottinger, ambassador to the emperor of China and first governor of Hong Kong.

The church was the subject of a very successful restoration scheme which was completed in 2000.

■ **References**
Brett (Belfast), pp 13, 33; de Breffny, p 146; Curl, p 13; Larmour, p 4; Rankin, p 58; RCB, plans by John Bowden and Welland and Gillespie.

GLASCAR PRESBYTERIAN CHURCH
Glaskermore, off A1 dual carriageway near Banbridge, County Down   *Presbyterian*

THIS CHURCH, situated in the heart of Brontë country, is interesting both structurally and for its associations with some fascinating characters. The congregation of Glascar was founded in 1756, with a meeting house being built in 1769. This was a building of stone and clay, with a thatched roof and rough benches on an earthen floor. A large circular hedge of beech in front of the present church marks the site of the pulpit of the original church.

During the ministry of the Rev John Rogers, the congregation decided to erect a new church. This was built in 1814, as the datestone on the facade testifies. As completed, the church was a rectangular galleried structure with an earthen floor and an open-trussed roof.

External staircases at either end gave access to the gallery. At this stage families had to provide their own pews, and this accounts for the variations in the sizes of the surviving family pews in the gallery. When first built the interior had no ceiling, the beams simply being exposed. Henry McFadden, a nineteenth-century sexton, recalled how, as a child, he sat up on one of the rafters above the gallery to allow older worshippers to have seats. The flat plaster ceiling, which is divided into six compartments, was probably installed about 1827. Further work was carried out between 1853 and 1861, when the pine pews were installed, and the side porches and minister's room were built.

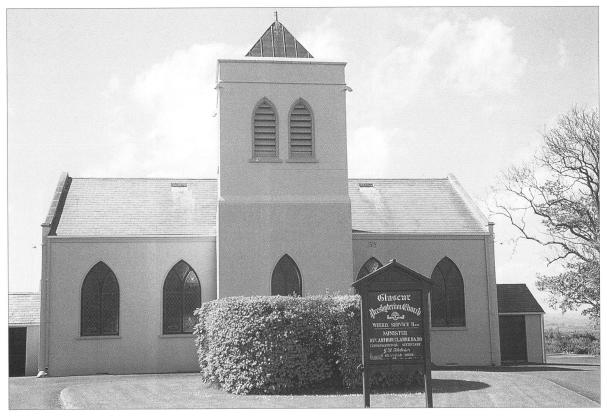

Glascar Presbyterian Church.

With the addition of the tower in memory of the Rev John Brown Lusk (died 1939), the church finally took on its present appearance. It is a five-bay structure with Y-traceried windows filled with coloured glass on the main facade, while the back wall has two storeys of regency-glazed windows. Also at the rear is the two-storey projection housing the minister's room and stairs to the gallery. The tower has pointed sound openings at its upper stage and is crowned by a squat pyramidal roof. At each end of the church is a porch leading to the central aisle, which runs the length of the building, and is intersected by the shorter aisle running from the back door. The base of the tower forms a 'sanctuary' area, entered by a shallow-headed archway placed on the long wall, with the pulpit set to one side. The rather elegant gallery which occupies three walls is panelled and carried on eight cast iron columns. An interesting facet of Glascar is that communion is still administered in the traditional manner, with long linen-covered tables placed in the aisles.

A number of clergy are commemorated by monuments within the church. A tablet under the gallery recalls father and son reverends John (who died in 1854 and was a moderator of the Seceders) and James Rogers. At the other end of the church Rev John Brown Lusk (died 1939) is remembered with an eloquently-worded monument.

The school-house at the church gates was built in 1848 on the site of the former school in which Patrick Brontë taught. He was dismissed from his position as schoolmaster in 1798. No record survives to explain exactly why, but local legend suggests that he was caught kissing one of his female pupils. Brontë had received his education locally from one Rev Mr McKee, who also instructed Mayne Reid, who went on to become a noted author. Indeed, for many years Mayne was a common Christian name in the area due to the fame of this local son.

Perched on top of a hill in a part of County Down rich in history, this pleasant church complements its surroundings.

■ References

Information supplied by Rev Arthur Clarke, minister of the church.

BANAGHER PRESBYTERIAN CHURCH
Ballyhanedin townland, County Londonderry

Presbyterian

THIS SOLID meeting house in 'the Grecian style of architecture' (Lewis) has many similarities with that at Ballykelly, and this is due to the fact that they were both designed by Richard Suter. As the datestone within the pediment suggests, it was completed in 1825, under the auspices of the Fishmongers' Company.

The church is constructed of coursed rubble with Dungiven sandstone dressings, and as at Ballykelly, the facade is well conceived, with the side walls receiving the same architectural treatment as the front. The facade is of three bays, the middle bay being occupied by a projecting pedimented porch with a segmental-headed doorcase. The flanking round-headed windows have Georgian glazing and keystones, and their springing lines are linked by the string-courses with the heavy framed pediment rising above. The church is five bays deep and has broad over-hanging eaves. At the rear is a single-storey extension running the breadth of the building, with an oculus window above.

The interior must have had a similar arrangement to that at Ballykelly, but was subject to 'Gothicising' in

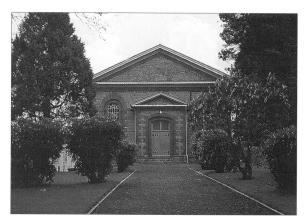

Banagher Presbyterian Church.

the 1860s.

Suter had the designs for Banagher and Ballykelly churches exhibited at the Royal Academy in 1827.

■ **References**
Curl, p 7; Lewis, Vol 1, p 176.

ARDTANAGH PRESBYTERIAN CHURCH (FIRST DROMARA)
One mile outside Dromara village on the road to Kinallen, County Down

Presbyterian

THIS IS a remarkably large church standing high in open countryside about a mile outside the village of Dromara. A number of changes have been made to Ardtanagh church over the course of the last thirty years, yet it is still a very fine building and a good example of a rural barn church.

Ardtanagh Presbyterian Church.

The facade of the church is of two storeys, and when it was built in 1826 it was seven bays wide, with three doorways each placed beneath a window. The roof is hipped, and the cornice is embellished with stone spherical finials at each end. In relatively recent times the number of bays has been reduced to five. This alteration, sadly, saw the removal of the outer bays which were, in fact, false windows designed to mask the external stairs to the gallery. The consequent blank expanse of wall and the substitution of unpainted render for the whitewashed harling serve to give the building a somewhat austere appearance. Happily, the Georgian Gothic sash windows have been reinstated in the windows.

Above the central doorway is a stone inscribed: 'Remember the Sabbath Day to keep it Holy. Erected by subscription 1826. William Craig Pastor'. To the left of this is a small stone preserved from an earlier church. The Rev William Craig presented a clock to the congregation which was fixed to the front of the gallery opposite the pulpit and was no doubt intended to aid himself and his successors to gauge the length of their sermons. Following his death in 1871 a fierce dispute broke out regarding the choice of a new minister, and court action had to be taken when one faction took possession of the meeting house illegally.

Internally, the church is a rectangular hall with the pulpit placed in the middle of the long wall and a semicircular-headed window on either side of it. There are three aisles, each leading from an enclosed porch accommodated within the body of the church. The gallery occupies three sides of the interior, the sides being rounded and the front breaking forward into a curve. The gallery fronts are divided into rectangular bays, long and short alternately. The whole structure is supported on columns with capitals and pedestals. The area under the gallery has rectangular windows, some of which have been filled with stained glass. Unfortunately the box pews have been removed: there had originally been canopied pews in the north-east and north-west angles. The pulpit has also been renewed, and there is something almost Romanesque in the round-headed panelling behind it.

This remains a very handsome building, set as it is, at the head of a steep path through its graveyard. Particularly charming, and easily overlooked, is the bell mounting on the eastern external gallery projection. No doubt this was the work of a local blacksmith and, although the bell is now silent, it would once have been rung by pulling the rope through one of the windows.

■ **References**
ASCD, p 338; Killen, pp 121, 122; UAHS (Mid Down), p 32.

BALLYKELLY PRESBYTERIAN CHURCH
Ballykelly village, County Londonderry

Presbyterian

THE TOWN of Ballykelly was built by the Fishmongers' Company of London, which had been granted land in the area by King James I in 1613. Having held land here since the seventeenth century, the company displayed no great building fervour until the 1820s, when a large number of improvements were carried out. Building work included a market house, an inn, the Lancasterian schools and the Presbyterian church.

The church was completed in 1827, built by James Turnbull, and designed by Richard Suter, the Fishmongers' own surveyor, at a cost of £4000. Rev WD Killen, writing of the histories of the Irish Presbyterian congregations, says, 'the present large and excellent church was erected at Ballykelly, at the expense of the Fishmongers' Company, an act commemorated in an elegant marble tablet, placed in a conspicuous position behind the pulpit'. He also comments that the building of this church 'gave an impulse to the cause of ecclesiastical architecture among the Presbyterians of the north of Ireland'. The church is extremely large and, like its slightly smaller partner at Banagher, is constructed of coursed rubble with Dungiven sandstone dressings. The two-storey facade is of three bays with a pedimented doorcase enclosed within a keystoned arch. The outer bays project slightly and the edges of the walls have quoins. On the ground floor are square-headed windows resting on brackets, while those above are segmental-headed. The frontage is crowned by a massive

Ballykelly Presbyterian Church.

pediment which is dated 1827. The string-course and broad eaves cornice are carried along the six-bay depth of the church.

The interior is galleried with two aisles, although the pews are not original. The gallery is carried on ten square timber columns. At the head of the church is the pulpit, which is approached on each side by a flight of steps, and has the appearance almost of a landing rather than an enclosed preaching stage. Behind it is the tablet to which Rev WD Killen referred. It is inscribed: 'By this tablet the Presbyterian congregation of Ballykelly records their gratitude to the Worshipful Company of Fishmongers,

London, for their liberality in erecting, completing, and presenting them with this Meeting House, March the 7th AD 1827'.

At the gate to the graveyard is a sandstone gatelodge with a hipped roof, which is also part of Suter's scheme.

■ **References**

Curl, p 7; Curl, JS, *The History, Architecture and Planning of the Estates of the Fishmongers' Company in Ulster* (Belfast, 1991), pp 63–4; OSM (Vol 25, Londonderry VII), pp 68–9; UAHS (North Derry), pp 27, 30.

MAY STREET PRESBYTERIAN CHURCH, BELFAST
May Street, Belfast   *Presbyterian*

THIS ELEGANT classical church is renowned for its associations with the great orator, Dr Henry Cooke, the first minister, for whom the church was built in 1829. If May Street Church is compared with Ardtanagh Church at Dromara, built three years before, the transition from the 'barn' church to the more assured classical style as employed here is clear. When the church was opened on 18 October 1829, Cooke was the preacher, taking as his text Psalm 77, v 3: 'Glorious things of Thee are spoken'.

The church was designed by W Smith and presents a facade of brick embellished with stucco. McComb's *Presbyterian Almanack and Christian Remembrancer for 1841* carries this description of the exterior which is still accurate today:

May Street Presbyterian Church.

‘

The front is of modern or Scamozzian Ionic, having two columns and four pilasters 28 feet high and fluted. The columns and interior pilasters form a piazza 36 feet long and 7 feet wide, over which rises a beautiful pediment. The front of the building is furnished with a regular architrave frieze and block cornice, which give it a light, pleasing, and at the same time, imposing effect.

’

Cooke's connection with the church is recorded on a stone tablet placed above the main entrance door in 1872.

Inside, two sweeping staircases to the left and right lead to a horseshoe gallery, 'appropriated to the accommodation of the poor', fronted with polished

mahogany. This is carried on ten Scamozzian columns and two half columns, and once continued round behind the pulpit to form a 'singing gallery', although it now stops short of the pulpit. There are box pews throughout, which curve gracefully at the top of each aisle. These were lowered about 6 inches at some stage in the nineteenth century, presumably in 1872, when the ceiling was sheeted in timber. It was at this time that the pulpit was altered. There was a great deal of resistance to replacing the octagonal pulpit from which Cooke had delivered so many sermons, and so the pulpit was simply extended by opening out the back panels to create a broader preaching space, with the old front projecting out at the middle. The area around the pulpit was reordered again around 1900 and in 1930, when a Binns organ was installed.

A number of memorials in the church are worth particular mention, especially the memorial archway to

Henry Cooke in the vestibule. This takes the form of a Roman triumphal arch, designed by John Boyd in 1872, showing a restraint and respect for its surroundings not always exhibited by Victorian architects. The memorial cost £380, exclusive of the medallion portrait of the cleric himself, which was the work of John Foley RHA and the gift of the ladies of the congregation. The Revs Lynd, McCaughan and Blue are also remembered in the vestibule by marble busts, executed by AM Shannon, each placed in a niche. Cooke is commemorated again in a stained glass window in the gallery, inscribed 'In memoriam, Henry Cooke, D.D., L.L.D. Born 1788, died 1868'. There is a corresponding window on the other side of the church to the memory of John Calvin, the gift of William McMeekin.

Next to the church is the two-storey school and session room of 1858–59, designed, once again, by John Boyd, which is in harmony with its older neighbour. It has high pedestals supporting four Doric columns. The Ionic fluted keystones certainly show a streak of individuality on the part of the architect. Given that his overall designing shows courtesy to the work of the original builders, this is perhaps his own little attempt at self-expression.

■ **References**

Brett (Belfast), pp 17, 42; Curl, p 14; Larmour, p 6; Williamson, J, *May Street Presbyterian Church Centenary* (Belfast, 1929), pp 25–9, 59–60.

HENRY COOKE (1788–1868)
Presbyterian minister

COOKE WAS minister of Killyleagh Presbyterian Church in County Down when he came to prominence through his opposition to the appointment of the Arian, William Bruce to the chair of Hebrew and Greek at Belfast Academical Institution. In his campaign against Arianism, Cooke also found himself in defiance of Henry Montgomery. Cooke was a conservative not only in religious matters, but also in politics; he was opposed to O'Connell's Repeal movement and the disestablishment of the Church of Ireland and what he feared would be the results for Presbyterianism. He was minister of May Street Presbyterian Church and his ministry is recalled by the Cooke Centenary Church on Belfast's Ormeau Road. Cooke was the preacher at the opening of the current Presbyterian Church in Portaferry. He is most popularly known in Belfast as the 'Black Man', because of the statue of him (actually of a green hue) outside the gates of the Royal Belfast Academical Institution.

Rev Henry Cooke ('The Black Man')

KILWARLIN MORAVIAN CHURCH
Kilwarlin, (sign-posted off the Moira Road) Hillsborough, County Down

Moravian

SET IN what is known locally as 'Zula's Hollow', this little church is more remarkable for the flamboyant gentleman who brought it about, than for any claim to architectural pretension. Moravian worship on this site began on 20 May 1754, about the time that John Cennick was founding churches elsewhere in Down and Antrim. Like most of the Moravian churches of this era, this must have been a simple thatched building, designed to meet the needs of a small community.

The halcyon period of Moravian fortunes at Kilwarlin came in 1834 with the appointment of Rev Basil Patras Zula as minister. Zula was a Greek prince who had had to flee his native land after resisting the Turks in the Greek War of Independence. On finding his way to Ireland, he married Ann Linfoot, under whose guidance he had put himself forward for the Moravian ministry. On coming to Kilwarlin, he found a congregation of five, and by the time of his death ten years later, he had increased this to

The unusual surroundings of Kilwarlin Moravian Church, laid out in the 1830s by Rev Basil Patras Zula.

150. Under his leadership a new church, manse and schoolhouse were constructed in 1835, and these buildings remain to this day.

Despite such domestic prosperity, Zula could never free himself from the fear of reprisals from his native land and he had the grounds of his church and manse laid out on the plan of the ancient site of the Battle of Thermopylae. The modern-day visitor to Kilwarlin must be rather startled by the unconventional landscaping of the church grounds, especially by the large central mound which greets those entering the front gates. Continuing this defensive trend, it is said that every room in Zula's manse was provided with two doors, one for entering and another for hasty exits. It is reported that one day Zula's wife saw him out on the road engaged in conversation with two foreign gentlemen, and, on being questioned by his wife, he simply said that he had to go to Dublin on urgent business. A number of days later she received news from Dublin that her husband had passed away. Those who accompanied his coffin back to Kilwarlin were rather puzzled by its great weight, and so they decided to open

it. To their horror, it was full of stones! We are told that, in spite of this, they said nothing and the casket was buried at Kilwarlin. It can be assumed that this is only a story and that his body rests below his tombstone in Kilwarlin Moravian graveyard. Such was the affection in which Zula was held that for a number of generations after his death, a great number of local children, both male and female, had the name Zula among their Christian names.

The church which Zula built is of four bays with the facade on the gable. The roof is surmounted by a bellcote, but most curious are the finials on the edges of the roof. These have the appearance of chimney pots, but are pinnacled rather like small crowns. A marble plaque within a semicircular-headed recess records the stages of the church's construction. The side windows are also semicircular-headed and are glazed with emblems of the Moravian faith, such as the Lamb of God with a banner. The manse is set under the same roof as the church, and continues on to the whitewashed and harled church hall, with its Georgian sashed glazing. To the rear of the manse is a two-storey projection known as 'Zula's Hide'.

The interior of the church is simple, and not dissimilar to the church at Ballinderry. There is a timber gallery at the back of the church, a central aisle flanked by bench pews and the pulpit on the end wall is flanked by balustraded staircases.

This little church, set in its unusual grounds, is an emotive place, bringing to mind the man who brought it into existence. It recalls a man who, detached from his native land, was able to evangelise and increase his flock, but lived in fear of his past, before finding his final resting place in this quiet corner of County Down, so far from his home.

■ **References**
Barry, pp 82–4.

LOWER BALLINDERRY MORAVIAN CHURCH
Lower Ballinderry, County Antrim
Moravian

'

The Moravian settlement at Lower Ballinderry was founded by the late Reverend John Cennick about 85 years ago. The chapel grounds, about 2 English acres, was then purchased for an unexpired term of years from a farmer, the late Ben Haddick.

'

THIS INFORMATION is from the Ordnance Survey Memoir of 1832–38, which also tells us that the first building on the site was thatched and paid for by English and continental Moravians. The Memoir goes on to state that the 1755 church was rebuilt in 1821, when goodwill seems to have prevailed, with donations from local clergy and 'persons of all religious denominations'. Disaster struck, however, for the church was destroyed in an accidental fire on Easter morning, 1835.

The church we see today was opened for worship on 16 June 1836, although the earlier foundation is recalled in the porch, which has a small circular window engraved with the date 1755. The building stands behind a long garden and graveyard, which formerly followed the Moravian custom of having all the tombstones laid flat. As with the Moravian settlement at Kilwarlin outside Hillsborough, the manse is attached to the end of the church, with communicating doors between the two. The entrance to the church is by a porch on the gable nearest the road, which is surmounted by a bellcote. The body of the church is of three bays of round-headed Georgian-glazed windows. Both the church and the manse sit beneath a continuous slated roof, a chimney stack marking the end of the church and the start of the manse, which has the appearance of a rural farmhouse with Georgian glazing.

The interior of the church is plain, the only ornament being found in the gallery at the back. This is panelled and dentilled, carried on four Ionic columns and

accessed by a tight spiral staircase. The central aisle, which is lined with pine pews, focuses on the pulpit and communion table. Emphasis is lent to the

Lower Ballinderry Moravian Church.

pulpit by a pedimented panel on the end wall, above which is a plaster arch with a key-block, supported on corbels.

With its own self-contained minister's residence and extensive gardens, this church gives the impression of having been built by a very self-sufficient religious community

■ **References**
Brett (Antrim), p 38; Craig, p 225; OSM (Vol 21, Antrim VII), pp 47–8.

GREAT JAMES STREET PRESBYTERIAN CHURCH
Great James Street, Derry, County Londonderry   *Presbyterian*

THIS FINE building, which is no longer used as a church, was built between 1835 and 1837 as the city's third Presbyterian church, and was often known as the Scots Church. The facade of the church, designed by Stewart Gordon, is rather tall with a narrow Ionic portico set at the top of a flight of steps flanked by scrolled retaining walls. Behind the portico is a semicircular-headed doorcase surmounted by a roundel which formerly bore the date 1837, but which now proclaims the building, not very convincingly, to be a glassworks of 1837! On either side of the portico are pedimented windows framed by Ionic pilasters which, due to the height of the steps, rest on a rather high plinth. Since conversion for commercial use a segmental-headed window has been broken through this plinth on either side of the steps.

The body of the church is of four bays lit by semicircular-headed windows, while the end wall has a large Venetian window, which internally had Corinthian columns and pilasters. There is a gallery around three sides of the interior, carried on fluted cast iron columns. Up to the time of the closure, the church was lined with box pews. The appearance of the interior owed much to a re-ordering carried out in 1863 by Boyd and Batt.

The former Great James Street Presbyterian Church, Derry.

Despite the fact that the church is now closed and used as a glassworks, it is quite clear that there was once a very hardy congregation here, as they endured a five-hour dedication service at the time of the opening of the church: no mean feat when you are sitting in a box pew.

■ **References**
Rowan, p 387; UAHS (Derry), p 31.

CRUMLIN NON-SUBSCRIBING PRESBYTERIAN CHURCH
Main Street, Crumlin, County Antrim

Non-Subscribing Presbyterian

HIDDEN OFF Crumlin's main street in a long graveyard, this church is very fine, and a visit to it is rather like taking a step back in time. The present church stands near the site of the earlier building of 1723. The facade is dated 1835 in Roman numerals, but from the church's appearance one would expect it to be much earlier. This is no doubt accounted for by the urban-rural architectural time-lag. It could well be that the church is modelled on the elliptical First Presbyterian Church in Rosemary Street in

Crumlin Non-Subscribing Presbyterian Church.

Belfast. The Crumlin minister, Rev Alexander, would have been familiar with this building, and despite shifts in architectural fashion, he must have decided upon this style for his new church. The actual date of opening was 17 September 1837, six months after Mr Alexander's death.

The church is built of rubble basalt with brick trimmings, shaped as an elongated octagon, with a projecting two-storey porch. (The present minister, who studied architecture, says that the only similar building, externally, that he has encountered is a charnel house in Italy!) The windows are Georgian-glazed; segmental-headed on the ground floor and semi-circular-headed on the upper floor. A broad doorway gives access into the porch, where the visitor can see the communion pewter and collecting shovels arranged over the mantelpiece. Access to the gallery can be had from either side of the porch.

Stepping into the body of the church, you almost expect to be joined by ladies in crinolines and men in frock-coats, such is the appearance and atmosphere of the building. The very individualistic arrangement of box pews survives, with an aisle circumnavigating the oval arrangement at the centre. The side pews follow the line

of this central oval. The horseshoe gallery above is carried on ten columns and two terminal pilasters. These all have Ionic capitals, pot-bellied bases and are painted in imitation of marble. The pulpit is hexagonal, painted white with gilded moulding on each face, and rests on a concave pedestal, which is also painted to look like marble. Two curved balustraded staircases give access for the preacher. Like many of the pews in the church, the pulpit retains its oil lamps. The ceiling is decorated with an acanthus roundel, surrounded by a circle of golden stars. In the gallery lie the remains of an organ, which had a very attractive white traceried case. This instrument would have been most unusual as it had pegged barrels which enabled certain hymns to be played in the absence of an organist.

In the graveyard is buried Rev Alexander, instigator of the construction of the present church, and founder of Crumlin Academy.

■ References
Brett (Antrim), p 52; UAHS (West Antrim), p 8.

CLOUGH NON-SUBSCRIBING PRESBYTERIAN CHURCH
Castlewellan Road, Clough, County Down   *Non-Subscribing Presbyterian*

BUILT IN 1837, the church is basically a three-bay hall lighted by semicircular-headed windows set in arched recesses. As with so many preaching houses the entire structure is lifted by the elegant facade, which in this case is dominated by two enormous granite Ionic columns, which stand 'in antis' on either side of a unique recessed semicircular porch. These columns, along with the two pairs of flanking pilasters support the entablature and the pediment. The side bays each have a segmental-headed recess, the upper half being occupied by a small sash window. Above each of these is a blind square-headed recess. The walls of the recessed porch are channelled to simulate masonry, and the doorway is embellished with a semicircular fanlight. A marble plaque set on the wall within this porch commemorates Rev James Shaw Brown, minister of the church 1930–39, who gave five years of his ministry to the congregation free of charge.

The interior of the church is of fairly conventional layout, with a flat plaster ceiling and a moulded cornice. The pulpit stands against the end wall and is flanked by a window on each side.

Immediately to the north-east stands the amazing Murland family vault, approached from ground level by a steep flight of steps. It is a sumptuous example of classical funerary architecture, being pedimented, with the added refinements of rusticated masonry and elaborate scrollwork.

Clough Non-Subscribing Presbyterian Church.

■ References
ASCD, pp 342–3; Curl, p 14; UAHS (East Down), p 26.

SCOTCH CHURCH, ARMAGH
The Mall, Armagh, County Armagh   *Presbyterian*

ARMAGH'S MALL proliferates with fine buildings of the eighteenth and nineteenth centuries, and among these is the Third Presbyterian Church, or Scotch Church. There had been a move to form a third congregation from 1837 and the first minister, Rev John McAllister, was installed two years later. At this stage there was no church, and worship was conducted in the Primitive Methodist Church in Abbey Street. The new church in the Mall was completed in 1840, although the facade bears the date

1837 in Roman numerals. The architect was William Murray, the cousin and apprentice of Francis Johnston, and the building cost £2500. The debt was cleared by 1845, due to Mr McAllister's exertions, travelling in Ireland, England and Scotland seeking support.

The facade is constructed of Armagh limestone, two storeys in height and three bays wide, the central bay being crowned by a pediment. This is supported on four Ionic pilasters, while two similar pilasters frame the facade

'Scotch' Presbyterian Church, Armagh.

Internally, the church holds no great surprises, being a four-bay rectangle with segmental-headed windows at ground level, round-headed at the upper level. There are two aisles and the pews are very idiosyncratically arranged on a shallow concave curve. The gallery rests on three cast-iron columns and its front has curious decoration which might be described as 'Celtic-esque'. The ceiling has a central plaster rose enclosed within an octagon of ribbing. This decoration was once more elaborate, but was modified during refurbishment.

Stained glass was installed in the 1970s. Rev David Graham and his wife, Mary, are remembered by the Good Shepherd window, created by the Harry Clarke Studios. The Good Samaritan window is in memory of William Elliot (died 1975).

■ **References**
Dixon, p 55; Killen, p 22; UAHS, *The Buildings of Armagh* (Belfast, 1992), pp 150–2.

and support the cornice. The central door is given emphasis by double scrolled brackets which support a cornice. Above is a round-headed window. The outer windows are segmental-headed, surrounded by rustication on the ground floor. The upper windows are square-headed and have lugged architraves.

BROOKEBOROUGH METHODIST CHURCH
Brookeborough village, County Fermanagh
Methodist

METHODISM HAS always prospered in County Fermanagh, and this church is a good example of a rural Methodist place of worship. It is a gabled hall, three bays in depth, the side windows having two lights with an oculus above. The facade has two tall and narrow round-headed windows flanking a central door, which is placed below an inscription plaque. This reads: 'Wesleyan Methodist Centenary Chapel AD 1839'.

The interior is plain, the only ornamentation being the cornice, which is decorated with acanthus leaves, and the three plaster ceiling rosettes. The two light pendants are particularly fine.

Brookeborough Methodist Church.

■ **References**
Rowan, p 149.

PORTAFERRY PRESBYTERIAN CHURCH
Steele Dickson Avenue, Portaferry, County Down

Presbyterian

THE OLD church on this site was a T-shaped meeting house of 1751 which had to be pulled down after being seriously damaged by the 'Big Wind' of 7 January, 1839. The architect chosen for the new building was John Millar, and it is thought that the selection of a classicist was due to the influence of the classical school attached to the congregation. Rev W Steele Dickson (who was imprisoned for his political radicalism before the 1798 Rebellion) founded this school in 1790. The building of the church was a truly congregational effort, with the stones being brought to the site by local farmers and businessmen. Henry Cooke opened the church on Thursday 2 September, 1841.

In appearance this is an amazing neo-classical church, and is quite unlike any other of its kind. Millar used the ancient Temple of Nemesis at Rhammus as his influence and produced a very robust Greek Revival structure. The stout unfluted Doric columns that carry the entablature of the structure rest on a high podium, giving the building a certain air of invincibility, which is enhanced by the fact that the columns are without bases. The gables are pedimented and are similar in appearance. In 1907 the spaces between the columns at each end of the church were glazed to create enclosed vestibules.

The solidity of the exterior is echoed in the ordered interior. The ceiling is compartmented and a U-shaped raked gallery occupies three walls. On each end wall are two Ionic columns, those at the pulpit end being partially obscured by the organ of 1917. The flanking stained glass

Portaferry Presbyterian Church.

windows commemorate those who served and those who died in the First World War. The church is four bays in depth with tall square-headed windows at gallery level, and smaller windows beneath the gallery. The building retains its box pews throughout.

This is a remarkable piece of architecture, and one that has always excited much comment. James Stevens Curl suggests that it would not look out of place in Helsinki or St Petersburg, and feels that it is one of the most distinguished neo-classical buildings in Ulster.

■ **References**

Bailie, WD, *Portaferry Presbyterian Church 1642–1992* (nd); Curl, p 14; UAHS (Portaferry and Strangford), p 12.

SAINT PATRICK'S CHURCH, MAGHERALIN
Magheralin village, County Down

Catholic

ST PATRICK'S CHURCH, built in 1843, is a rather rare example of a classical building constructed as an Ulster Catholic church. This was the style of architecture more usually associated with Presbyterianism at this time, and indeed Magheralin church would look like many Ulster Presbyterian churches if the cross was removed from the gable. Following emancipation there may have been a number of Catholic churches built in the style, but many of these were subsequently rebuilt in a more flamboyant Gothic idiom. Perhaps its rural location ensured the survival of this particular church.

This is not the first place of worship on this site, as the Ordnance Survey Memoir of 1834 describes the previous building, which dated from 1777, and suffered the misfortune of being burnt in 1798. It was, however, 'shortly afterwards reroofed and repaired by subscriptions'. According to the memoir this church was a T-shaped building, of whinstone with Gothic windows.

The facade of the present church is simple and dignified, being of whinstone (perhaps salvaged from its predecessor) and dressed with freestone. The two entrance doors are set in the sides of the pedimented porch, which is supported on four pilasters. The pediment itself is filled with black mosaics and a gold cross. This was built in the late 1980s replacing the former stuccoed porch which had two outer pilasters and two Ionic columns. This was probably added to the church later, although the new porch is fitting and contributes to the overall classical simplicity of the building. The facade proper is composed of four stone pilasters supporting the entablature of the pediment, which is really little more than a gable framed in stone and crowned by a cross. Beneath the cross is an inscription plaque which says, 'Ad majorem Dei gloriam AD 1843'. At ground floor are brick-framed recesses on either side of the porch, while above are four semicircular-headed windows, again framed in red brick. The church is four bays in depth and again composed of tall semicircular-headed windows with brick dressings. The facade is flanked on either side by an arched gateway.

Changes have been made in relatively recent years and there is little that is particularly outstanding about the interior of the church, although it is seemly and well cared for. The church is basically a two-aisled hall, with an integral sanctuary and a shallow gallery. There is dark woodwork throughout. The only ornate piece is the communion rail which is composed of Romanesque arches and extends outwards into the body of the church. The windows throughout are of coloured glass decorated with religious symbols and intertwining Celtic designs. A new sacristy, which cannot be seen from the road, was built at the back of the church in 1996.

St Patrick's Catholic Church, Magheralin – a rare example of a nineteenth-century classical Catholic church.

■ **References**
OSM (Vol 12, Down III), p 110; UAHS (Craigavon), p 9.

GILFORD FREE PRESBYTERIAN CHURCH
Dunbarton Street, Gilford, County Down

Free Presbyterian

THIS IS a pleasant building on an elevated site at the top of a flight of steps on the town's main street. Built in 1843 as a Methodist church, it first appears on the Ordnance Survey map of 1860. Since its construction it has also served as an Elim Pentecostal Church, and since 1990 has been the home of the Free Presbyterian congregation.

The gabled facade is of stucco and has three bays, the central bay being occupied by a flat-roofed porch incorporating a round-headed window with attractive glazing bars. The tall flanking sashed windows with margined panes are set within semicircular-headed recesses. Two plaques adorn the building; one formerly read 'Methodist Church', but only the latter word survives, while the other plaque bears the date of construction.

Gilford Free Presbyterian Church.

BANBRIDGE NON-SUBSCRIBING PRESBYTERIAN CHURCH
Downshire Road, Banbridge, County Down   *Non-Subscribing Presbyterian*

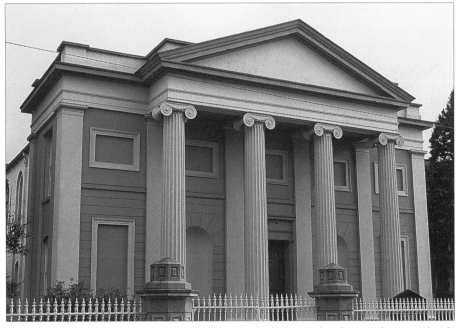

Banbridge Non-Subscribing Presbyterian Church.

THIS DIGNIFIED church was built between 1844 and 1846 by the Presbyterians, although it is now a Non-Subscribing congregation. The stuccoed facade, which is raised on a granite plinth, is five bays wide, with the three central bays fronted by the portico, composed of four fluted columns with Ionic capitals. Behind this are six unfluted pilasters with moulded capitals and bases. The entrance door is flanked by two semi-circular-headed niches; these in turn are flanked by blind square-headed recesses. Above, each bay is occupied by a blind rectangular recess with moulded architrave. At the other end of the building is a pedimented feature with narrow flanking wings (accommodating the old school room and the session room), all adorned with pilasters. On the ground floor there is a centrally placed door with a rectangular fanlight and above a semicircular-headed window, both enclosed within a tall round-headed recess. The sides are six bays wide, the terminal bays being broken forward and pilastered with windows at each floor set in square-headed recesses while the ground storey windows are segmental-headed and those above semicircular-headed.

The interior is arranged in the traditional Presbyterian meeting house manner; on entering the building, the visitor comes into a vestibule with a curved staircase on either side leading to the large U-shaped gallery. This runs around three sides of the interior and is carried on rather delicate-looking cast iron Ionic columns. The panelled gallery extends beyond these columns and the soffit is coved and plastered. As is the norm in this type of church, the pulpit is centrally positioned on the end wall, flanked by doors to the rooms behind. The pulpit is a fine tall piece of woodwork approached on each side by curving flights of thirteen steps with cast iron bannisters, and is flanked by a pair of tall lamp holders. Beneath, and just in front, is the seat for the clerk, while behind is a recess three bays wide, the entablature of which is supported on Ionic columns and is an integral part of the ceiling cornice. The ceiling itself is compartmented and centred by an elaborate radiating central rose. There are box pews throughout flanking the two aisles and a good Walker organ stands in the gallery.

Time has, thankfully, done little to diminish the architectural qualities of this church, and it stands as an excellent example of what a good neo-classical meeting house looked like in a prosperous market town in the nineteenth century. However, although it is one of the best, it must also rank as one of the last of the Presbyterian churches in Ulster to be built in this style, as congregations became architecturally aware and affluent, and looked to the greater air of spirituality which Gothic architecture was felt to give to any denomination.

■ **References**
ASCD, pp 339–40; Curl, pp 13–14; UAHS, pp 11, 13.

FORMER DONEGALL SQUARE METHODIST CHURCH, BELFAST
Donegall Square East, Belfast   *Methodist*

JOHN WESLEY preached in Belfast for the first time on 23 July 1756 in the town's market house. The first Methodist society in Belfast was founded in 1763, meeting in an old slaughter-house. After a period of meeting in private houses, a chapel was built in Fountain Street in 1786. In 1806 a place of worship was erected on the present site in Donegall Square. This was a plain square building seated with wooden forms, on the north side of which stood the preacher's lodge, known locally as 'the salt-box'. With an increase in numbers, it was decided to provide a larger church, and much debate on its siting ensued. However, the original site was maintained, largely because Alderman William McConnell promised £1500 towards the building if the congregation remained in Donegall Square.

Alderman McConnell laid the foundation stone for the present building on 2 July 1846. The architect was Isaac Farrell of Dublin, and the builder was James Carlisle, later the benefactor of the vast Methodist church at Carlisle Circus. As with Farrell's churches at Dublin and Coleraine, the style of architecture chosen was a very solid classical form. The front consists of a broad pediment carried on six Corinthian columns. Behind this is a rusticated arcade at ground level, and five blind square-headed recesses above. At the time of church's opening it was graced with a very valuable organ. This was an eighteenth-century instrument of some rarity, having been built by John Snetzler for the Church of Ireland Cathedral at Armagh, at the instigation of Archbishop Richard Robinson. When the cathedral was

The former Methodist church in Belfast's Donegall Square, before redevelopment.

given a new instrument in 1842, the Snetzler organ went to the Tontine Rooms in Armagh, before being bought by the Belfast Methodists in 1849. Tragically, when it came to the Donegall Square church, it was destroyed by fire on the evening it was first played. The fire also caused extensive damage to the church interior, which was reconstructed by James Carlisle, and completed in 1850.

Subsequent to the closure of the church in the early 1990s, the main body of the building has been demolished and only the facade survives, incorporated into a larger office development. The retention of the facade is little compensation for the loss of what was a very fine structure. The church was six bays long with semicircular-headed windows and the window on the pulpit wall was similar, except that it was flanked by two smaller rectangular windows. The church had two aisles lined with box pews, with a gallery running around three sides of the building. The pulpit was enclosed within a curved communion rail and the display pipes of the organ occupied the end walls of the gallery. The ceiling, which was replaced in 1949, was compartmented and rose from vaults on the side walls. The organ has now found a new home in the University of Ulster at Jordanstown.

The destruction of this handsome church has left this side of Donegall Square very much the poorer.

The facade of the church is all that remains after commercial development of the historic site.

■ **References**
Brett (Belfast), p 28; Curl, p 18; Larmour, p 11; Wesleyan Historical Society: *Donegall Square and Belfast Methodism* (Belfast, 1994).

JOHN WESLEY (1703–91)

Founder of Methodism

IN 1739 Wesley, an Anglican clergyman, experienced an intense religious experience which influenced him to begin a ministry of itinerant preaching which occupied the rest of his life. He preached tirelessly, usually in the open air, often encountering hostility. He visited Ireland regularly, travelling on horseback through the countryside and continued to do so well into his eighties. Despite some opposition by the

Anglican clergy and people, he was graciously received by Bishop Hervey of Derry and Archbishop Robinson of Armagh. His followers were nicknamed 'Methodist' because of their methodical devotion to religious study. Wesley always worked within the Church of England, although by the end of his life it became apparent that Methodists would become a distinct denomination.

Rev John Wesley

COLERAINE METHODIST CHURCH
Circular Road, Coleraine, County Londonderry

Methodist

METHODISM FIRST found a footing in Coleraine in 1774 when the Rev John Price travelled to the town from Derry to preach. The momentum that his preaching generated was increased when John Wesley himself preached in the town in 1778, 1785 and 1787. Wesley said of the townsfolk that they were 'good old soldiers and entirely after my own heart'. By 1801 a chapel along with a preacher's house had been completed in Preaching-house Street (now called Queen Street). This served the congregation well until the opening of the present gracious building in 1854.

The plans for this new church were drawn up by Isaac Farrell of Dublin in 1852. Farrell made two sets of designs, and the rejected ones bear many similarities to his church at Donegall Square in Belfast. The Coleraine church was built by local contractor Samuel Kirk, while the stuccowork, seen to great effect on the facade, was the handiwork of Thomas Boyle, also of Coleraine. The facade is composed of a Corinthian hexastyle portico, 'in antis', with the walls placed forward between the two sets of outer pilasters to provide more internal accommodation. These walls are banded for about half their height and are pierced by square-headed recesses which have moulded architraves. There is a vestibule area in front of the massive entrance door, and this is set back behind two large Corinthian columns. Above all this is the pediment, which has a dentilled cornice. Farrell had intended that the composition should be completed with curved flanking walls with attached pavillions, but sadly these did not materialise.

The body of the church is five bays deep, the windows being round-headed and set in sandstone surrounds. The interior is a galleried hall with a shallow apse. Cast iron columns with Corinthian capitals support the gallery, and have the added force of very decorative brackets on the

Coleraine Methodist Church.

soffit. The ceiling is coved with groined arches over the windows and the criss-cross ribs, which spring from this coving, are decorated at the intersections with acanthus leaves. This ceiling was particularly mentioned by the *Coleraine Chronicle* on 16 September 1854, when it was reporting the opening of the church. It also went on to state modestly that the mahogany pulpit was one of the most beautiful to be found in the country. Behind the pulpit are three semicircular-headed windows which were filled with stained glass in 1960.

It has been said of Farrell's classical designs for the Methodist church that they represent the tail-end of an architectural genre, and this may be true. However, of the number of churches for which he was responsible, the Coleraine church is perhaps his most imaginative and externally much more three-dimensional than, for example, that at Donegall Square in Belfast.

■ References
Rowan, p 206; UAHS, pp 14, 16.

THOMAS STREET METHODIST CHURCH, PORTADOWN

Thomas Street, Portadown, County Armagh   *Methodist*

WESLEYAN MEETINGS in Portadown had already commenced by the time John Wesley first visited the town in April 1767. The first chapel was built close to the site of St Mark's Parish Church. In 1832 a new church was built at the top of Thomas Street, and this still exists as commercial premises. It is a pleasant structure, built of coursed basalt with very pretty Georgian Gothic glazing. Increased attendances at services as a result of the 1859 revival added impetus to plans to build a new and larger church further down Thomas Street. Completed in 1860, this is the present Methodist place of worship in the town.

The interior of the present Thomas Street Methodist Church in Portadown.

The former Methodist church in Thomas Street, Portadown.

The church is built of blackstone trimmed with brick, but the ornate classical facade, which extends round the side of the building for one bay, is of stucco. Four very tall Corinthian columns support a pediment with a dentilled cornice which extends the breadth of the facade. Behind the portico, and at the angles and terminal points of the frontage, are fluted Corinthian pilasters. The facade is divided horizontally by a decorated frieze, above which are five square blind recesses. Access is by a central entrance door, or by two semicircular-headed side doors.

Given the rather hard external appearance of the church, the interior is a delight. There is the usual three-lobby arrangement in the vestibule area, with access to the gallery by balustraded staircases. There are pews lining either side of the two aisles, those at the back of the church retaining their doors, which are glazed and have a progressive increase in height. The side walls have four sets of paired windows, segmental-headed on the lower

level and semicircular-headed at gallery level. The gallery is extremely elegant, being an oval running the entire circuit of the building. Its front has a series of elongated oval openings, with a dentilled cornice and gilded foliage at the base. Fourteen barley-sugar columns with gilded Corinthian capitals carry the structure. The six-panelled ceiling is equally colourful with its details picked out in crimson, yellow and blue. The cornice is composed of an egg and dart motif with dentils above. The shallow barrel-vaulted ceiling above the organ is divided into eight panels, each with a very attractive plaster ceiling rose. On the parapet of the gallery at this point is an unusual music stand, supported on four miniature carved wooden harps. The pulpit, below the organ, is of highly polished wood and is octagonal with a projecting bowed front. The visual build-up of communion table, pulpit and organ is particularly impressive.

The church boasts a number of simple, but pleasing, classical monuments, with three dedicated to the Shillington family. In the gallery is a memorial to Rev Adam Averell, President of the Primitive Wesleyan Methodist Society, who died in 1847 in his ninety-third year.

■ **References**

Green, WJ, *Methodism in Portadown* (Belfast, 1960); UAHS (Craigavon), p 3.

ENNISKILLEN METHODIST CHURCH
Darling Street, Enniskillen, County Fermanagh

Methodist

METHODISM TRADITIONALLY tended to be more robust in areas without a strong Presbyterian tradition, and this accounts for the large number of Methodist churches in County Fermanagh. Methodism in the county was fostered largely through the preaching of Trooper William Price, 'a retired soldier who never retired from the service of his Lord'. Price began his work in 1762 and continued to travel and preach for thirty-two years. Progress was not easy though, as Wesley noted while preaching in the town in 1769: 'the large number of hearers – some civil and some rude and almost all totally unaffected'. Such was the antagonism shown towards Wesley, that the military had to save him from attack when he came to Enniskillen again in 1773. So serious were further incidents that a number of preachers were killed. When the authorities began to take action to prevent disturbances, the Methodists felt confident enough to build their first chapel (in what became Wellington Place) in the town in 1780. When Wesley returned again in 1787 he noted that 'the lions have turned to lambs'. In 1793 a new chapel with a thatched roof was built. Methodism in Enniskillen was gaining momentum due to visitations to prisons, conversions of condemned men and preaching in Irish. In 1845 it proved necessary to build yet another church in what is now called Wesley Street. Finally, with the added impetus of the 1859 revival, a site was purchased in Darling Street for the present church. The laying of the foundation stone by the Earl of Enniskillen took place on 17 June 1865 to the sound of the ringing of the Church of Ireland church bells.

The new church, opened in February 1867, was described as 'a splendid example of Corinthian style architecture'. The church was designed by WJ Barre, and although a fine building, it is rather archaic, being built in a neo-classical style at a time when many churches were embracing Gothic architecture. The facade is tall, being of two storeys and five bays and the ground floor windows are segmental-headed; those on the upper level are round-headed and all have keystones. There are six fluted Corinthian pilasters carrying a tall entablature with a dentilled cornice. Projecting forward is a lofty pedimented portico with four fluted Corinthian columns and a balustrade crowns the facade.

As with most churches of the 'preaching' denominations, of this architectural style, the interior is very much an auditorium, with a gallery with a

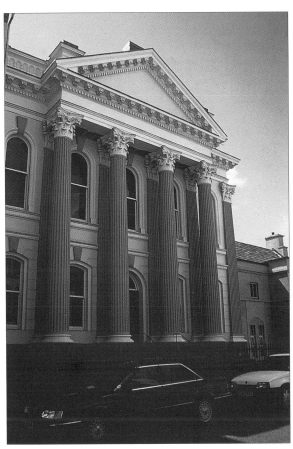

Darling Street Methodist Church, Enniskillen. The Methodists continued to employ the classical style at a time when most churches were built in Gothic.

pot-bellied front extending in a U-shape and carried on ten cast iron columns with Corinthian capitals. The pews which line the two aisles were once box pews, but the doors were removed and replaced with bench ends early in the twentieth century. On the back wall of the gallery are three round-headed arches which admit light from the front windows. Indeed, the entire interior is extremely well-lit with five bays of paired windows on the side walls; segmental-headed below and round-headed above. An elaborate cornice runs the circuit of the interior, while there is an exquisite plaster arch in which the organ sits.

Although it is a late neo-classical building, it is, nonetheless, a good example of its type.

■ **References**
Curl, p 18; UAHS (Enniskillen), pp 28–9.

ST MARY'S ORATORY, BUNCRANA
St Mary's Road, Buncrana, County Donegal

Catholic

St Mary's Catholic Oratory, Buncrana.

BUILT AROUND 1890, this represents a very late usage of the neo-classical style of architecture, particularly at a time when Gothic was much more favoured.

The facade is dominated by the portico with a steep pediment depicting Mary and the infant Jesus, topped by a cross. The entablature bears the inscription: 'Sancta Maria Ora Pro Nobis', and is carried on four Corinthian columns which sit on square panelled plinths. These columns are reflected on the facade proper by four pilasters, and the compostion has terminal pilasters supporting a dentilled cornice. Between the pilasters are moulded panels and roundels surrounded by festoons. The entrance door is round-headed and has a fanlight. Round-headed windows flank the portico.

Internally, the church is very long, with seven bays of paired windows. The decoration has a rather sparing neo-classical quality, with a compartmented ceiling and plaster rectangular panels on the walls, some of which are filled with the painted stations of the cross. These stations are the work of A Mariani and date from 1896. The simplicity of the interior serves to lend visual weight to the rather good reredos, which is composed of a dentilled pediment carried on two Corinthian columns. The pediment is filled with a representation of the Holy Spirit as a dove surrounded by cherubs.

■ **References**
Rowan, pp 154–5.

7
First Fruits Gothic Churches

THE BOARD of First Fruits was established in Ireland in 1711, when it was decided to use the first fruits (or annates) of the first year's revenue of a benefice or bishopric to provide funds for the building and repair of churches and glebe houses. However, these resources were woefully inadequate and there were so many churches in a state of disrepair by 1777 that the Irish parliament voted an annual grant to the Board of First Fruits for church building. These grants far outweighed the revenue from annates, and without them the board would have been destitute. The grant made by parliament for 1777–78 was £6000, and the annual sum fluctuated between this and £1500 until the end of the eighteenth century. After the Act of Union, when the Church of Ireland was united with the Church of England, parliament voted roughly £4850 each year for seven years. These funds were doubled in 1808 and 1809 and levels rocketed to nearly £60,000 per annum from 1810–16. Although this was reduced by half in 1817–21, the vast majority of First Fruits churches date from the first quarter of the nineteenth century. In addition the treasury could lend the board up to £50,000 interest free. Government assistance was absolutely vital to the board, given that between 1801 and 1821 its own revenue amounted to little more than £400 per annum.

With this financial help from the government, the board proceeded to make grants to parishes for the building of new churches. These grants tended to be of £500, which were often supplemented by a local benefactor. Due to the small amount of money available to parishes to build new churches, the materials chosen were often very cheap, with the result that the board had later to be approached again for funds for repairs. A case in point is Ballyphilip Parish Church in Portaferry, which was built in 1787 with a spire which became dangerous and had to be removed in 1810. With improved finances the board was in a position to offer substantial loans as well as making gifts. Frequently the churches built by the board took the form of a hall with a western tower in a simplified Gothic idiom, and this genre became recognised as a style in its own right, 'First Fruits Gothic'. Of course, the idea of a rectangular hall with a square tower appended to it was not a new one: Archbishop Richard Robinson and the Earl-Bishop of Derry had both constructed such churches in their ecclesiastical domains. However, it is the simplification of these and the sheer weight of numbers which renders appropriate the label of 'First Fruits Gothic'. The alert traveller will be aware that examples of this type of church can be found throughout Ireland.

Architecturally, the First Fruits churches were not especially inspiring, but they did provide a centre of worship in many places which lacked resource or a wealthy patron. Typical churches of the genre can be seen at Bushmills, County Antrim and Maghera, County Down. One particular observer, CL Eastlake, who decried the debased ecclesiastical architectural style which was employed, described a visit to such a church:

'

Enter and notice the tall neatly grained witness-boxes
and jury boxes in which the faithful are impanelled;
the 'three decker' pulpit placed in the centre of the
building; the velvet cushions which profane the
altar; the hassocks which no-one kneels on;
the poor box which is always empty. Hear how
the clerk drones out the responses for a congregation
too genteel to respond for themselves.
Observe the length, the impeachable propriety,
the overwhelming dullness of the sermon.

'

Clearly, Eastlake, like so many others, wanted to see a revival both in the fortunes of Gothic, that most Christian of styles, and in the ceremony of the church. However, it is unfair to dismiss the First Fruits churches as merely being sham Gothic halls. This may have been the case where resources were few, but in other areas we see a more muscular, 'spikier' type of Gothic, for example, at Monaghan and Cavan. In his excellent thesis on the Gothic revival in Ireland, DS Richardson draws comparison between St Mark's, Newtownards, and Francis Johnston's Chapel Royal at Dublin Castle. St Mark's is not just a glorified hall, for it has all the clearly demarcated elements of a true Gothic church: a tower, nave, transepts and a chancel. It is obvious from this church that the board was able to employ competent

architects and to appreciate this we need only look at Derryloran Parish Church in Cookstown (tower only surviving), designed by John Nash. By 1813 the principal architect to the board was John Bowden, and by 1830 there was an architect for each archdiocese of the Church of Ireland: William Farrell for Armagh; John Semple and his son for Dublin; James Pain for Cashel and Joseph Welland for Tuam. With the demise of the Board of First Fruits, Welland, who had been trained by Bowden, became the architect to the ecclesiastical commissioners.

The historian FSL Lyons has stated that the cultural differences in Ireland in the nineteenth century were reflected by religion and in turn by the architecture which each denomination employed to express its own tradition. So, dotting the countryside with Anglican churches was a physical manifestation, particularly after the Act of Union, of the Anglo-Irish ascendancy, as well as meeting the need for new churches. Many of the rural examples of the First Fruits churches are very simple, but it is unfair to dismiss them because of this. Most of them are very seemly buildings, often containing items of great interest, and to those who worship within them they represent old forms of architecture serving a very real purpose in their spiritual lives.

■ **References**
Eastlake, CL, *A History of the Gothic Revival* (London and New York, 1872), p 177; de Breffny, pp 145–50; Richardson, pp 184–5; 193–202.

BALLYPHILIP PARISH CHURCH
Off High Street, Portaferry, County Down   *Church of Ireland*

A PRETTY and unassuming church approached by two avenues which meet at a courtyard at the church door, this building dates from 1787 when the Board of First Fruits contributed £500 towards its cost. (The entire cost of the structure was £800 18s 9d.) When first built the tower had a spire, but this became dangerous and was removed in 1810. Writing of the church in 1837, Samuel Lewis described it as a 'neat modern edifice', indicating that even without the spire the church was in good order – the ecclesiastical commissioners had made a grant for repairs in 1836.

The church is built of rubble, although the upper section of the tower is rendered, no doubt to conceal the scars from the dismantled spire. The tower itself is

extremely squat, having battlements and corner pinnacles, with curious minature mullioned windows on the upper stage. A wooden structure, almost concealed behind the battlements, houses the bell. Rather than being appended to the church, the tower actually rises from the gable. The nave is three bays in depth with Georgian Gothic sashed glazing in all the windows, except that on the north-east, which is filled with stained glass. Later additions to the structure include the chancel and south transept, and plans for these survive, being dated 1861 and 1864 respectively.

At the time of these alterations to the fabric the opportunity was taken to remove the old pews and provide new chancel furniture. Perhaps the most pleasant of these fittings is the reader's seat with its poppyhead finials. The three-light east window contains a representation of the Ascension of Christ and is signed by Meyer of Munich. In the south transept stands the Conacher organ, which retains its hand bellows and 'mouse', used to indicate to the blower just how much air was in the instrument.

To the left and right of the chancel arch are the monuments to Rev John Robert Echlin (died 1891) and his wife Mary Anne (died 1871). The Rev Echlin was descended from Bishop Robert Echlin, Bishop of Down 1612–35. In the nave are good classical monuments to Hester and James Randal Donaldson (died 1807 and 1825 respectively) and John Savage (died 1825). The oldest tablet is that dedicated to the family of Patrick Savage (last date is 1725), which was brought here from the previous parish church. The west end has a curved gallery carried on four cast-iron columns, which is possibly contemporary with the pitch-pine roof.

Ballyphilip (C of I) Church, Portaferry.

■ **References**

de Breffny, p 136; Lewis, Vol 2, p 463; UAHS (Portaferry and Strangford), p 14.

CAVAN PARISH CHURCH
The Mall, Cavan, County Cavan

Church of Ireland

SITED AT the top of Farnham Street, this is a rather fine First Fruits church, attributed to the board's architect, John Bowden. The town's former place of worship was the old abbey church and a petition to the Lord Lieutenant, the Duke of Richmond, dated 1809, requests the move to a new site: 'The church was rebuilt in 1816, for which purpose the late Board of First Fruits granted a loan of £4000, and the remainder of the expense was defrayed by private donations'. It seems that plans were drawn up by a William Elsan; yet the *Gazetteer of Ireland* of 1842 claims that Bowden was the architect. Given his very obvious links with the board, there is every reason to accept this as fact.

The church is cruciform in shape with a four-storey west tower, all built in coursed rubble sandstone. The church is generously sized as it served as the place of worship for the town's garrison. As is evident from the appearance of the building, the transepts are later, probably about 1860, when a 'restoration' took place. A single-storey porch gives access to the foot of the tower and has its own buttresses, crocketed pinnacles and crenellations. The parapets of the vestibule and nave are also topped by crenellations, with crocketed pinnacles at the angles. The three-pointed nave windows have hoods with dripstones. There are crenellations and pinnacles on the tower parapet, from which rises the octagonal spire.

Cavan (C of I) Church.

The vestibule accommodates a north-south running passage with a door at each end, designed to ease the flow of people entering and exiting the church.

As with most garrison churches, the nave is very wide, covered by a rib-vaulted ceiling. The sandstone arches to the transepts very clearly mark them out as later, as the other internal decoration is in plaster. Interestingly for a Church of Ireland church, there is no central aisle, but rather two side aisles, running from the back doors. The pews are not original, and date from the Victorian restoration. However, the woodwork of the U-shaped gallery, which is carried on quatrefoil columns, is original.

The church possesses one of Ireland's three monuments by Sir Francis Chantrey. Here the Earl of Farnham is commemorated by a memorial of 1826, which shows the dying earl about to take his final leave of his distraught countess. This cost 1000 guineas, and would have cost a further £200 had Chantrey carried out the countess's wish for a more elaborate marble background. Other monuments of interest include that to Nathaniel Sneyd, MP, 'whose valuable life was terminated by the hand of a maniac at noonday'. He was shot in 1833 by one John Mason in Dublin's Westmoreland Street. In the gallery is a memorial to Rev Joseph Storey (died 1838), showing a heaven-bound angel above a sorrowing figure at an urn.

■ **References**

Lewis, Vol 2, p 319; UAHS (Cavan), pp 14, 16.

ST MARK'S PARISH CHURCH, NEWTOWNARDS

Church Street, Newtownards, County Down   *Church of Ireland*

UNTIL THIS church was completed in 1817, Anglican worship in Newtownards was conducted in the medieval priory church. The present church came into being at a cost of £5446. The Board of First Fruits gave £831 plus a loan of £3692, while the remainder came from the Londonderry family of Mount Stewart, whose arms appear over the west door. The rector of the parish at the time was Rev Marcus Cassidy and it has been suggested that the church was dedicated to St Mark, in recognition of his Christian name.

Built in Perpendicular Gothic, the church has been likened to Francis Johnston's Chapel Royal at Dublin Castle and there are a number of similarities both inside and out, particularly in the external carving and the internal ceiling and woodwork. As first built the church was cruciform, but in 1865–66 the north transept was demolished and replaced by an aisle which virtually doubled the size of the building.

The west tower is of four stages, with weathered buttresses and a pinnacled parapet, and carries a graceful octagonal spire. All the pinnacles on the building have rich carving, being festooned with an amazing array of female, clerical and kingly heads. This decoration underlines the parallels with the Chapel Royal. The entire circuit of the roof is battlemented and is punctuated by pinnacles at the top of angled buttresses. The walls of the church have a slight batter. The main nave and south

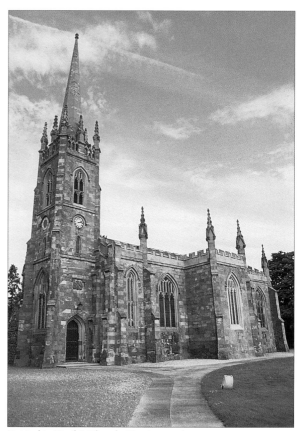

St Mark's (C of I) Church, Newtownards.

transept windows are of three lights with Perpendicular tracery, while a narrow lancet occupies the westernmost bay of the nave. The windows of the later north aisle are fairly faithful copies of the original and may incorporate some of the old tracery, for it is evident that the pinnacles have been re-used from the old walls.

Internally, the north aisle throws the building off balance, although it emphasises how small the original church must have been. The south transept served as the vestry room until 1865 and the triple-decker pulpit stood in front of it. The north transept (which no longer exists) was the Londonderry family pew. From the porch the nave is approached through a passage running under the gallery. Flanking this passage are large enclosed pews which provided seating for the rector and the churchwardens. The Gothic detailing of these pews is very fine and the ribbed plaster ceilings are of particular note. As a reminder of the longevity of Christian worship in the area, an old carved stone, brought here from Movilla Abbey, is built into the south nave wall. Pilasters run up the nave walls and support the intersecting ribs of the painted and gilded vaulted ceiling. This arrangement is reminiscent of other large First Fruits town churches, such as those at Cavan and Monaghan. The shallow south transept now serves as a baptistry and has a very colourful medieval stained glass window, decorated with intricate patterns and religious figures. This is reckoned, by some, to have come from the old priory, but is more likely to have been purchased on the Continent by the Londonderrys, as they had similar glass installed in the chapel at Mount Stewart. After 1865 the south transept was their family pew and so they may have been anxious to enrich it with this rare glass. The glass in the six-light window in the chancel was erected as a First World War Memorial.

The symmetry of the nave was destroyed by the addition of the north aisle, which is linked to the old church by four pointed arches resting on circular columns, but it seems that some attempt was made to marry the two parts. Although the aisle roof is trussed, the pews and windows do at least replicate those of the older section. There is a rose window on each gable of the aisle, and the Conacher organ stands below the eastern one.

DS Richardson feels that St Mark's may actually have been designed by Francis Johnston, although there is no documentary evidence to support this. He goes on to say that 'the exterior is a most exceptional piece of Perpendicular design, probably the best of its date in the British Isles'.

Medieval stained glass in the south transept of St Mark's, Newtownards.

■ References

Richardson, pp 196–8.

MAGHERA PARISH CHURCH

Three miles outside Dundrum, following sign-posts for Maghera round tower, County Down *Church of Ireland*

Maghera (C of I) Church – a very typical Board of First Fruits church.

THIS LITTLE church of 1825 is a fairly typical example of the hall and tower churches erected by the Board of First Fruits, which in this instance contributed £500 towards the building. It was most likely to have been designed by the board's architect, John Bowden.

The architecture is rudimentary Gothic, being basically a hall of three bays of lancet windows with a western tower. This tower is rendered and rises in three stages, having a pointed door, a thin lancet with lattice glazing and a belfry window. The angles of the tower have buttresses which are inset at each stage and rise to a battlemented parapet capped by pinnacles with little finials. The nave is also rendered and was extended in Victorian times by the addition of a three-bay south aisle of random granite. Inside, this division is marked by arches carried on granite columns.

There is something rather appealing in the simplicity of this church and those like it. Nestled away in quiet corners of our rural landscape they seem to represent how a church should look in the popular imagination.

■ **References**
UAHS (Mourne), p 44.

ST PATRICK'S PARISH CHURCH, MONAGHAN
The Diamond, Monaghan, County Monaghan

Church of Ireland

LEWIS RELATES that this church was erected in 1836 on the site of an earlier structure and cost £5330. Of this, £1100 was a legacy from the Dowager Lady Rossmore; £1000 was bequeathed by a Mrs Jackson; £2000 came as a loan from the Board of First Fruits. The board was usually associated with the construction of simple hall and tower churches, but they liked to be more ambitious in the larger towns, as we see here, and at Cavan and Newtownards.

According to Lewis, the church is 'later English' in style and is composed of a rectangle with crenellations and divided into six bays of tall pointed windows by a series of buttresses topped by pinnacles. At the east end is a shallow chancel, and a buttressed and pinnacled three-stage tower with a needle spire stands at the west end.

Over the entrance door on the north side of the tower is a plaque with a bishop's mitre, above which is the clock erected in 1902 to mark the coronation of King Edward VII. In the porch is the crudely-lettered gravestone of Oliver Ancketell (died 1666). The church has many features in common with those at Cavan and Newry, having a broad interior with a gallery around three sides, and very similar treatment of the ceiling. Ten clustered columns and four half-columns carry the gallery and continue to support the ceiling vaults and to divide the nave from the north and south aisles. The ceiling is ribbed and has six elaborate gilded bosses placed at the intersections of the ribs. As at Cavan, there are two aisles rather than a central one, and the church's military connections may explain this; this layout enabled large processions to take place more easily. The box pews, sadly, only survive at the head of each side aisle, but there are interesting canopied pews at either side of the chancel arch. These are of dark colour, with clustered columns supporting the canopies, which have Gothic pendant tracery and crocketed pinnacles. The left-hand canopy is decked with a baron's coronet, and that on the right with a mitre. By their very position these pews reflect the local secular and sacred powers. Alas, neither pew is seen to any advantage as they are placed behind the alarmingly large white Victorian pulpit and reading desk.

St Patrick's is rich in memorials, particularly with a military leaning, and the walls of the chancel have an especially good array of wall monuments. Mary Anne, Baroness Rossmore (died 1807) is commemorated by a

St Patrick's (C of I) Church, Monaghan.

work by Thomas Kirk which shows 'The Parting Glance', as her grieving husband has to be torn away from his dead spouse. Even the dog is shown having a good cry! Another emotionally-charged memorial, the work of Lewis of Cheltenham, recalls Lady Augusta Rossmore (died 1840). The sculptor shows a distraught Baron Rossmore (the same gentleman shown in the previous monument) looking longingly at the empty chair once occupied by his second wife. 'The Soldier's Funeral' is the subject of another Kirk memorial in the chancel, and remembers the Honourable Charles Westenra (missing in action 1824) of the 8th Hussars, who was, on 23 January 1824, 'found wanting at their roll call'. Kirk depicts two hussars leading the unfortunate hussar's horse with its vacated saddle.

At the west end of the gallery is the fascinating monument to Henry Craven Jesse Lloyd, killed in 1879

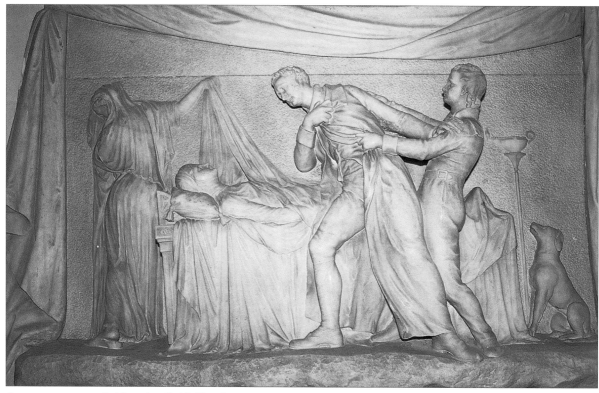

Rossmore monument in Monaghan Parish Church.

by the Zulus at Islandula. The memorial is canopied, with a relief at the centre showing two soldiers at the grave of their fallen comrade, while the Boers approach. Framing the relief are attendant figures; a soldier on the left and two Zulu warriors with assegais and shields to the right. At the base of the memorial is a reliquary containing the (presumably posthumous) medal awarded to Lieutenant Lloyd. Death in a far-off land is also recalled in the south gallery monument to Captain John Owen Lucas, who was killed at Ferozeshah in 1845. This shows drums, bayonets, spears and two elephants. This was the work of Joseph Robinson Kirk, whose father fashioned the monuments in the chancel.

The east window is of three lights and contains stained glass in memory of the third Baron Rossmore who died in 1860. The top section of the window contains the Rossmore arms and is mirrored at the opposite end of the church by the carving of the arms on the top of the organ case in the gallery. These carved, painted and gilded arms, though now darkened by age, have a soldier and a horse as supporters. The organ was built by Telford in 1865, although the case has the appearance of being earlier.

St Patrick's was completed three years before the demise of the Board of First Fruits, but by its elaborate nature demonstrates that where there was financial patronage from another source, a building of some grandeur could be constructed.

■ **References**

Potterton, p 57; UAHS (Monaghan),
pp 11–14; Lewis, Vol 2, p 384.

8
Tudor and Early Gothic Churches

FOLLOWING THE 1829 Catholic Emancipation Act there was greater scope for architectural adventure in church building among the nonconformists. The momentum in church building which the Catholic church should have had from this time was stunted somewhat by the catastrophe of the Famine, but nevertheless there was a concerted move and desire to provide better places of worship. Writing in 1798 in the *History of Winchester*, Father John Milner said that Gothic was a Catholic, not an Anglican style. Catholic churches in Ireland in general had tended to be built as classical structures, shunning the 'Anglican style', but there was a feeling that Gothic was an essentially Christian architecture and in the period from 1829 to about 1850 we can see a faltering start and then a gain of momentum towards a full embracing of Gothic in Ulster. This trend can be detected in all the denominations.

Since the mid eighteenth century the Church of Ireland had produced what were essentially classical churches with Gothic detailing. This continued into the 1830s with the simple Gothic encouraged by the Board of First Fruits. In 1829 Thomas Bell published his work, *On the Revival of Gothic Architecture in Modern Times*, and in so titling it he appears to have coined the term 'Gothic Revival'. The mode of Gothic employed in the 1830s and 1840s, as with First Fruits Gothic, is Perpendicular and the degree of competence with which it was applied varied from church to church. A timid use of Gothic can be seen at the Methodist church of 1835 at Tandragee, now sadly divested of its original tracery. With its rather two-dimensional use of buttresses, finials and battlements

this church belongs to a little family of buildings which includes the Faith Mission at Ballymena, Banbridge Catholic Church and the vanished Seceders Church in College Square North in Belfast. At Tandragee the architecture seems to lack confidence, for behind the Gothic facade is a very sober classical interior. Much more self-assured is the fine church of St John at Killowen, which has an inspired articulation of tall Perpendicular traceried windows, crenellations and turrets and generally the air of a Tudor college; an architectural suggestion much more fully developed at St Malachy's, Belfast.

Crumlin Presbyterian Church of 1839 by the classicist John Millar is a charming Gothic church, and along with the pretty 'Tudoresque' Dunluce Presbyterian Church, built in 1845 by Lanyon, represents an early Presbyterian foray into Gothic architecture at a time when this denomination was still utilising the neo-classical idiom. Once again, these early dissenting examples of Gothic are somewhat two-dimensional, although extremely picturesque.

Further impetus was gained by the formation in 1838 of the Down and Connor Church Accommodation Society within the Church of Ireland. The society existed to provide grants to build churches in parishes where it was felt that a place of worship was needed. The young Charles Lanyon offered his services to the society free of charge and the churches that resulted from this arrangement tended to be variations on two basic designs. Among such churches were those of Muckamore, Killagan, Hollymount, Upper and Lower Kilwarlin, Craigs, Groomsport, Ballyclug, Glynn and Raloo.

Crumlin Presbyterian Church, designed by John Millar.

One of the prime movers in the society was Richard Mant, Bishop of Down and Connor, who was concerned that liturgical correctness should be reflected in church buildings, and provision made for the proper administration of the sacraments. He felt that new churches should have better provision for kneeling at prayer, and that particular emphasis be given to the witness and participation in the eucharist. The study of ecclesiastical (and therefore primarily Gothic) architecture, was promoted by the Down and Connor and Dromore Architecture Society, founded in 1842 with substantial input from Mant. The move towards better standards in sacramental worship which he and the Architecture Society wished to see was severely criticised in some quarters as 'Popery', allied to a suspicion of high church Tractarian tendencies. An example of the extremism of views can be seen in the case of the ordering of the chancel at Tyrella Parish Church, which called for an enlarged space around the holy table as well as a separate lectern. The outcry that this engendered eventually finished the Architecture Society, for the low

church element feared what they perceived to be a diminution of the place of the word of God.

Looking at the first tentative steps towards a Gothic revival across the denominations there is plainly a progression from a cautious approach to an eventual realisation that it represented a style which enhanced devotion and sacramental worship. Thomas Duff provided the Catholics of Newry with a fine granite cathedral of English Perpendicular Gothic complete with side aisles, a clerestory and vaulted ceilings; the whole edifice enriched with turrets, battlements and pinnacles. This was built between 1825 and 1828, just before emancipation, but, with a better understanding of Gothic architecture and a more ecclesiological approach, this Perpendicular form would give way to Decorated Gothic. This change in perception and scholarly advance is materially conveyed by the structure of the Catholic cathedral at Armagh. This was begun in 1838 to the designs of Thomas Duff, but work ceased due to the Famine when it would have appeared lacking in compassion to continue building while so many church members were dying. After the Famine Duff was dead and JJ McCarthy was appointed in his stead in 1851. Duff's cathedral was to have been Perpendicular and had been built as far as the top of the aisle walls, although the mullions had not been built. McCarthy chose to retain the shape of the cathedral, but altered the style to Decorated Gothic. He removed the triple-tower arrangement and gave the building more of a vertical thrust by adding two steeples to the frontage. Duff's Tudoresque ogee-arched doors survive in the ground level of the cathedral, but a Decorated structure rises above them. This cathedral is a material expression of the transition from Tudor and early Gothic to a full High Victorian Gothic Revival style.

■ **References**

ASCD, p 50; de Breffny, p 251; McBride, pp 7–15.

ST MARY'S PARISH CHURCH, NEWRY
John Mitchel Place, Newry, County Down

Church of Ireland

ANGLICAN WORSHIP in Newry had been conducted in the old parish church of St Patrick since 1578. Indeed, St Patrick's is claimed to have been the first Protestant church built in Ireland after the Reformation. However, in 1811 an act was passed by parliament for the provision of a new church. One of the reasons why this need arose was the 'decayed and ruinous' condition of the old building.

Work on the new Gothic parish church of St Mary, designed by Patrick O'Farrel and supervised by Thomas Duff, commenced in 1811, but was hindered by a shortage of money. Among a number of schemes to raise the necessary funding was an unsuccessful application for a grant from the Board of First Fruits. Eventually an act of parliament was employed which levied a tax on property in Newry. The Catholic cesspayers in the town did not oppose this levy on the understanding that the promoters of the bill would assist in the building of the Catholic cathedral in Hill Street, which they did. By the time St Mary's was completed in 1819, it had cost a total of £12,566.

As completed, the church consisted of the present aisled nave with an eastern tower and spire and a chancel flanked by a room either side at the west. In 1886 the chancel was lengthened and the side rooms increased in size by Sir Thomas Drew. The building is constructed of granite, with internal dressings of Bath limestone. The buttressed tower is of four stages, crowned by gabled pinnacles and graced with a 60-foot spire. On the north, south and east faces of the tower are pointed doors, each with a fanlight containing interesting Gothic tracery. At first-floor level each face of the tower has a hooded window. Above this and beneath the clock is a sculpture of a mitred abbot in his alb, sitting in a chair, with one hand raised and flanked by two yew trees. This makes visual reference to the position of Lord Kilmorey as the lay abbot of Newry and Mourne, while the yew tree refers to the Irish name of the town, *an tlúr* – 'the yew tree'. The three dials of the clock are enclosed within diamond-shaped panels. The clock was made by Edward Smith of Dublin in 1827 and presented by the Earl of Kilmorey. At third floor level are windows with two cinquefoiled and transomed lights. The internal divisions of the church are marked externally by weathered buttresses and those at the angles have gabled pinnacles. The aisles are lit below gallery level by windows of two-

St Mary's (C of I) Church, Newry.

pointed lights with chamfered jambs in a four-centred head, while those above are taller with two-centred heads. A vestibule links the tower to the body of the church and gives access to the galleries. Internally this vestibule takes the form of a vaulted passage leading through the foot of the tower, with doors to the left and right.

The interior of St Mary's is spacious and light and consists of north and south arcades of five bays. The quatrefoil columns in the aisles are made of wood and carry galleries around three sides of the building. The arches span each bay of the nave arcade and also divide each bay of the aisles at gallery level. Above, the columns support the ribbed and vaulted plaster ceiling, the intersections of which are enriched with elaborate bosses. The gallery stops one bay short at the western end of each aisle. In 1886 the chancel was extended to cover an area of 29 feet by 21 feet, approached from the nave by a flight of steps. The large chancel window is of five cinquefoil ogee lights with vertical tracery in a two-centred head. The stained glass in the window depicts five scenes from the parable of the Good Samaritan in the lower section; above are St Patrick, the four archangels and the four evangelists. The uppermost section shows the Ascension. The window is in memory of Rev Thomas B Swanzy (died 1884), whose son, Dean HB Swanzy, later became rector and was responsible for compiling the diocesan clerical succession lists. During this period the encaustic tiles were laid on the chancel floor and the ceiling above was sheeted in pine. At the same time the box pews throughout the church were removed and replaced by the present bench pews and memorial choir stalls were provided by the Swanzy family, again in memory of Rev Thomas Swanzy.

St Mary's is especially notable for its splendid collection of monuments, some of which were brought here from St Patrick's Church. Three are the work of John Smyth (c1773–1840), of which that commemorating Sarah Hamilton on the north wall of the nave is the simplest, being a white marble wall tablet with cornice. More ambitious is the nearby memorial to Acheson Thompson (died 1818) which has a full-length figure of Religion leaning on an urn and pedestal, while an upturned torch, symbol of death, rests on the opposite side. The most outstanding monument in the church is undoubtedly that commemorating Major-General Henry Davis on the west wall of the south aisle. It is claimed that this monument cost over £1200, and given its sheer size (occupying most of the wall) this is easy to believe. It is a superb example of Smyth's work, which compels attention, constructed of white marble and freestone and depicts the Major-General in a medallion portrait surrounded by military trophies, above which Fame stands blowing her trumpet.

Perhaps more interesting for the man it commemorates than for its design is the memorial on the north wall of the nave to Trevor Corry (died 1781). He was the British Consul at Danzig and was created a Polish baron by King Stanislaus Augustus. The monument itself, the work of W Spence of Liverpool, is pedimented with crossed palm branches.

On the south wall of the nave is a monument by Kirk of Dublin to James Wright (died 1817). The inscription tablet is flanked by fluted pilasters surmounted by a pedimented panel containing the figure of a woman seated beneath a weeping willow. To the left is a draped urn, and to the right, a lily.

Below the gallery on the east wall of the nave, is a monument to Isaac Corry, the Chancellor of the Exchequer for Ireland, who died in 1813. There is a marble sarcophagus covered in drapery, thoughtfully pulled to one side to reveal a cartouche of arms and a medallion portrait of the departed. On the same wall above the gallery is the fine monument to John and Elizabeth Pollock (died 1785 and 1774 respectively), which has moulded architraves rising from consoles to a fluted frieze and moulded cornice supporting a pediment, broken to accommodate an urn. The inscription tablet is decorated with foliage sprays and crossed bones. Above the inscription is a circular panel enclosing an angel with a torch and beneath this is a panel with crossed palm branches. The family must have been slightly less than pleased with the work of the mason who lettered the monument, as the inscription is extremely crooked.

The church possesses a fine set of four wooden-handled brass collecting shovels. Two of these are inscribed, 'The gift of Mr John Rakestrow'. The other shovels were given by the churchwardens, George Guy and James Halyday.

■ **References**

ASCD, pp 331–3; Reside, SW, *St Mary's Parish Church, Newry* (Newry, 1933), pp 9–17, 21–2.

ST JOHN'S CHURCH, KILLOWEN
Kyle Brae, Coleraine, County Londonderry   *Catholic*

WELL SITED ON a hillside overlooking the River Bann and the town of Coleraine, St John's is one of the finest Catholic churches of its period.

The present church building, which was completed in 1834, was built largely due to the exertions of Father Daniel O'Doherty, with financial assistance from the Irish Society. The building is Tudoresque in appearance and is built in Perpendicular Gothic. It is constructed of rubble basalt with freestone dressings. The main facade facing the town is of five bays, with the largest window being the central five-light window. This is framed by slender octagonal flanking turrets pierced by blind Gothic arcades. The parapet of the church is capped by crenellations and there are stone crosses on the gables. The architect is said to have been J Kirkpatrick.

When first constructed, the church had the rather traditional internal arrangement of having the altar placed on the long wall of the building, with a door on each gable. Despite being such a fine church, the original floor was made of packed earth. Alterations during the course of the years have given St John's a longitudinal internal layout. Among these changes was the installation of a holy water stoup from the old Cistercian monastery at Macosquin. The most recent changes to the interior

St John's Catholic Church, Killowen.

were in 1990 when the building was reroofed and the present sanctuary fittings installed. These replaced the elaborate Gothic reredos, although the new fittings are simple and appropriate, being made of light oak with basic Gothic detailing. The east window depicts the Crucifixion and was installed by Meyer of Munich.

This is a remarkably fine church and the articulation of its architectural elements is reflected in the later church of St Malachy in Belfast.

■ References

Mullan, D, and Donnelly, P, *St John's, Coleraine* (Coleraine, 1992), pp 156–7.

TANDRAGEE METHODIST CHURCH
Market Street, Tandragee, County Armagh

Methodist

THE FACADE of this church represents an early attempt at rudimentary Gothic architecture at a time when most dissenting places of worship were still employing the classical idiom. Having said that, the body of the church is still very much a classical church. The facade is rather two-dimensional, but it is pleasing for what it represents and has architectural parallels with the Faith Mission Hall in Ballymena, which was built as a Non-Subscribing Presbyterian church.

A plaque over the main front window is inscribed 'Wesleyan Chapel 1835', which is quite an early date for a Methodist church built in this style. The facade is of stone with a central gabled section which has a doorway with a shallow pointed fanlight. Above this are a large pointed window and the datestone. Flanking this central section are two more similar windows. When first built, the windows were filled with Perpendicular Gothic tracery, but this was removed to allow the installation of modern stained glass. The front has four very thin buttresses, each capped by pinnacled finials, linked by not very convincing battlements.

Given that there is a Gothic facade, it is a little peculiar to find a classical interior. The body of the church is entered through an airy vestibule with pretty plaster ceiling roses. On the staircases to the gallery are stained glass windows in memory of John Wesley and Robert Strawbridge, the founder of Methodism in the United States of America. The minister's room over the vestibule is lit by a large window depicting sowers and reapers at work in spring and summer and is inscribed,

Tandragee Methodist Church before the removal of tracery from the windows.

'The world is my parish'. Three segmental-headed windows at ground floor and three round-headed windows at gallery level light the interior. Presumably these were once filled with sashed glazing, but now regrettably contain uPVC windows. The U-shaped gallery occupies three of the walls and is carried on seven fluted Ionic columns, while the pulpit and the Conacher organ in its Gothic case dominate the end wall. The ceiling has a simple coved cornice, and the light pendant hangs from the central ceiling rosette.

The interior is unremarkable, though seemly; it is the early attempt at a Gothic facade which renders the church of interest.

ST MALACHY'S CHURCH, BELFAST
Alfred Street, Belfast

Catholic

St Malachy's Catholic Church, Belfast.

PERHAPS ONE of the best-known Catholic churches in Belfast, this was the third church built in the city for that denomination. The need for a new church arose when St Mary's and St Patrick's could no longer cope with growing numbers of worshippers.

The present splendid Tudor Revival structure owes its genesis (as a memorial in the porch records) to a bequest of £3000 left by Captain Thomas Griffith (died 1838). The bishop of the diocese, Dr Denvir, needed a cathedral and it was proposed that St Malachy's would serve this purpose. In fact, Bishop Dorrian was consecrated here in 1860. The architect for the church was selected by competition, the work being given to Thomas Jackson, whose former partner, Thomas Duff, had produced churches in the Tudor Gothic idiom at Armagh, Newry and Dundalk. The foundation stone of St Malachy's was laid on the patronal festival, 3 November 1841 and Primate Crolly dedicated the church on 15 December 1844.

The church is cruciform, the actual interior being rectangular, but with projecting porches and a rear sacristy. King's College Chapel, Cambridge, may well have influenced Jackson's design. The exterior is constructed of red brick with stone trimmings painted a pastel shade to complement the brick. The main facade is dominated by the two-storey porch composed of a Tudoresque doorcase with a window above, which is flanked by the arms of the dioceses of Down and Connor

and those of Dr Denvir. On the gable are stepped battlements, crowned by a cross. Vertical emphasis is given to the front by the soaring flanking turrets which have castellated tops looking rather like rooks on a chessboard. The terminal wall of each arm of the church is treated in a similar manner. Battlements run the entire length of the parapets, with pinnacles placed on the corner buttresses. The castellated tower, which is not really visible at close quarters, replaced a spire of 1868.

For the magnificent interior, Jackson employed the device of rural Catholic churches, in that the altar is set on the long wall. As with the rural churches, a raked gallery, carried on eight cast quatrefoil columns, occupies three walls of the interior. The Telford organ stands in a recess at the back of the gallery and is contemporary with the church. The crowning glory, literally, of the interior is the superb 'Strawberry Hill' ceiling which has been likened to that of Henry VII's chapel at Westminster Abbey and is composed of plaster pendants and vaults, which enliven what would otherwise have been a flat expanse. The walls have pilasters which run from the half-pendants which abut the walls.

When the church was renovated in 1926 the original oak sanctuary furnishings were removed and the present marble altar, pulpit and rails (some of which survived a more recent re-ordering) were installed, the gift of Hugh and Sarah Donaghy. The octagonal pulpit rests on eight squat circular columns and has carvings of the Agnus Dei and Christ preaching. Above the pulpit is a traceried and crocketed canopy, which is particularly Tudor in feel. The altar employs a variety of coloured marbles and the frontal depicts Christ in the tomb. At the same time as the installation of these fittings, the sanctuary arch was given a screen of Perpendicular tracery. The three-dimensional quality of this has been heightened in recent years by the placing of the altar within a deep arched recess. The reredos paintings depict Christ carrying the cross, Mary with two odd-looking cherubs, and St Malachy. These were the work of Felix Piccione, a refugee from the Hapsburg-ruled Italian states.

■ References

St Malachy's Church, Belfast, Centenary Record (Belfast, 1948), pp 7–11; Brett (Belfast), pp 19, 23, 45; Larmour, p 10; UAHS (Joy Street and Hamilton Street area), pp 9–10.

PATRICK DORRIAN (1814–85)
Catholic Bishop of Down and Connor

BORN IN Downpatrick and trained in Maynooth, Dorrian became coadjutor Bishop of Down and Connor in 1860, and was enthroned as bishop in 1865. During his episcopate Belfast witnessed great industrial growth and a marked increase in the Catholic population. Dorrian met this challenge by building new Catholic churches, the most notable being St Patrick's in Donegall Street. He also gave encouragement to religious orders and was involved in the provision of new schools. He was buried in St Patrick's, where he is commemorated by a monument in the chancel.

Bishop Patrick Dorrian

FAITH MISSION HALL, BALLYMENA
High Street, Ballymena, County Antrim

Faith Mission

THIS LITTLE building, designed by Thomas Jackson, represents a naive example of Gothic architecture, built before a serious Gothic revival had got underway in Ulster. It was built in 1845 as a Remonstrant Presbyterian church and has many physical similarities to the now-vanished Scottish United Secession Presbyterian Church in College Square North, Belfast. Like that church, and the Methodist church at Tandragee, the Gothic style here is rudimentary in the extreme, but has a simple charm and marks a wavering attempt to move from the traditional nonconformist use of classical architecture.

The facade is of three bays, battlemented, with thin buttresses capped by pinnacles, the central pair being angled. The glazing patterns are very pretty, the two outer windows being latticed and the oculus window over the central door having elaborate glazing.

Of the interior, only vestiges remain, the building having been converted into two floors. Balustraded staircases (which presumably gave access to the gallery) remain and there are a number of Gothic doorcases.

■ **References**
Dixon, p 55; UAHS (Antrim and Ballymena), p 16.

Ballymena Faith Mission.

ST PAUL'S PARISH CHURCH, CASTLEWELLAN
Main Street, Castlewellan, County Down

Church of Ireland

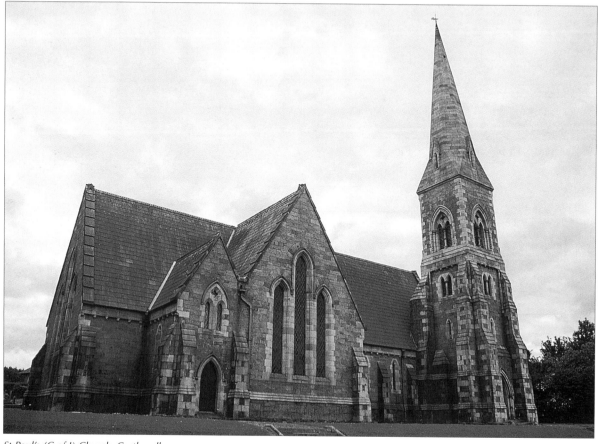

St Paul's (C of I) Church, Castlewellan.

ON 1 DECEMBER 1853, Dr Knox, Bishop of Down, Connor and Dromore, consecrated St Paul's, Castlewellan, as a Proprietary Chapel within the parish of Kilmegan. Under an act of parliament landowners were permitted to build new churches auxiliary to the parish system, provided their upkeep could be maintained. It was the Annesley family that built St Paul's, although it was some time in the planning. Following the death of the third Lord Annesley, his brother-in-law, Rev JR Moore, managed the family estates. It was he who, in 1847, invited Charles Lanyon to provide plans for a church building. In the event it seems that it was Lanyon's partner, WH Lynn, who was actually responsible for the plans, and he has left us with a very fine early Victorian Gothic church.

Lynn encountered problems during the design stage over the proposed crosses for the gables. Rev JR Moore was happy enough to have them, but advised the architect to incorporate the crosses within circular shapes, saying, 'there is a feeling against crosses, if a circular one like a wheel could be put next the road, people who have hot heads and bad eyes might take it for a chimney'. There are now no crosses and this is not the only indication of a local dislike for 'Puseyism' or high church tendencies; a look in the vestry room reveals a short flight of steps which once led from this room straight into the pulpit. This arrangement allowed the clergyman to vanish from sight and change from a white surplice into a black preaching gown.

Set well back from the road at the head of a broad

The Annesley family pew in Castlewellan Parish Church.

lawn, the church is of cruciform shape and solidly built of Ballymagreehan granite with ashlar dressings. At the north-west corner is a four-stage tower surmounted by a slender broach spire with a weather-vane. There are graduated buttresses, inset at each stage, stopping just below the belfry windows. The crest of the roof carries a decorative ridge. On each gable of the church are triple lancets with taller central windows; these have hood mouldings adorned with rather comical carved heads. The nave is of four bays of narrow pointed windows divided by buttresses, although there is one less window on the north due to the position of the tower and entrance door. At the far side of the north transept is the organ chamber, which was formerly also a porch enabling the Annesley family access to their pew without troubling them to mix with the rest of the congregation. The church has a pleasant Conacher organ.

The yellowish glass of the west window admits light to the nave, while modern stained glass in the smaller windows depicts saints. The oak pews have finely carved poppyhead bench ends at the top and bottom of the aisle and quatrefoil heads on those in between. Some of the pews retain their doors. In the north transept is the Annesley family pew, which is a large box pew with matching upholstery, carpet and tablecloth. On the table sit prayer books belonging to various members of the family. Unusually for this type of pew, there is no fireplace, although the discovery of a chimney flue in the south transept suggests that the Annesleys possibly once sat there. The transeptal windows with their purple, yellow, orange and green diamond panes were made by Clokey of Belfast to the design of Lady Mabel Annesley in memory of her brother, the sixth earl. By contrast, the glass in the east window is a rich tapestry of Celtic patterns. The crossing of the building is supported by four sets of piers, composed of seven clustered columns which support the ceiling vault. The nave, transept and chancel roofs are constructed with timber trusses. The east wall of the chancel has a fine sandstone arcade with a central canopy above a pointed opening. Other decoration on this reredos includes three angels and chevron mouldings, which are also to be found elsewhere in the church. Throughout the building the floors are laid with glazed tiles, but those in the chancel are particularly good and incorporate the symbols of the four evangelists with the pelican at the centre representing Christ. A setting of tiles just before the holy table depicts the Lamb of God taking away the sin of the world.

An interesting fact about worship in St Paul's is that from the time of the disestablishment of the Church of Ireland in 1869 the clergy continued to use the Church of England Prayer Book, a practice which persisted into the reign of Edward VII. St Paul's became a parish church in its own right in 1977.

■ References

Greer, RF, unpublished historical notes on the church; McBride, pp 25–6; UAHS (Mournes), pp 25–8.

9

The High Victorian Period

AS HAS BEEN noted, early attempts were made to utilise Gothic for Ulster churches, as far back as the seventeenth century and 'Planters' Gothic'. A brief look at the Catholic cathedral at Newry shows it to be an embryonic attempt at a Gothic Revival structure, and also how the development of the Catholic cathedral at Armagh places it at the threshold of High Victorian Gothic church architecture. There are many reasons why the mid nineteenth century saw a fuller and more correct use of the style. Relaxation of the penal code meant that it was no longer necessary to keep Catholic places of worship as low-key structures. It appears that there was an element of architectural rivalry between the Catholic and Church of Ireland churches, best seen in Letterkenny, County Donegal, where the massive Catholic cathedral towers over its older and smaller Anglican counterpart. As industrialisation increased, so too did the prosperity of worshippers in the Catholic and nonconformist denominations, and this contributed to greater resources being available for the construction of churches.

Comparing the Gothic elements used in the mid to late nineteenth century with the 'Gothick' of a century before, the chief difference we can see is that a scholarly or 'ecclesiological' approach was now employed, and the most influential writings on the subject advocated a move away from 'picturesque' Gothic. Important writings on the subject included John Britton's *Architectural Antiquities of Great Britain*, EJ Wilson's *Specimens of Gothic Architecture* and *An Attempt to Disseminate the Styles of English Architecture from the Conquest to the Reformation*. This latter work was written by Thomas Rickman and Charles Pugin. Pugin's son, Augustus Welby Northmore Pugin, is regarded as one of the greatest exponents of true Gothic architecture. He felt it to be the most Christian of styles, and that no other should be used. Augustus Pugin expounded his ideas on Gothic with a scholarly antiquarian approach in his book, *True Principles of Pointed or Christian Architecture* of 1841. He felt strongly that an ecclesiastical architect had to work with his faith as well as his architectural knowledge and ability. It was, in Pugin's view, essential that the architect understood and embraced the church's liturgy, rubrics, rites and ceremonies. In some of our Ulster churches we are aware that the architect worked with a visualisation of the outward signs of faith. It is little wonder then that the Catholic architect, JJ McCarthy, is often referred to as the 'Irish Pugin', for he claimed that a 'Catholic architect must be Catholic in heart'.

In England, *The Ecclesiologist* journal was scathing of architectural developments in Ireland, stating that 'ecclesiology in Ireland is far more backward from various causes than it is in England'. Despite this criticism, there was a growing interest in ecclesiology and this manifested itself particularly within the Catholic church and the Church of Ireland. Societies were formed with the express purpose of studying and promoting ecclesiastical architecture. As we have already noted, the Church of Ireland had the Down and Connor and Dromore Architecture Society, formed in 1842 with substantial input from Bishop Richard Mant (a member of the Cambridge Camden Society, which was a by-product of the Oxford Movement). The formation of such a society

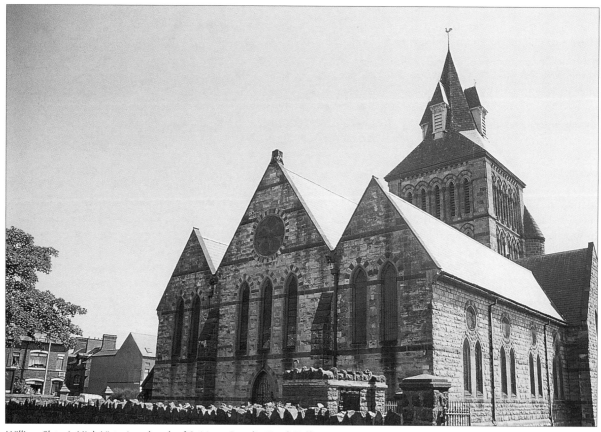

William Slater's High Victorian church of St Mary, Crumlin Road, Belfast.

was welcomed by the *Ulster Times*, which supported Gothic architecture with its 'exalted and noble feelings which are so devotional in their character'. Unfortunately this was not a common viewpoint and many evangelicals and low churchmen feared the implications of 'high' elements, given that the Cambridge Camden Society was seen by many as supporting the Catholic spirituality of the Oxford Movement. While in England the Cambridge Camden Society did want to reintroduce features which had been dispensed with at the Reformation, such as confessionals, rood screens or holy water stoups, the Down and Connor and Dromore Architecture Society had no idea of following suit. They were concerned rather to give the sacraments of baptism and Holy Communion more visual emphasis. The Architecture Society was eventually shaken into submission by a petition with 1300 signatures of those concerned about doctrines from England creeping into the Church of Ireland. Mant said that the petition would not finish the society, but it had to be renamed the Harris Society and became a sterile body offering no further innovation or disturbance. The important factor in these events is that an interest had

been established in ecclesiology within the Church of Ireland, and as long as high church elements were excluded, Gothic architecture was used enthusiastically in the construction of churches from the mid nineteenth century.

Extensive church building took place right across the denominations, particularly in Belfast where the population had risen to 119,393 by 1861 and 208,122 by 1881. New churches were also constructed in the larger and more prosperous towns, and often this necessitated the replacement of an older building, or substantial reconstruction as at St Patrick's Church of Ireland Church, Coleraine.

Belfast gained some very fine and idiosyncratic churches at this time, with a number of renowned architects vying with each other to produce outstanding buildings. The Belfast Church Extension and Endowment Society was set up in 1863 'to provide church accommodation and pastoral care' for members of the Church of Ireland who had moved to Belfast to seek employment. The first church to be built by the Church Extension Society was St Mary's, Crumlin Road, to the designs of William Slater, who was also responsible for the Church of Ireland cathedral at Kilmore, County Cavan. Slater was able to accommodate a congregation of 700 within St Mary's by incorporating broad side aisles grafted onto a cruciform plan with an apsidal chancel. The most outstanding feature of the exterior is the massive central tower with its broach spire pierced by tall lucarnes. The choice and manipulation of building materials, white Scrabo stone banded with red Scottish stone, is very High Victorian in feel. The relish for the polychromatic treatment of church buildings can be seen elsewhere in Belfast at St Matthew's, Shankill Road; University Road Methodist Church; St Mark's, Dundela, and at the startling Methodist church at Carlisle Circus. Of course, it will be noticed that some of the High Victorian churches in Belfast are Romanesque as opposed to Gothic, such as Elmwood Avenue and Sinclair Seamen's Presbyterian churches and University Road Methodist Church. The nonconformists seem to have gone for eccentricity rather than ecclesiology, although there was an element of scholarship, as evidenced by the influence of John Ruskin's *Stones of Venice*. Utilitarian considerations came into play for the Methodists, and this accounts for the cleverly-hidden halls under 'pattern book' Romanesque churches at Donegal and Ballymoney. Such Gothic churches as were built by the Presbyterians and Methodists still clung to their own liturgical requirements, having two aisles and a central pulpit, rather than the Gothic, and therefore Catholic, arrangement of a central aisle leading to an altar or holy table. The nonconformists, it has been said, never became leaders of architectural fashion, but at this period their aesthetic conservatism did lessen and they had the will and the resources to display more adventure in their buildings.

The firm of Lanyon, Lynn and Lanyon, fired by the versatility of Charles Lanyon and the imagination of WH Lynn, produced some very fine High Victorian churches, while the firm of Welland and Gillespie designed a number of churches for the ecclesiastical commissioners, although without the same sparkle. An early death robbed Ulster of the great promise shown by WJ Barre, an architect capable of injecting his churches with remarkable individuality. He was responsible for the chancel of the Anglo-Catholic church at Ballymoyer, County Armagh, which has the most obvious ecclesiological features of a Church of Ireland church of the High Victorian era. Its font, which is placed prominently under the tower, was designed by William Butterfield and has a covering hood, which is extremely rare in Ulster. One of the dripstones on the east window is said to represent the Blessed Virgin Mary. It was not everywhere in Ulster that an Anglican architect could have got away with this! St Anne's Church of Ireland in Dungannon was designed by Barre in 1865 and shows his mastery of the High Victorian Gothic idiom. Indeed, Alistair Rowan has detected qualities in this church akin to the work of William Burges. St Anne's is an almost aggressively Gothic church, and has a very solid looming appearance, with a large rose window and broach spire.

Some of the province's finest Catholic churches were built in the second half of the nineteenth century, and the formation of the Ecclesiological Society nurtured the desire for more spiritually-driven architecture. The society strove to study the architecture of the past and 'to apply the result of their investigations to the wants of the Church'. It was not the church building alone which concerned the society, but also the fittings of stained glass, sculpture and paintings, all of which were now to be found in abundance in Gothic churches, recreating the conditions of worship of medieval Christian Europe. When designing his churches, JJ McCarthy made particular use of the Decorated idiom of the fourteenth century, and this can be seen at Monaghan Cathedral; Carrickmacross Catholic church, County Monaghan; and at his finest Ulster church, St Patrick's, Dungannon.

William Butterfield's Church of Ireland church of St Mark's, Dundela, provides us (at least externally) with an ideal of a High Victorian church, with its unique tower and striking use of coloured sandstone. DS Richardson feels that everything which follows St Mark's is an anti-climax, for here we find a richness of design coupled with a visual expression of the need for sacramental worship. Allied to this is the importance of the church as the only example in Ulster of one of the most talented High Victorian architects.

When we compare the superb churches of the High Victorian era with the buildings constructed as places of worship in the first quarter of the nineteenth century, we can detect a remarkable transformation. All the major denominations embrace of the Gothic Revival to a greater or lesser extent, and perhaps for the first time the differences between the religious traditions, as expressed by their churches, became less marked.

■ References

McBride, pp 7–23; Richardson, pp 482, 544; Rowan, pp 257–8; Sheehy, pp 5–29; *Ulster Times*, 8 October 1842.

HOLY TRINITY CHURCH, COOKSTOWN
Off the main street of Cookstown, County Tyrone

Catholic

THIS CHURCH, set high above the broad thoroughfare at the centre of Cookstown, has the distinction of having been designed by JJ McCarthy. Like all of his work, the building displays his great attention to detail. The intention to build a church here was revealed in the *Builder* in 1854, and the cost was then expected to be £5000. The church envisaged at that stage was slightly bigger than actually built, although this is still a substantial edifice. Work continued up to the time of the church's consecration by Most Rev Dr Joseph Dixon on 3 June 1860.

Holy Trinity consists of a nave and chancel with aisles, a south porch and sacristy to the north-east. The facade, seen from the narrow drive from the street, is dominated by the west tower and spire, which are Early English Gothic in style. The entrance door has carved heads serving as stops for the hood moulding, while above is a blank niche, obviously wanting a statue. Rubble dressed with sandstone has been used for the construction of the church.

Behind the ordered symmetry of the facade is a five-bay nave with sanctuary, the pointed arches being carried on circular pillars, a favourite of McCarthy. There are five clerestory windows to the nave and four smaller trefoil ones to the sanctuary. The roof is of open timber-work highlighted by the gold stencilling of religious symbols onto the red-painted panels above the decorative cornice. The windows in the aisles are two-light, whereas the east window is of five lights and filled with glass by Hardman, which depicts the Virgin Mary. Much of the carving in the church is by Purdy and Outhwaite of Dublin. The reredos behind the high altar is the work of Lane of Birmingham and Dublin.

There is an interesting juxtaposition between this McCarthy church of the nineteenth century and Laurence McConville's convent chapel of 1965 next door. The chapel sits at an angle of 45 degrees to the old convent. It is clad in Portland blocks decorated with crosses, and incorporates the work of Michael Biggs, Patrick Pye, Benedict Tutty and Patrick McIlroy. It is indeed rare to find two such diverse pieces of architecture side by side.

Holy Trinity Catholic Church, Cookstown.

■ References
Builder, 10 June 1854, p 305; Hurley, p 55; Rowan, p 215; Sheehy, pp 45–6; UAHS (Dungannon and Cookstown), p 33.

NEWTOWNARDS METHODIST CHURCH
Regent Street, Newtownards, County Down *Methodist*

METHODISM HAD been growing in Newtownards since the visit of John Wesley in 1758, when he preached to an attentive crowd at the bowling green in the town. In 1807 a place of worship was built, which was subsequently sold to the Reformed Presbyterians. Such was the growth in Methodist numbers that another church had to be built, and this was opened on 22 December 1822, with considerable help from other denominations.

The present church was dedicated on 12 November 1854 and was the first of a group of Ulster Methodist churches built to a standard pattern. It is five bays in depth, one of which is a later addition, and has a stuccoed Romanesque facade. The entrance door is round-headed and has the construction date in the fanlight. Stucco piers divide the bays of the frontage, the door being set below a two-light window with an oculus beneath a hood moulding. The outer two windows are narrow and round-headed. The facade is topped by a pagoda-like bellcote.

■ **References**
The Methodist Churches of Newtownards and Comber (Newtownards, 1954), pp 7–12.

One of a set of four: Newtownards Methodist Church.

COOKSTOWN METHODIST CHURCH
Loy Street, Cookstown, County Tyrone

Methodist

THE SECOND of the 'pattern book' Romanesque Methodist churches, this was built in 1858 and replaced an earlier church in the town. On the facade of this freestone church is a plaque brought from its predecessor, which reads: 'Primitive Wesleyan Methodist and Sunday School Bible and Missionary Societi [sic] Meeting House 1825'.

■ **References**
Rowan, p 216.

Cookstown Methodist Church.

BALLYMONEY METHODIST CHURCH
Seymour Street, Ballymoney, County Antrim   *Methodist*

THIS CHURCH, built in 1861, is constructed of rubble blackstone with sandstone dressings, such as the corbel-table and the scallop-capped columns. The church hall is cleverly placed in the basement of the church, which makes full use of the drop in the ground level.

■ **References**
UAHS, (North Antrim), pp 41–2.

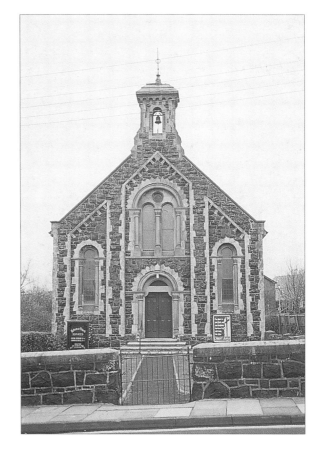

Ballymoney Methodist Church.

DONEGAL METHODIST CHURCH
The Diamond, Donegal, County Donegal   *Methodist*

DESCRIBED BY Alistair Rowan as having an 'entertaining design', this building is contemporary with the rest of this group of Methodist churches and follows just the same pattern. As at Ballymoney, the church sits on top of a hall. Rowan likens the bellcote to a Victorian country-house chimney!

■ **References**
Rowan, p 239.

Donegal Methodist Church.

SINCLAIR SEAMEN'S PRESBYTERIAN CHURCH
Corporation Square, Belfast
Presbyterian

The nautical interior of Sinclair Seamen's Presbyterian Church, Belfast.

PERHAPS ONE of the most imaginatively furnished churches in Ulster, Sinclair Seamen's Presbyterian Church dates from 1857, when the foundation stone was laid by Lord Moncrieff, Lord Advocate of Scotland. However, the church had its beginnings with the interdenominational organisation known as the Seamen's Friendly Society, which built a chapel and school in Pilot Street in 1836. Ten years later the chapel, known locally as 'the Bethel', came under the jurisdiction of the Presbyterian Church. An increase in numbers in the congregation moved the Sinclair family to erect the present church in memory of John Sinclair, with the express wish that it 'be considered as specially called on to watch over the spiritual interest of seamen frequenting the port'.

The church was designed by the firm of Lanyon and Lynn, and readily displays Lynn's interest in the writings of John Ruskin. Built in the Venetian style, with Romanesque and Gothic elements, the building could evoke thoughts of the great Mediterranean seaports that some of the nautical worshippers would have visited. The striking campanile stands in the angle of the main church building, which is L-shaped, and the two are linked by a 'bridge of sighs' which gives access to the gallery. The facade to Corporation Square contains a rose window placed above four Romanesque windows.

It is the interior furnishings that really elevate the building. The Rev Samuel Cochrane (ordained in 1902), sought to create a church building which reflected the church's commitment to the spiritual needs of seafarers. Visitors to the church are welcomed by semaphore flags laid into the tiling on the floor. The pulpit was installed in 1903 as a memorial to Rev D Berkley, and twenty years later had a carved prow of a ship, the *Mizpah*, added to the front. The pulpit, and the organ behind, are hung with port and starboard lights, those on the pulpit having served a practical purpose on one of the Guinness barges

on the Liffey. There is also a main mast light on the pulpit. From such a preaching platform it is easy to visualise the minister steering his flock 'o'er the world's tempestuous seas'! There is a brass wheel and capstan which came from an American ship, and was retrieved by two members of the congregation after spending a number of years at the bottom of the ocean. At harvest each year the figure of a sailor stands at this capstan in full naval garb.

The font is actually a binnacle adapted for baptismal use by the Rev Samuel Cochrane and placed in the church as a memorial to his mother, and is inscribed with the words 'consecration', 'dedication', 'initiation' and 'thanksgiving'. His father is commemorated by stained glass depicting the four evangelists, incorporated in one of the porches. On one of the walls is a brass bell from *HMS Hood*. This was also rescued from the bottom of the sea and is now used to herald the start of evening service by ringing 'six bells'. Although the church retains its original collecting shovels, a series of model lifeboats now serve to lift the collection.

Even the wall monuments in the church reflect the sea, being shaped as an anchor, a lifeboat, a rudder, a bell and a lighthouse. The stained glass speaks of the sea through scriptural references such as, 'The sea is His and He made it' (Psalm 95 v 5) and 'The winds and the sea obey Him' (Matthew 8 v 27). Particularly pleasant are the windows in the bridge of sighs, which show the four seasons. The war memorial windows beneath the gallery were erected in 1919 and show a soldier, a sailor and an airman. Laid up here are the flags of disabled ex-servicemen.

The actual layout of the church is rather individualistic, the basic plan being a double-aisled church with a gallery at the back, but there is a single-aisled transept looking towards the pulpit which is placed in the corner as opposed to centrally. To the left of the pulpit is the communion table with its carved decoration of an anchor and a bell.

With such interesting nautical fittings adapted for religious purposes, along with superb models of ships displayed around the interior, Sinclair Seamen's Church stands as a remarkable and tangible reminder of the congregation's ministry to the sailors who used, and still use, the port of Belfast.

■ **References**

Brett (Belfast), p 18; Larmour, p 30.

ELMWOOD PRESBYTERIAN CHURCH, BELFAST (NOW THE ELMWOOD HALL)
Elmwood Avenue, Belfast   *Presbyterian*

THIS IS a highly individual building and it comes as no surprise to find that it was designed by an amateur architect rather than a professional one. This is perhaps why it is such a flamboyant structure, free from some of the strictures of conventional church architecture.

In the winter of 1858 the decision was taken to form a new congregation in this part of Belfast. The period 1858–59 saw the formation of about four or five new Presbyterian congregations, and it may be assumed that this upsurge was due in part to the revival of 1859, and also the rise in the population of the developing industrialised city. (In 1861 the Presbyterian population in Belfast numbered 42,229.) R Workman invited parties interested in forming a new congregation to his house on 5 November 1858. At this meeting Robert Corry offered the members a building site for a church on University Road, on the corner of Elmwood Avenue. Accordingly, he and a number of others, including John Corry were asked to submit plans for the church. John Corry was a keen amateur architect, having been the builder of the Presbyterian college to the designs of Charles Lanyon. By 15 March 1859 he had submitted plans for a galleried church capable of holding 750 people. The contract for the building work was given to Henry Martin of Great Victoria Street and the foundation stone laid on 28 May 1860 by George H Stuart of Philadelphia. It is interesting to note that a sealed bottle was placed in the foundations containing: the names of all those connected with the foundation of the new church; 1859 General Assembly minutes and report of assembly proceedings with regard to the 1859 revival; the report of the Belfast Town Mission; McComb's Almanac for 1860; the *Banner of*

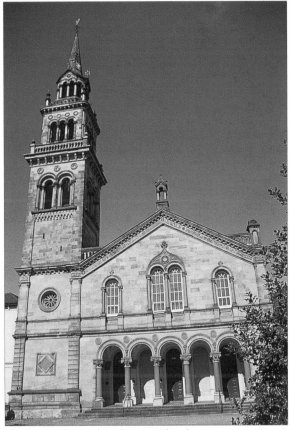

The former Elmwood Presbyterian Church.

Ulster and *Belfast News-letter* for the day, and a few coins bearing the image of Queen Victoria.

In reporting these events, the *Belfast News-letter* remarked that the 'church will be an ornament to the neighbourhood. The plans will differ considerably from any with which we are acquainted'. They were right. The exterior of the church is striking, employing and welding together quite an array of architectural features giving a facade which can be described as Lombardo-Venetian in style, and like Sinclair Seamen's Church elsewhere in the city, deriving inspiration from the writings of John Ruskin. The body of the church was faced with Scrabo sandstone, while a yellower sandstone was used for the tower, completed in 1872. The tower has something of the appearance of the tiers of a wedding cake, being of three stages, each pierced by openings framed by columns with finials at the corners of the lower two tiers. The whole edifice is crowned by a short needle spire with a rooster weather-vane. The front of the church is broad and has a loggia of five arches, the capitals of which have a strong botanical theme. Above these are circular discs of coloured marble let into the wall. At first floor level there are central coupled windows, flanked by outer single semicircular-headed windows, all with hoods. This treatment of the windows is repeated on the Elmwood Avenue elevation, with the added distinction of an arcade beneath two circular windows. The gable of the facade has a rather jaunty little minaret, completing the vertical thrust of the design.

Having closed as a church, the interior is bereft of its rich dark pulpit and pews, and now serves as the base for the Ulster Orchestra. Indeed, so different is this building from most conventional churches that, with its ecclesiastical fittings removed, it is rather difficult to visualise it as a place of worship. Most splendid of the internal decorations is the ceiling divided into eighteen panels, each enriched with a geometric plaster rosette, all very suitably painted. The amateurism of the design can be seen in the way the compartmenting of the ceiling does not tie in with the layout of the windows below. On the front wall three Romanesque arches mark where the pipes of the organ once stood, with the pulpit in front, as there are two doors beneath the arches which obviously gave access to the minister's room. The walls are wainscoted to a height of about 4 feet, while the side walls each have three sets of paired windows resting on elaborate corbels. The stained glass has been removed and replaced by elongated Georgian glazing, which looks rather bland in this particular setting. There is a raked gallery supported on two Corinthian columns and two terminal pilasters, while the gallery front is composed of a row of narrow Romanesque arches. Next door to the church is the former manse, also to the designs of John Corry.

Elmwood Presbyterian Church has proved more fortunate than many former churches, and in its present role is well maintained and serves an excellent purpose in the cultural life of the city, and, indeed, the province.

■ **References**
Brett (Belfast), p 21; de Breffny, p 144; Dewar, J, *A History of Elmwood Church* (Belfast, 1900), pp1–8; UAHS (Queen's University area), pp 27–9.

ADAM CLARKE MEMORIAL METHODIST CHURCH, PORTSTEWART
Heathmount, Portstewart, County Londonderry   *Methodist*

AS WITH the Methodist Church in Portrush, this church is in memory of Adam Clarke (c.1760–1832), the great promoter of Methodism in Portstewart and Portrush. Clarke was a great classical scholar and spent his life preaching in England and Ireland, and is credited as having filled the void left by the death of John Wesley. In fact, this church is built on a site which Clarke had purchased to build himself a house for his retirement but he died of cholera in England before work could start.

The church which we see today was opened on 4 July 1861, having been built to the designs of WJ Barre, and it was a very unusual building. No doubt it was this individuality which gained Barre the commission following a competition. Dunlop, in his book on the life of Barre, describes the church as a Gothic building with 'the walls of the nave carried up to give the external effect of a very large tower, with the chancel and porch bays projecting like choir chapels'. Pictures of the church as built show a broad and squat tower with five pointed openings, the whole embellished with crenellations, pinnacles, flying buttresses and a corner turret. Re-

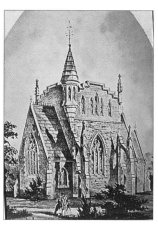

Portstewart Methodist Church as originally built.

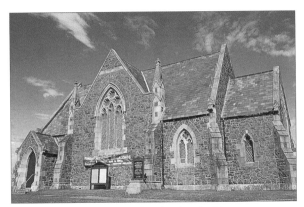

Portstewart Methodist Church today, bereft of its ornate stonework.

grettably, this was damaged in a storm in December 1884 and some sections were removed, and all was swept away during alterations in 1914, leaving the building as it is now. It is built of uncoursed basalt with sandstone trim and takes the form of a nave with a single-bay chancel. The large west gable, which was formerly the base of the tower has a large three-light window, as does the chancel. There are weathered buttresses at the angles of the church.

■ **References**
Dunlop, D, *A Memoir of the Professional Life of William J Barre Esq* (Dublin, 1868); Rowan, p 460; UAHS (Coleraine and Portstewart), p 35.

ADAM CLARKE (c1760–1832)
Methodist theologian

BORN IN County Londonderry, Clarke became a Methodist in 1778 and embarked on a prolific career as a preacher, much in the same vein as John Wesley, although, unlike Wesley, he was never ordained. He received training in a school for Methodist preachers at Kingswood in Bristol and came to the attention of Wesley. Due to his gifts as an orator, he was given responsibility for a number of preaching circuits and was known as the 'boy preacher' because of his youth. Many regarded Clarke as the natural successor of Wesley, and he was president of the Methodist conference on three occasions. An outstanding preacher and theologian, he was also a gifted linguist and did much to promote the Irish language. He intended to retire to his native Portstewart, but died of cholera, which he contracted at the opening of a new chapel in Liverpool. He is recalled in the churches named in his honour in Portrush and Portstewart. That in Portstewart is actually built on a site previously owned by Clarke and where he intended to build his retirement home.

■ **References**
Dwyer, F, *Georgian People* (London, 1978).

Adam Clarke

UNIVERSITY ROAD METHODIST CHURCH, BELFAST
University Road, Belfast

Methodist

ON 15 SEPTEMBER 1862 the four Methodist circuits of Donegall Square, Frederick Street, Wesley Place and Willowvale took the decision 'to erect a chapel in some eligible situation in the neighbourhood of the Botanic or University Roads'. As a plaque in the church porch states, the foundation stone of the building was laid in April 1864 and worship commenced on 23 April the following year.

The church was designed by WJ Barre and cost £2500. Like the Sinclair Seamen's Church and Elmwood Presbyterian Church, the building demonstrates the influence on architecture of John Ruskin's book *Stones of Venice*. The high square Lombardic brick campanile dominates its corner site and complements its sister towers of the nearby Moravian and Crescent churches. The facade is constructed of polychrome brick with twin semicircular-headed doors on the ground floor, above which are five Romanesque windows. The large central window was originally circular but, since its destruction in 1973, has been replaced with the present arrangement. To the left is a curious slated turret, the windows of which indicate the internal stairs to the gallery. As the galleries were built three years after the completion of the church, this may well be a later addition to the facade.

Internally, the church is a two-aisled galleried structure, lined with pine pews and dominated by the progressively-tiered arrangement of communion table, pulpit, choir seating and organ. The communion rail and choir railing are composed of a series of Romanesque arches. There are ten segmental-headed windows in the lower storey of the church, and fifteen Romanesque windows inside pointed hoods at the gallery level. The gallery, which occupies three sides of the interior, rests on nine cast-iron columns and has an elaborate front of scrolled metalwork. The windows throughout are filled with geometric designs. Only two have illustrative stained glass, and these depict Dorcas carrying out acts of charity, and the Good Samaritan. These are in memory of members of the Clawson family. Eight heavy decorated corbels support the sheeted pine ceiling, which is divided from the walls by a plaster frieze.

University Road Methodist Church is a remarkable building, constructed in a flamboyant style and representing a departure from the classical idiom, which had been the norm for Methodist church architecture. As late as 1865 the Methodist church in Enniskillen had

University Road Methodist Church, Belfast.

been built in an uncompromising classical style. However, it has to be appreciated that architectural tastes in the country would have lagged behind the city and also that this Methodist congregation had a lot of visual competition from the other denominations in the area. Indeed, the university section of Belfast is uncommonly well-endowed with idiosyncratic ecclesiastical architecture. The towers and spires of this part of this city all contribute to a very exciting skyline.

■ **Reference**
Brett (Belfast), p 32; Larmour, p 25;
UAHS (Queen's University area), p 12.

ST PATRICK'S AND ST BRIGID'S CHURCH, BALLYCASTLE
Moyle Road, Ballycastle, County Antrim
Catholic

PERHAPS ONE of the initial interesting facts relating to this church is that it was designed by the priest/architect Fr Jeremiah McAuley, pupil of Thomas Jackson and designer of St Peter's Cathedral in Belfast. Built in 1870 of a bright gold-coloured stone from the Pan Rocks quarry, the church is, according to O'Laverty, in the style of 'Gothic and twelfth century'. The present overall appearance of the church is due to imaginative and far-reaching alterations made to it by architect Paddy Byrne in 1993.

The most outstanding feature of the exterior is the soaring octagonal spire, which was added in 1890 and may not have been part of McAuley's design. This spire holds an important place in the history of modern communications, for in 1898 it was used by Marconi as a mast to link Rathlin Island with the mainland by the first radio broadcast. The gable has a triple lancet, while the tympanum of the west door is filled with a depiction of the Crucifixion.

Internally, with the re-ordering and extensions of 1993, most notably the addition of transepts, the church has a relatively harmonious mixture of old and new. This is first apparent on entering the porch, where the glass screen incorporates old sections of stained glass. In the nave, four pointed arches on each side are carried on round columns with five clerestory windows above. The roof, which rises from beams between the windows, is rather elaborately trussed. The ceilings of the aisles and new transepts are simply sheeted.

The sanctuary presents a contrast between old and new, with the old fittings retained behind a quasi-Gothic brass and glass screen. The old altar has crocketed canopies of Caen stone, and a Pieta. It was sculpted by

Daniel O'Connell Gilliland. The walls of the sanctuary are beautifully decorated with rich mosaics showing the Descent from the Cross and the Madonna and Child. The patronal saints of the church, Patrick and Brigid, are pictured on either side of the triple lancet east window. The side chapels are linked to the sanctuary by archways and are also covered in mosaic. Each chapel is lined

Catholic church of St Patrick and St Brigid, Ballycastle. Marconi used the steeple as a mast for the world's first radio broadcast.

with a reredos with very 'busy' panels depicting biblical scenes. A modern representation of the Madonna and Child is suspended from the roof of the Lady chapel.

Internally and externally the work of 1993 adds to, rather than detracts from, the appearance of the church, and the very broad Gothic windows are filled with vibrant colours which give a striking contrast to the Victorian glass elsewhere.

■ References
Brett (Antrim), p 66; O'Laverty,
Vol 4, pp 432–3; UAHS (North Antrim), p 50.

JAMES O'LAVERTY (1828–1906)
Catholic priest and historian

A NATIVE of the Lecale area of County Down, O'Laverty trained for the priesthood at Maynooth and was ordained in 1851. After serving curacies at Ahoghill and Portglenone, he became the parish priest of Holywood. During his time in the parish he set up a national school and built a church dedicated to St Colmcille. A noted historian and antiquarian, he regularly wrote for the *Ulster Journal of Archaeology* and was a member of the Royal Irish Academy. He is particularly remembered for his historical account of the parishes in the diocese of Down and Connor. When Monsignor O'Laverty died in 1906 he was buried in the Holywood cemetery in a tomb which he had designed himself.

Monsignor James O'Laverty

ST MICHAEL'S CHURCH, ENNISKILLEN

Darling Street, Enniskillen, County Fermanagh   *Catholic*

BUILT BETWEEN 1870 and 1875, St Michael's was designed by John O'Neill, whom Hugh Dixon describes as 'one of the most distinguished Catholic architects working in the north of Ireland in the nineteenth century'. The church is a very vigorous structure in the French Gothic Revival idiom, but sadly the tower and spire as designed by O'Neill were never built. The church enjoys a precarious site; conventional from the street, but behind there is a massive drop in ground level, and when seen from the south the church appears as a great hulking mass, with 40 feet of under-building beneath the sanctuary. As the church frontage is hemmed into the streetscape, it looks as though the rest of the building is trying to make a bid for freedom! The west (side) wall of the church has a walkway under a series of flying buttresses, and there is a very medieval feel about this confined space. The buttresses were an addition of 1921, necessitated by the mean-spiritedness of a neighbour who at the time of the church's construction would not allow scaffolding on his land, and subsequently the wall began

to give way.

The frontage has three doors, the central of which has a hood and decorated tympanum flanked by niches. The flanking doors have clustered columns supporting the hoods which have integral trefoil designs. A canopied statue of St Michael stands between the two tall lancet windows. Above these is a rose window, similar to that on the right of the facade. O'Neill's original design had called for a tall banded and crocketed spire, but this was never executed. As a result the front had a truncated appearance, as the tower stump ended below the gable. In the early 1990s a belfry stage and slated broach spire were added. Although there is no doubt that the church needed a spire, what it got is really not lofty enough to give the building the heavenward thrust that all its other proportions would demand.

The church is thirteen bays long, the pairs of windows being punctuated by buttresses. With square-ended side aisles and an apsidal sanctuary, St Michael's has a basilical plan. The roof has scaled slates with bands of different colours, and is crowned for its entire length by a cast-iron cresting. Inside, the nave is composed of five pointed arches carried on round sandstone pillars which have foliated capitals, out of which peer carved faces. The trussed roof rises from colonettes at clerestory level. Divided from the nave by an arch carried on tall columns the height of the building, the sanctuary has a polygonal end pierced by five windows. The marble high altar of 1882 is Italian Gothic and has a lofty central spirelet, flanked by two shorter ones carrying angels at the summits. The frontal with its Pietà has been moved forward to meet current liturgical requirements. Old photographs of the church show the sanctuary area and the soffits of the nave arches as having painted decoration, which has now gone, unfortunately. However, painted scenes from the life of Christ survive in one of the aisles.

St Michael's was built as a result of panic in the previous church, which dated from 1802–3. It was so crowded on a particular Sunday in 1867 that the galleries began to creak alarmingly under the weight of the congregation. The injuries which ensued in the rush to vacate the building brought home very forcibly the need for a bigger church.

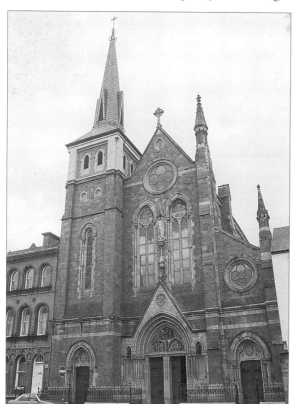
St Michael's Catholic Church, Enniskillen.

■ **References**
UAHS (Enniskillen), pp 26–8.

CHRIST CHURCH, DERRIAGHY
Derriaghy Road, Lisburn, County Antirm

Church of Ireland

BY 1837 the seventeenth-century church on this site had become structurally unsound. The Ordnance Survey Memoir describes it as 'an oblong edifice, one storey high and slated … The side walls are not perpendicular, they vary in thickness and are spreading either from age or bad architecture'. The unsatisfactory condition of the church and the growth of the congregation meant that the need for a new church had to be addressed. In 1864 the rector, Rev Henry Stewart, reported that the ecclesiastical commissioners had promised £2000 towards the cost of a new church, but only if the parish made a contribution. Work was not put into hand immediately due to difficulties arising over the siting of the new church. This contentious issue was eventually settled and William Charley of Seymour Hill House laid the foundation stone on 24 July 1871. Construction work cost £3600 and was completed in time for the service of consecration on 17 October 1872.

Christ Church was designed by William Gillespie of Welland and Gillespie and his drawings still exist, dated 11 April 1871. The church is unusual, particularly in the treatment of the west end. Gillespie's plans for the west elevation show quite an ordered design, belying the eccentric three-dimensional qualities of the completed building. The square tower is remarkable, being extremely thin and surmounted by an equally slender spire. The sound windows occupy about half the height of the tower and hold a bell made by Sheridan of Dublin, and loudspeakers give it a little assistance. It is said that this bell was destined for the Catholic church at Hannahstown, but due to an error at the foundry, it ended up here. Maybe the loudspeakers are needed to make it heard in Hannahstown! The tower and spire stand at an angle of 45 degrees to the body of the church, and are balanced at the other side of the facade by a semicircular projection with a conical roof. The two are linked in between by a lean-to roof which forms a porch, the eaves of which have carved foliage. Above this is a large circular window. Just to confuse us as to the style of architecture to which this church belongs, the wall is surmounted by a crow-stepped gable, characteristic of Scottish buildings. On the north and south walls are two broad four-light pointed windows, as well as a single lancet.

Perhaps one of the most remarkable features of the interior is the dark groined and vaulted timber roof which

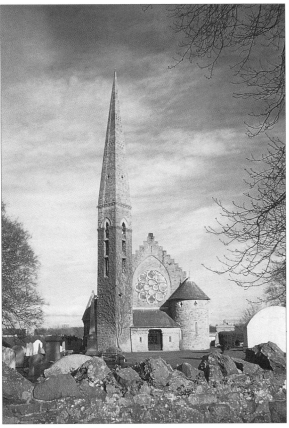

Christ Church (C of I), Derriaghy.

rises from colonettes supported on carved corbels. In the sanctuary area there are two corbels decorated with angels, proclaiming between them, 'Glory be to thee, O Lord Most High'. The six-light east window is in memory of William Charley of Seymour Hill (died 1872). The gallery at the west end is of timber and is carried on two slender columns. Two monuments survive from the former church, one on the south side of the nave to Rev Edward Higginson (died 1828) and one on the north to Rev Philip Johnston (died 1833). The church possesses an unaltered example of an organ built by Norman and Beard of Norwich.

■ References
Barr, WC, *Derriaghy: a Short History of the Parish* (Belfast, 1974), pp 51–4; Brett, p 65; Dixon, p 20; OSM (Vol 8, Antrim II), pp 102–3; RCB, drawings by William Gillespie.

ST PATRICK'S CHURCH, DONEGALL STREET, BELFAST
Donegall Street, Belfast

Catholic

A FORMER very pretty 'Gothick' church on this site was opened at a service of great interdenominational harmony in 1815. It was demolished to make way for the present vigorous Romanesque church, constructed between 1874 and 1877. This was designed by Timothy Hevey, although his partner, Mortimer Thompson, also had a hand in it. The church's weather-beaten sandstone steeple is a familiar landmark in this part of the city, as is the sound of its bell which reverberates through the surrounding streets.

With the tower and spire sitting astride the western gable, St Patrick's is a grand example of Victorian Romanesque revival with French overtones. It is constructed of soft red sandstone, dressed with a lighter sandstone, and the decayed appearance of this gives the building a greater air of antiquity than it deserves. A statue of St Patrick by Neill and Pearse of Dublin peers down on worshippers from the central tympanum, while a large rose window dominates the stage above. This window is accommodated within a semicircular hood which is supported on tall Romanesque columns. On either side are weathered buttresses which terminate in angels whose task it is to hold up the pinnacles. The tower itself has an arcaded base, upon which rests an octagonal belfry stage, flanked by four tall pinnacles. The spire is pierced by lucarnes on its cardinal faces, and is crowned by a wrought-iron Celtic cross.

In 1996 the interior of the church was extensively damaged by an accidental fire, and the opportunity was taken to highlight some of the beauties of the interior during the course of the restoration work. Given the rather brooding appearance of the outside, the interior is spacious and bright, with a new light-coloured timber ceiling and beautiful painted ceilings to the apse and side chapels. The nave has a clerestory set above round-headed Romanesque arches carried on circular polished granite pillars, while there are broad side aisles and apsidal side chapels and sanctuary. The north side chapel contains the very beautiful triptych of Sts Patrick and Brigid and the Virgin Mary, painted by Sir John Lavery.

Angels again appear in the nave, acting as corbel stops, and the heavenly host is depicted in the sanctuary ceiling which is illuminated by a stained glass top-light. The old high altar with its crocketed canopies and flashes of coloured marble remains in situ, and the new altar and ambo fit unobtrusively into their surroundings. The glass

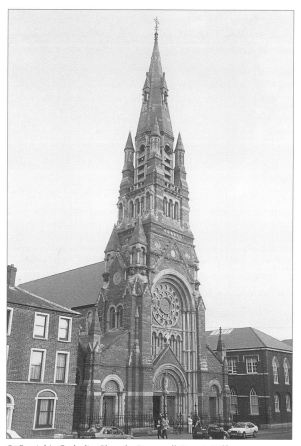
St Patrick's Catholic Church, Donegall Street, Belfast.

of the clerestory windows is clear, but there is painted and stained glass elsewhere in the building. The seven sanctuary windows display Christ and six saints, while the south chapel windows show the neighbouring Christian Brothers school and the old St Patrick's of 1815. The only monument in the church is that in the north aisle which commemorates Bishop Dorrian, who is buried in a vault under the sanctuary.

■ References
Larmour, p 44.

126

CARLISLE MEMORIAL METHODIST CHURCH
Carlisle Circus, Belfast

Methodist

GIVEN THE manner in which Carlisle Circus has lost its once impressive array of sacred and secular buildings, this dilapidated church stands as a forlorn testimony to another age when vast city centre churches were required for a resident population.

Alderman James Carlisle, who also had a hand in the construction of Donegall Square Methodist Church, had this building erected in memory of his only son, who died aged 18. The church was completed in 1875 to the designs of WH Lynn, and has been described as possibly Belfast's ugliest church. Admittedly, there is little grace about the building, but it might be fairer to say that it has a jarring aspect, principally due to the choice of materials; light Armagh limestone juxtaposed with pink Dumfries sandstone. At worst, when the stonework was cleaner, the building must have had a rather startling appearance.

The church is an example of Early English Gothic Revival style, but it is the sheer size of the building which is most impressive. The spire rises to a height of 198 feet and is a well-known landmark, especially to those using the nearby Westlink. It is octagonal, of limestone with sandstone at the corners and pierced alternately with one and two hooded louvred openings. The roof is steeply pitched and slated with Westmoreland slates. Externally the church appears to be cruciform with aisles, although inside the pews were laid out on a common plane, broken through by a central aisle with aisles to the east and west. The pulpit stood at the head of the central aisle, while an aisle to the north linked the north-west and north-east doors. The ceilings of the nave and aisles are sheeted with timber fixed to decorative purlins running between timber ribs. The ribs are fixed to main truss ties and bear stone corbels above arched supporting walls. Wall finishes throughout the church are rendered, but the arches, columns and the quoins are in dressed sandstone.

There were fourteen groups of stained glass windows throughout the church, the most interesting being the New Testament depictions in the east aisle and the five chancel windows, which displayed a pre-Raphaelite influence. The Conacher organ was a massive instrument and, following the closure of the church, sections were taken to Cooke Centenary Presbyterian Church in Belfast, while the 32-foot pedal pipes went to Salt Lake City in the United States of America.

Carlisle Memorial Church closed in 1980, and although the adjacent halls have been put to other

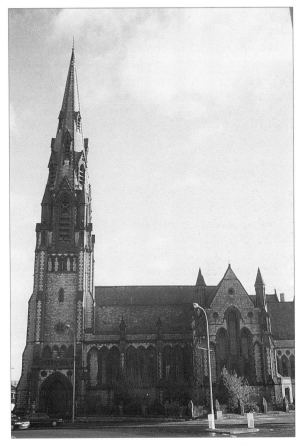

The former Carlisle Memorial Methodist Church, Belfast.

purposes, the church itself stands empty and unkempt. This is a sad situation in which to find such a building, but unfortunately one which is becoming all too common for urban churches bereft of congregations.

■ References
Brett (Belfast), pp 42, 51; Larmour, p 43.

ST PATRICK'S CHURCH, NEWTOWNARDS

Upper North Street, Newtownards, County Down   *Catholic*

THE FIRST Catholic church at Newtownards was erected in 1812 at Clay Holes, outside the town, on a site provided by the first Marquis of Londonderry. With the increasing size of the congregation a new church was needed and this came about in 1846. This in turn proved inadequate to cope with the number of worshippers and the *Newtownards Chronicle* of 7 August 1875 records:

St Patrick's Catholic Church, Newtownards.

'

On Tuesday 3rd August shortly after 12.00, the Rt Rev Dr Dorrian, the Roman Catholic Bishop of Down and Connor drove over from Holywood for the purpose of laying the foundation stone of the new Catholic chapel – the gift of the Most Hon the Dowager Marchioness of Londonderry. The stone was laid in the presence of a large and mixed assemblage composed of persons of various denominations.

'

Elizabeth, wife of the fourth Marquis of Londonderry, was a convert to the Catholic faith, and paid the entire cost of the new church, as well as presenting many of the fittings. She chose the architect herself, Joseph Aloysius Hansom of the London firm of Hansom and Son. Among the triumphs of this firm are the design of the famous cab and the plans for Arundel Cathedral. The church at Newtownards was completed in 1877 and dedicated on 24 October of that year by Bishop Dorrian.

As designed, the church is composed of a central nave flanked by aisles; shallow transepts which are almost engulfed within the main structure; an apsidal sanctuary, with an apsidal chapel to the north; and a sacristy to the south. The church is built of Scrabo stone with Dundonald stone dressings. There is a squat central lantern tower, abutted by a rather jaunty circular turret with a conical roof. There is a central rose window on the west gable and three windows on the aisles, while above, at clerestory level, is a row of quatrefoil windows. The transepts are lighted by triple lancets and the sanctuary by a group of nine narrow windows. A statue of St Patrick stands in a niche above the south-west door. The arches of the nave are pointed and are carried on sandstone quatrefoil pillars. The arches at the crossing are of the same material, but higher. The crossing is lighted by the

windows of the tower, the internal height of which is exposed at this point.

The interior of the church was re-ordered in 1988, with the provision of a new altar and ambo base, carved in Donegal granite. The altar is circular and decorated with the Christian symbol of the fish, while the circular font has a wave design, symbolic of the waters of the River Jordan where Christ was baptised. An altar of 1876 still remains in the Blessed Sacrament Chapel to the north of the sanctuary, and communication between these two areas exists by means of an archway with a single central column. The windows throughout the church are filled with simple coloured glass, but it is thought that the small circular window in the baptistry may be glazed with fragments of glass from the town's medieval Dominican priory.

St Patrick's Church owns a magnificent chalice, which has quite a remarkable history. The eighth Duke of Norfolk had acquired a set of Flemish church plate of c1735, which included a splendid large chalice. In 1872 the Duke had a new chapel built at Arundel, which was designed by Joseph Hansom, and here lies the connection with Newtownards. At about the same time, the architect was working on the church at Newtownards for Lady Londonderry, and she obtained a copy of the Norfolk chalice for her new church. The chalice subsequently managed to find its way into secular ownership before being returned to the church in 1987. It is inscribed: 'Ex Dono Elizabethae Marachionissae De Londonderry MDCCCLXXVI' [1876].

St Patrick's is indeed a fine building, and was

worshipped in by members of the Spanish Royal family, friends of the Londonderrys. A story is told of how one particular parish priest decided to make his royal visitors welcome by taking the trouble to learn a few words of greeting in Spanish. On being regaled thus at the church door, one of the royal visitors commented to her interpreter that sadly she didn't understand, as she had no knowledge of the Irish language!

■ **References**
Solemn Dedication of St Patrick's Church, Newtownards (Belfast, 1988).

ST PATRICK'S CHURCH, DUNGANNON
Northland Row, Dungannon, County Tyrone   *Catholic*

'

This building now in the course of erection, is the parish church of Dungannon, the chief town of the County Tyrone. It has been undertaken principally through the exertions of the Very Rev Dean Slane.
It is built entirely of the fine warm-coloured yellow sandstone of the district. The roofs are panelled in wood interiorly. The tower and spire will rise to a total height of 195 feet and will form a conspicuous object in the surrounding landscape. The design is by Mr JJ McCarthy, RHA, architect; and Mr Thomas Byrne of Belfast is the contractor.

'

SO SAYS the *Builder* of 4 March 1871, and accompanies this statement with a plan and an engraving of this impressive church, which was finally dedicated on Trinity Sunday, 1876. Although the church was designed by the great JJ McCarthy, many of the internal fittings were the work of his son, Charles.

The exterior is dominated by the magnificent soaring spire, which is 'French Gothic' of the thirteenth century. At the foot of the north side of the tower are two doors, and in the tympanum of each are scenes from the life of St Patrick. On the left Patrick is shown as a shepherd on Slemish Mountain, while on the right he is depicted dreaming of his call to return to Ireland. The tympanum of the main west door has Patrick preaching to his followers, and that of the south door shows him baptising a king. The west facade is flanked by the tower to the north and an aisle with two-light window to the south. Above the hooded central doorway there is an arcade of seven arches, four of which contain thin windows, and the remaining arches have pedestals for statues which appear not to have been executed. At the top of the facade

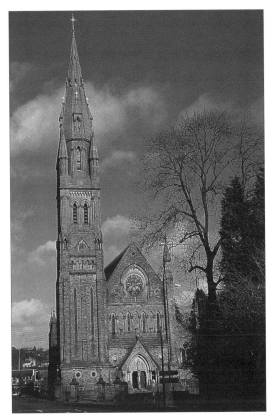

St Patrick's Catholic Church, Dungannon.

is a rose window within a pointed arch.

The side walls are of five groups of triple lancets on the aisles, and above are twelve clerestory windows. On the south side, a door and a flight of steps are accommodated within this arrangement. On the north side the aisle terminates in a gabled chapel, while this is reflected by the sacristy on the south. This sacristy has the added refinement of a conical turret with a battered base. On the east external wall of the chapel is an inscription in stone which explains the dedication of the church: '+ Deo

Sub Invocatione Sancti Patritti'. The east wall of the chancel is composed of two tall pointed windows divided by a buttress with accommodation for a statue. Above this is a rose window, and the whole is flanked by buttresses capped by scaled pinnacles. A decorative ridge runs the length of the roof.

Inside the church the theme of the life of Ireland's patron saint is continued in the engraved glass of the inner doors, which show Patrick at Slemish, Slane, Saul and Cruachan. The interior is entered through three pointed arches with foliated capitals on polished marble columns sitting on stone plinths with the organ gallery rising above. The church is very tall, of five bays plus the chancel. The arches are carried on tall, but stout, circular columns with capitals decorated with foliage and heads. The second capital on the south side represents the elements of earth, air, fire and water, and also has a monkey. The clerestory windows are in pairs and are divided by the pine shafts which support the hipped roof, which is composed of square panels painted turquoise. The aisle walls are of sandstone and have a timber lean-to roof.

The high altar stands behind a fine set of marble rails, which have metalwork gates depicting the Agnus Dei and the pelican in her piety. The high altar, of Caen stone, is the work of Charles H McCarthy and the reredos has a central graduated spire with flanking cusped arches with crocketed canopies, terminating in a statue under a spirelet at each end. On the front of the altar proper is a carving of Christ in the Holy Sepulchre. The high altar and the Sacred Heart altar to the north date from 1889. There is a chapel to the Blessed Virgin Mary at the end of the south aisle.

The sanctuary windows depict the life of Christ from His baptism in the River Jordan to the Ascension. There is a good modern window, the work of DI Branie in the Sacred Heart Chapel, which illustrates the life of Mary. To the north of this are three windows in memory of Very Rev Patrick Quin, which depicts St Patrick baptising Hiedelm the Red and Ethne the Fair. Windows in the south aisle commemorate 100 years of the Sisters of Mercy in Dungannon (1894–1994). Very Rev Felix Dean Slane is remembered by three windows showing Columba, Patrick and Bridget. Also in the south aisle is a set of windows with St Celsus, St Malachy and St Oliver Plunkett about to be executed at Tyburn.

St Patrick's has been described as one of McCarthy's most ambitious town churches, and it certainly illustrates his mastery of Gothic architecture. Given the sheer size of the building and the grandeur of its design, it may be lamented that its siting was not more prominent.

■ References

Builder, 4 March 1871, pp 166–7; Rowan, p 258; Sheehy, pp 64–6; UAHS (Dungannon and Cookstown), p 19.

ST MARK'S PARISH CHURCH, DUNDELA
Holywood Road, Belfast
Church of Ireland

'THE FOUNDATION stone of St Mark's Church at Dundela, Sydenham, a fashionable suburb of the town, has been laid by His Grace the Lord Primate'. So says the *Irish Ecclesiastical Gazette* of 24 October 1876. This foundation stone can be seen in the south side of the choir.

St Mark's was designed by the famous Tractarian architect William Butterfield (1814–1900) and bears the hallmark of his strong beliefs, both architectural and liturgical. The church was built in two phases, the first consisting of the nave, aisles and tower in 1876–78; and second, the chancel and transepts in 1889–91. The cost of the work was £14,000. The parish of Dundela owes its origins to the Belfast Church Extension and Endowment Society which set out to provide new churches for the rapidly expanding port of Belfast. Thus a new parish of Dundela was created out of Holywood parish, and a new church was needed to replace what had been a chapel-of-ease. Unlike the majority of Belfast churches of this period, St Mark's was not designed by an Irish architect. It was a bold and self-assured decision to select Butterfield as the architect, given that his Tractarian leanings would not have been popular in the Church of Ireland. The result, however, is a very happy one, and Sir John Betjeman said that the church represents 'Butterfield at his best'. The building is marked by a number of

St Mark's (C of I) Church, Dundela, as first built, minus the chancel.

idiosyncrasies characteristic of Butterfield, particularly in the scales on the tower roof, and in his handling of the baptistry. Butterfield was absolutely meticulous in his attention to details, and forty drawings exist for the chancel alone, even down to the designs for the boot-scrapers.

The exterior of the church gains its imposing nature not only from the soaring rectangular tower, but from the bold use of red Dundonald sandstone banded with lighter contrasting stone. The west tower is of four stages, has buttresses as far as belfry level, and is abutted on the south side by a stair turret. There are two pointed sound windows with cusped tracery on the east and west faces, with a single one on north and south. The scaled stone mansard roof, topped by an elaborate finial, adds a touch of individuality to the design and gives a rather continental feel to the Gothic architecture. The nave is composed of four pairs of coupled two-light windows, which alternately have cinquefoils and hexafoils. Beneath, the aisles have four bays of three-light trefoil-headed windows. A glance at the change in the colour of the slates on the roof indicates the later construction of the chancel and transepts. Each transept has buttresses and a large

three-light window, while there is a similar, but larger, east window on the chancel. Each gable is topped by a cross.

The interior is as Butterfield designed it, but it is sadly bereft of the rich decoration which elevated so many of his church interiors. The nave and aisles are divided by four pointed arches of sandstone, carried on alternating round and octagonal banded pillars. Above the intersections of the arches are roundels, which would have been intended to contain some kind of decoration. Corbels cut the tops of these roundels and support colonettes at the clerestory level, holding the trusses of the fine hammer-beam roof, which has angels by Smith of Clapham. Particular note has to be taken of the manner in which Butterfield handles the baptistry and chancel, described as one of his 'most rewarding experiments in spatial interpenetration'. The baptistry is a remarkably large space, occupying the foot of the tower and illuminated by two large windows. Among those baptised here was the author and Christian apologist, CS Lewis, whose grandfather, Rev Thomas R Hamilton, was the first rector of St Mark's (1875–1900). Only a rather slight supporting column divides the baptistry from the nave of the church, and this accessibility is reflected at the eastern

The interior of St Mark's, Dundela.

end by the broad arch which marks the entrance to the chancel, and which gives emphasis to the holy table. Butterfield designed all his churches to lend weight to the importance of the sacraments of baptism and communion for, like all Tractarians faithful to the Book of Common Prayer, he appreciated that these were 'generally necessary to salvation'. Physical accessibility to the sacraments was felt to be an aid to accepting them spiritually.

The reredos makes striking use of coloured stone, and bears the sacred monogram in mosaic, made in 1890 by Minton. The glass in the east window was dedicated in

1913 in memory of Isabella Kelso, Lady Ewart (died 1905), and bears the inscriptions, 'I am the vine' and 'Ye are the branches'; these are reflected in the visual imagery. Christ is depicted here as the spring of life. Shrigley and Hunt of Lancaster provided the glass in the baptistry. The window in the upper south aisle, showing Christ blessing children, was designed by Michael Healy and commemorates Rev Thomas R Hamilton. This was the gift of CS Lewis and his brother Warnie, in memory of their grandfather. The church organ, which stands in the north transept, is a four-manual instrument built by Compton.

In the tower hangs a grand ring of ten bells cast by Taylor of Loughborough, the gift of the Newell family, which were dedicated on St Mark's Day, 1955.

This is an extremely important church, being one of only two Butterfield churches in Ireland, the other being at St Columba's College in Dublin. St Mark's also represents an Anglican high church tradition which never really gained a firm foothold in Ireland.

■ **References**
Beckett, JC, *St Mark's Church, Dundela, 1878–1978* (Newtownards, 1978); Brett (Belfast), p 40; Larmour, p 44; Thompson, P, *William Butterfield* (London, 1971), pp 63, 73, 131, 142, 181, 249, 341, 381, 432, 475.

ST PATRICK'S PARISH CHURCH, COLERAINE
Church Street, Coleraine, County Londonderry   *Church of Ireland*

ALTHOUGH COLERAINE Parish Church presents a striking example of Victorian Gothic architecture, this building has in fact had a long evolution. It seems that there has been a church here since the mid fifth century, when legend states that Patrick himself built a place of worship at Cuilrathain – the 'ferny corner'. This church, and whatever buildings may have succeeded it, was plundered on many occasions. In 1613–14 the Honourable the Irish Society, the planters of the county, rebuilt the church in a more substantial form, as a a rectangular structure of four bays. Subsequent additions included a tower and the present south transept, and an idea of how this church looked can be gleaned from a depiction of it on a window in the nearby town hall. A weathered block of sandstone on the north wall of the church is said to be where a cannonball struck the building during the siege of the town in 1641.

In 1851 the work of shaping the church which we see today began under Joseph Welland, architect of the ecclesiastical commissioners. Welland added a chancel and a new south aisle with a porch. Eleven years later a north transept was added, making the church cruciform in shape. The final overall appearance of the church was the result of rebuilding carried out in 1883 by Sir Thomas Drew, with an addition of 12 feet to the nave, a north aisle, an extension to the north transept and the introduction of a clerestory. Coursed basalt was used, trimmed with Dungiven and Draperstown sandstone. The nave is six bays long, with transepts which are unequal in size, that on the north being double-gabled. The windows are fifteenth-century in design, with three-light windows in the aisles. The most striking feature of the exterior is the powerful four-storey sandstone tower, rising to a height of 114 feet. It has inset buttresses,

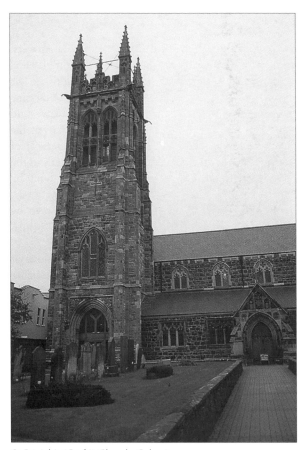

St Patrick's (C of I) Church, Coleraine.

interior is the ugly mass of the sound system now suspended from the nave roof. During the work, foundations from a church of perhaps the fourteenth century or earlier were uncovered, along with evidence of burial within the building. The conserved foundations are now visible through a large glass screen let into the floor in the north aisle. The sandstone columns of the nave vary in shape and have foliated capitals, while the walls of the chancel are lined in sandstone, above cusped panels of Bath stone. Alterations were also made to the chancel arrangements during the work of 1995–96. The opportunity was taken to extend the three chancel steps out into the body of the church more, and provision was very cleverly made for a movable sectioned communion rail.

A number of the monuments in the church are of some interest and recall the long tradition of worship here, and the connection between Coleraine and the Irish Society. At the west end of the building is the Hamilton Memorial, recalling the brothers who fought for James II in the seventeenth century. One of them, the sixth Earl of Abercorn, left the king's army to defend the besieged city of Londonderry. In the north transept can be found the monument to Sir Tristam Beresford (died 1673), the first mayor of Coleraine. It carries many of the symbols of death such as an hourglass, an upturned torch and skull. The words 'memento mori' are surmounted by a chilling winged and crowned skull. In the south transept Elizabeth Dodington (died 1610), wife of Sir Edward, armourer and Captain of the King's Fort at Dungiven and designer of Derry's walls, is commemorated by a tablet flanked by pilasters and topped by a heraldic cartouche. Nearby, Ann Munro (died 1647) is lamented by some sorrowing cherubs (which have been mutilated at some stage), while Mary Heslett's memorial is decorated with a skull and crossbones, an hourglass and gravedigger's tools, which were needed, in her case, in 1697.

Much of the stained glass in the building is fine, particularly the west window in memory of a William John Church which shows the life and work of St Patrick. The Irish Society window in the north transept recalls that organisation's long connection with secular and spiritual matters in the town. Indeed, until the disestablishment of the Church of Ireland, the society had the right to nominate the rector of the parish. In the chancel, the east window depicts New Testament saints alongside early Irish missionaries, and was erected to commemorate the ministries of James Dunn O'Hara and his son, Henry Stewart O'Hara, first dean of Belfast.

The disused graveyard surrounding the church is full

pinnacles, crockets and gargoyles. The sound windows are glazed with transparent louvres, allowing the sound of the eight bells to escape. Internal lighting makes the tower into an impressive feature at night, almost giving it the appearance, from a distance, of a lighthouse. Although the tower is a dominant feature in the general townscape, we can only imagine how forceful its impact would have been had Drew added his intended spire. There is fine carving in the pediment of the south porch, showing the Holy Spirit as a dove; the arms of the archdiocese of Armagh; the arms of the dioceses of Down, Connor and Dromore; those of Rev Henry Stewart O'Hara, rector at the time of rebuilding; and the pelican in her piety, the symbol of Christ's blood shed for us. All of this carving is the work Charles McGowan of Coleraine.

The interior of the church was extensively altered during renovations of 1995–96 and by and large these changes have been successful. The pews have been removed and replaced by rows of upholstered seats which follow roughly the lines of the traditional pew arrangement. Perhaps the only really jarring note in the of beautifully carved tombstones, reminding us of the individuality of each burial place when the skills of local masons had to be employed, long before machined black marble had made its appearance.

Coleraine Parish Church, although containing remnants of earlier building phases, stands as a seemly and well-conceived example of Victorian church architecture.

■ **References**

Drew, T, *A brief History of the Church of St Patrick, Coleraine, with some account of its proposed restoration* (Dublin, 1883); Rowan, p 204; UAHS (Coleraine and Portstewart), pp 11–14.

10
Celtic Revival Architecture

THE CHURCHES of the eighteenth and nineteenth centuries in Ireland took the form of structures designed in idioms which were adaptations of English models, or which merely followed rather utilitarian lines. Since the arrival of the Normans in the twelfth century, Irish ecclesiastical architecture had tended to be directed by influences from outside Ireland, and even the native architects, often working for the establishment, chose styles fashionable elsewhere. The architecture of the ancient Irish church, which had extended its influence as far as the realms of Charlemagne, had become relegated to the sketch books of the romantic amateur artist.

It took a political reawakening in Ireland to resurrect the allied ideas of a national history, folklore, arts and architecture. In the political sphere Daniel O'Connell gained mass support for his Repeal Association, which favoured the return of a parliament to Dublin under the British crown. With his skilful appreciation of politics, O'Connell was perceptive enough to harness the emotional appeal of cultural nationalism. The 'Monster' rallies he held to further the repeal movement were staged at Tara and among the ruins of Glendalough. Where the appreciation of such places and remains of Ireland's past had largely been the preserve of gentlemen antiquarians, such as George Petrie, a wider number of people now saw the need for a popular understanding and enjoyment of the country's heritage. This cultural nationalism was harnessed by the Young Ireland movement, and a desire grew to make Ireland's heritage more accessible to all. Allied to this was a belief that a distinct cultural identity would help to foster the desire for political separatism.

A prime mover in the Young Irelanders was the journalist, Thomas Davis who, along with Gavin Duffy and John Blake-Dillon, founded *The Nation* in 1842. This journal was filled with romantic poems and ballads of a nationalist and historical nature.

Just how powerful visual images became can be seen by a perusal of the frontispiece of Martin Haverty's *The History of Ireland, Ancient and Modern* (1867). This is

Frontispiece of A History of Ireland: Ancient and Modern (Dublin, 1867) by Martin Haverty.

loaded with ecclesiastical images and allegorical reference. We can see a round tower, a familiar symbol of the ancient Irish church and also three saints, Patrick, Columba and Bridget who are shown in Catholic clerical dress. The Catholic Church did embrace the Celtic Revival in the design of many of its churches, but so too did the Church of Ireland which claimed a direct line of descent from the church of St Patrick.

The impetus given to church architecture by this Celtic reawakening can be seen by the following statement from the *Irish Catholic Directory* of 1845:

'

We hope yet to see the day when the zealous piety
of the people, guided by educated taste, will once more
cover the face of the 'Island of saints' with structures
that shall emulate the sacred splendour of the august
fanes which were the boast of 'Cashel of the Kings' or
of holy Mellifont, and whose ruins remain to attest the
ruthless atrocity of our Saxon invaders.

'

The importance of *The Nation* cannot be underestimated, for it gave JJ McCarthy 'the first impulse to revive the Irish Gothic in ecclesiastical buildings'. Increased appreciation of ancient Irish ecclesiastical architecture became apparent in the number of societies founded to nurture its study. The Church of Ireland had the Down, Connor and Dromore Church Architecture Society and the St Patrick's Society for the Study of Ecclesiology, while the Catholic equivalent was the Irish Ecclesiological Society. Ireland now saw the beginning of a period of church-building which employed Hiberno-Romanesque features married to round towers and swirling Celtic tendril decoration, shaped by varying degrees of scholarship. St Patrick's, Jordanstown, has been described as the first attempt to revive the ancient architecture of Ireland. The particular interest of this church lies in the fact that its inspiration came from the twelfth-century church of St Finghan at Clonmacnoise, County Offaly. With a fine Hiberno-Romanesque doorway and rather correct round tower, it is more scholarly in its approach than many Celtic Revival churches, but the apse, never a feature of the ancient Irish church, strays from the Celtic style. Timothy Hevey's Sacred Heart church of 1877 at Dunlewey, Co Donegal, is harsher in appearance and even less correct, but demonstrates how the Celtic Revival had inter-denominational appeal. More successful is Hevey's

Hiberno-Romanesque church of St Eunan at Raphoe, County Donegal.

The idea of a Celtic Revival gained further impetus in 1893 with the foundation of the Gaelic League, with its mission to re-establish an Irish identity. By the end of the century and well into the twentieth century a number of Celtic Revival churches had sprung up throughout the country. Some, such as St Jude's at Ballynafeigh, Belfast, were fairly conventional churches with a round tower as their only concession to the Celtic idiom. At the other extreme is St Matthew's, Woodvale, Belfast, with its yellow-brick round tower and an amazing 'shamrock' layout.

In the 1920s and 1930s there was a resurgence of church buildings in a pre-Norman Romanesque style. The results often took the form of heavy-handed Romanesque doorways and attached round towers, as at Artasooly, County Armagh. The Catholic church at Ederney, County Tyrone, while a fine building, has been cited as an example of the very loose adaptations of the country's architectural past. More successful, but not without its faults, is the Catholic Church of the Four Masters of 1935 in Donegal town. Of similar vintage is the Church of Ireland St Patrick's Memorial Church at Saul near Downpatrick. This church is built of Mourne granite, with a nearly convincing round tower and fine stained glass. However, a fault of both these churches, as with all of their Celtic Revival predecessors, is that round towers were never originally attached to church buildings as they were for defensive use. This criticism may seem pedantic, as the architects did have to use the foot of the towers as vestries or belfry access and they had to be functional as well as decorative. The artists involved in the decoration of many of these churches of the Celtic Revival provide a strand which can be traced in modern Irish ecclesiastical architecture, and can be seen in the symbolic Celtic designs found in modern churches; witness, for example, the recent works of Oisin Kelly at Sion Mills and Burt. And, of course, with a Celtic Revival in church architecture there was a tangible reminder of the unbroken thread of Celtic spirituality from ancient times to the present day.

■ **References**
Sheehy, pp 13–4.

ST PATRICK'S PARISH CHURCH, JORDANSTOWN
Jordanstown, off the A2 between Belfast and Carrickfergus, County Antrim   *Church of Ireland*

THE SITE for this church was a gift from William Lyons and his sister, Sarah, in 1865. The Archdeacon of Connor at this time was Charles Chichester Smythe, whose brother, General James Smythe, was a noted antiquarian. It was the general who instigated the building of the new church at Jordanstown in the Celtic style and a visitor to the church can easily appreciate what a success this venture was.

The inspiration for the design was the twelfth-century round tower and church of St Finghan at Clonmacnoise, County Offaly, with which General Smythe was familiar. The parish was fortunate in that Sir Charles Lanyon was a parishioner, serving as a churchwarden and parochial nominator on a number of occasions. It was his partner, WH Lynn, who was responsible for the planning of the church, which was consecrated on 15 August, 1868.

Jordanstown Parish Church has been described as 'one of the prettiest Celtic Revivalist churches in Ireland'. The only element of the building which does not glean its inspiration from Hiberno-Romanesque sources is the apsidal sanctuary. However, the internal use and decoration of this part of the church is a decided visual bonus. The exterior is of white Scrabo sandstone, with bands of red sandstone. The tower, which is based on an ancient Irish round tower, stands at the junction of the south aisle and the sanctuary. One of the most notable features of the exterior is the south-west porch with its Romanesque doorway, but more particularly, the splendid tympanum of 1932 showing St Patrick as a shepherd boy on Slemish. This is the work of Rosamund Praeger, from Holywood, County Down, and reminds us of the great artistic talent so often found in Ulster.

Inside, the church walls are lined with warm pink and black brick, supporting a pitch pine roof, matching the pews which are made of the same material. The south aisle is divided from the nave by an arcade of four arches carried on pillars of blue limestone. The sandstone capitals are of the heavy cushion type and each is carved with a separate design. Internally the most charming part of the church is the sanctuary, rich in both furnishings and decor. The reredos is composed of three hooded Romanesque arches, each framing a mosaic Celtic motif. On either side of the reredos is an arcade of four arches, decorated with brightly coloured mosaics, some of these representing the symbols of the four evangelists. The excellent Clayton and Bell windows in the wall above

St Patrick's (C of I) Church, Jordanstown.

show the Irish saints Patrick, Comgall, Brigid and Columba. Patrick is shown in episcopal dress, casting the snakes out of Ireland. St Comgall is seen blessing those going out to preach; Brigid gives bishops' robes to the poor and Columba boards his boat to spread the gospel in Scotland. Each window has a border based on designs from the Book of Durrow. The remarkable pair of prayer desks of 1912, the work of Purdy and Millard, are supported by angels, one clutching a palm and the other a trumpet. Conacher and Co of Huddersfield built the organ which fills the small north transept. The east end of the south aisle has been panelled and adapted for use as a side chapel in memory of Rev Kenneth Smythe, a former rector of the parish.

Inside and out, St Patrick's is a bright and inspiring church and represents one of the province's most successful attempts at Celtic Revival architecture in the nineteenth century, and is an example which is much admired.

■ References
Brett (Antrim), p 68; Dixon, p 66; Larmour, p 101; McCappin, W, *St Patrick's Church, Jordanstown* (Belfast, 1993), pp 13–17, 19–40.

SACRED HEART CHURCH, DUNLEWEY
Below Errigal mountain at Dunlewey on the R251, County Donegal *Catholic*

SET IN wild countryside next to the looming mass of Errigal Mountain, the dark basalt walls of this church make it appear rather forbidding.

Sacred Heart Church was built in 1877 at the expense of William Augustus Ross of Mayfair, who had shortly before bought the Dunlewey estate. Presumably he built the church either as an act of piety or charity. The architect was Timothy Hevey (1845–78), who had worked in the office of Pugin and Ashlin and had begun his own practice in the north of Ireland.

The church is constructed of rock-faced basalt, banded with lighter stone and local marble. The building is composed of a nave with an apse under a continuous roof, with a round tower to the north-west and a vestry at the south-east. The roof has two bands of paler slates. The round tower, while only a loose representation of its ancient forbears, does at least demonstrate the increasing awareness of the architecture of the ancient Irish church. On the facade is a marble statue of Christ, placed between two thin semicircular-headed windows, all set above the round-headed doorcase. At the corners are buttresses surmounted by finials. The side walls each have four semicircular-headed windows, while the apse is lit by three similar windows.

Internally, the church is rather plain, having a vaulted ceiling of pine sheeting and bench-like pews. The nave is relieved only by the traditional stations. At the entrance to the apsidal chancel are two pairs of Romanesque columns and there are two half-columns on either side of the easternmost window. The new sanctuary fittings are made from natural stone.

Catholic church of the Sacred Heart, Dunlewey.

■ **References**
Rowan, p 269.

ST PATRICK'S CHURCH, DONEGAL TOWN
Donegal, County Donegal *Catholic*

DESCRIBED AS being 'Neo-Irish-Romanesque', St Patrick's Church, otherwise known as the Church of the Four Masters, was designed by Ralph Byrne and constructed between 1931 and 1935. The Four Masters were Brother Michael O'Clery (a native of County Donegal), Fearfeasa O'Maolchonaire, Cuchoigcriche O'Clerigh and Cuchoigcriche O'Duibgheannain and they began their work of collecting Irish history and hagiographies in January 1635 and completed *The Annals of the Kingdom*

of Ireland in August 1636. This church, which recalls their work, was built 300 years later and is constructed of pinkish Barnesmore granite, being cruciform in shape with double transepts and a slight batter to the walls. The references to ancient native ecclesiastical sources extend to the round tower at the north-west corner and the very steep pitched roofs topped by Celtic crosses on the gables. The windows in the nave and transepts are tall lancets, the shape of which seem to form the outline of a round tower.

Catholic church of the Four Masters, Donegal.

On the west front is a large rose window incorporating a Celtic cross in the glazing pattern and edged with chevron mouldings. Below this is a Romanesque doorway with chevron moulding in its hood. There are similar doors in the transept porches.

The chevron pattern is repeated in the decoration of the interior. The nave and aisles are divided by columned arcades, while the barrel vaults are supported on colonettes which have cushion capitals. The vivid colours of the stained glass contrast with the rendered internal walls.

■ **References**
Rowan, p 23.

ST PATRICK'S MEMORIAL CHURCH, SAUL
Sign-posted one mile outside Downpatrick, County Down
Church of Ireland

APPROPRIATELY, THERE is a late and relatively successful example of a Celtic Revival church at Saul, the cradle of Irish Christianity. Patrick built a church here at 'Sabhall' in 432 on the site of a barn given by the local chieftain, Dichu. In 1130 an abbey was built, fragments of which still stand to the west of the present church. Yet another church was built in 1788 and this served as the parish church until its demolition to make way for the present building which commemorates the foundation of Christianity in Ireland.

The foundation stone of this new church was laid by Archbishop Charles d'Arcy on Ascension Day 1933 and the building was dedicated on All Saints' Day of the same year. The architect was Henry Seaver (died 1941) who is commemorated by a simple plaque inside the church. Situated at the end of an avenue of yew trees in the midst of beautiful rolling countryside, the church has quite convincing physical characteristics of an early church. It is rectangular with a steeply pitched slated roof and has a small chancel as well as a round tower with a conical cap at the south-east corner. Round towers would originally have been detached from the church, but no matter. The church is constructed from Mourne granite, which gives it a glistening effect on a bright day.

As with ancient churches, the interior is dark and intimate, having five very small round-headed windows with clear glass on each side wall. The little west gable oculus above the entrance door incorporates St Patrick's cross in its glass. The chancel is separated from the nave by a round-headed arch and is even darker, giving a

St Patrick's Memorial (C of I) Church, Saul.

mystical and devotional Celtic air. The fine stained glass chancel window depicting Patrick with his crozier is the work of Katherine O'Brien of An Túr Gloine and it seems almost to float in its dark setting. The roof of the church is composed of dark timber trusses. The ancient square font, which rests on four circular shafts came from Burnchurch, County Kilkenny, to mark the 1500th anniversary of Patrick's arrival at Saul. The fine organ was built by Wells Kennedy of Lisburn.

Although the church is a simple representative of Celtic Revival architecture, it seems to gain credibility and vigour from the historical associations of its situation. This is an emotive place which turns the thoughts of the visitor to far-off times when Ireland's patron saint began his evangelising work from this little corner of Down.

STAINED GLASS

THE CLERICS and monks of the early Irish church knew the value of imagery. Promoting the spread of Christianity to an illiterate people made it difficult to teach from the Bible. The earliest missionaries in Ireland used the high crosses to educate their new flocks about stories from the Old and New Testaments. The crosses we now see in the Irish countryside are covered in time-worn stone images, but these were once crisp and brightly painted. By the use of these pictures the monks were able to explain the contents of the Bible to their new converts. In later centuries, stained glass served the same purpose in churches, by providing colourful depictions of events in the scriptures.

Whereas English churches still retain vestiges of medieval glass which survived the hands of iconoclasts, Ireland can boast virtually no stained glass made prior to the eighteenth century. This is due to lack of resources to provide this in the first place, reformers who thought it idolatrous, the destruction wrought during the Cromwellian period and the desire for Protestant simplicity in church buildings.

Where medieval glass does exist, it takes the form of a few salvaged fragments, such as those found in the Catholic church of St Patrick in Newtownards, which are said to have come from Movilla Abbey. The Church of Ireland church in the same town claims to have glass from the same source. All Saints' Church, Antrim, has two panels of continental glass depicting the Virgin and Child, saints Hieronimus and Carolus and the martyrdom of St John the Baptist: all obviously of an

St Nicholas in the guise of Santa Claus in the baptistry window at Carrickfergus Parish Church.

early date. The simple Kilcoo Church of Ireland parish church at Bryansford, County Down, has a series of very interesting sixteenth-century Flemish glass roundels. These were given to the church by the Earl of Roden, who had given similar glass to Dundalk Parish Church. The seventeenth-century window in St Nicholas', Carrickfergus, is Flemish in origin and was brought to the church from a disused family chapel in County Meath.

During the seventeenth and eighteenth centuries Church of Ireland and Presbyterian churches did not generally have stained glass as their theology denied the need for religious images. In the case of the Catholic church, stained glass windows were not an option due to financial constraints and the low profile imposed during the penal period. Such stained glass as did exist was probably brought secretly from the Continent.

The one existing example of eighteenth-century glass, and it is painted rather than stained, is at Hillsborough Parish Church. The upper section of the east window depicts a dove, representing the Holy Spirit, surrounded by a group of winged cherubs. This window is the work of Francis Egington, based on the designs of Sir Joshua Reynolds, the first President of the Royal Academy. Egington also made the east window for the primate's chapel in Armagh, although this was removed during the Victorian period.

By the nineteenth century it became commonplace to install stained glass in new church buildings, and this applied to most denominations. Gone was the primary purpose of teaching biblical stories to the illiterate and instead the windows were presented in memory of local worthies or members of the congregation. Having said that, the subject matter of these windows was invariably of a biblical nature. Much of the stained glass provided in Victorian churches was made by Meyer of Munich, and examples of the work of this company can be found in the Catholic Cathedral in Armagh.

The most important development in Irish stained glass in the twentieth century was the founding of An Túr Gloine (the tower of glass) by Sarah Purser. This studio was to produce a variety of talented Irish artists, whose work can be found in churches and public buildings throughout Ireland. The works of Harry Clarke and Evie Hone impress the observer by the vast contribution they make to Irish churches, breaking the stylistic mould of what had preceded them.

Design for a stained glass window by Clokey of Belfast. It is not known if this design was ever executed.

Given here is a brief guide giving examples of the Ulster works of the major stained glass artists and their location.

CLARKE, Harry (1889–1931)

Carrickmacross Catholic Church, County Monaghan
Dominican Convent, Falls Road, Belfast
Letterkenny Catholic Cathedral, County Donegal
St Patrick's Purgatory, Lough Derg, County Donegal

GEDDES, Wilhelmina Margaret (1888–1955)

Belfast: Presbyterian Assembly Buildings, Fisherwick Place
Rosemary Street Non-subscribing Presbyterian Church
St John's Church of Ireland Church, Malone
Townshend Street Presbyterian Church
Inver Church of Ireland Church, County Antrim
Monea Church of Ireland Church, County Fermanagh

HEALY, Michael (1873–1941)

Billy Church of Ireland Church, County Antrim
Castlerock Church of Ireland Church, County Londonderry
Enniskillen Convent of Mercy, County Fermanagh
Layde Church of Ireland Church, County Antrim
Letterkenny Catholic Cathedral, County Donegal
Magheralin Church of Ireland Church, County Down
St Mark's Church of Ireland Church, Dundela, Belfast
Warrenpoint Catholic Church, County Down

HONE, Evie (1894–1955)

Dominican Convent, Falls Road, Belfast
Fahan Church of Ireland Church, County Donegal
Kingscourt Catholic Church, County Cavan
St John's Church of Ireland Church, Malone, Belfast

GLENAVY, Lady (1881–1970)

Carrickfergus Church of Ireland Church, County Antrim
Enniskillen Convent of Mercy Chapel, County Fermanagh
Magheralin Church of Ireland Church, County Down

PURSER, SARAH (1849–1943)

Enniskillen Convent of Mercy, County Fermanagh.

For more modern glass, the churches of Liam McCormick are worth visiting, as they contain examples of stained glass by Patrick Pollen, Patrick Pye and Imogen Stuart (Milford Catholic Church, County Donegal) and Helen Moloney (Cresslough Catholic Church).

■ References

Whyte, J, and Wynne, M, *Irish Stained Glass* (Dublin, 1963); Snoddy, T, *Dictionary of Irish Artists: the Twentieth Century* (Dublin, 1996.)

Window by Helen Moloney at Creeslough.

11

Late Victorian and
Edwardian Church Architecture

INDUSTRIALISATION IN Ulster in the second half of the nineteenth century created the need for new places of worship for all denominations. Following its disestablishment in 1869, the Church of Ireland found itself trying to maintain a large number of buildings with reduced resources. As a result, its building activities outside Ulster declined. However, along with the other denominations, it had to meet the demands of the new industrialised populations in the north. What is particularly striking is the individuality and eccentricity of the designs for the churches which were built at the end of the Victorian era and during the Edwardian period.

At the tail-end of the High Victorian Gothic genre are the fine Catholic churches at Strabane and Omagh from the hand of William Hague, a keen exponent of French Gothic. His Ulster masterpiece has to be the Church of the Sacred Heart in Omagh, which gleans its inspiration from the great cathedral of Chartres. The Catholic church at this time was in a confident position and was financially capable of building vast Gothic churches. The other denominations were by now tending to move away from more conventional ecclesiastical architecture and even those that still employed the Gothic idiom were laden with eccentricities and architectural fancy. One such church is the former Crescent Presbyterian Church in Belfast with its tall campanile whose belfry openings occupy nearly half the height of the structure. Equally surprising is the nearby Elmwood Non-Subscribing Presbyterian Church, a church of the Presbyterian ethos decked out like an Anglican parish church. Perhaps the most perplexing of all is Ballynafeigh Methodist Church of 1899, which has frequently defied an architectural label.

In some quarters church architecture began to follow trends in other aspects of the arts. The influence of the Art Nouveau movement manifests itself in Vincent Craig's Presbyterian churches at Ballywatt, County Antrim, and Portstewart, and most notably at Blackwood and Jury's church at Hillhall, County Down. This latter church has close physical similarities with Frederick Wheeler's Mount Vernon Hospital Chapel at Northwood in Middlesex. Writing of this English church, AS Gray comments that Art Nouveau was rarely found in churches, which makes our few examples all the more valuable. Increasingly we find the personal experiences of the architect percolating strongly into his work, and here we think of how Alfred Forman's Methodist churches, by their internal layout, reflect his interest in amateur dramatics. The Church of Ireland church in Sion Mills takes its inspiration from a sacred building in Italy which the architect, WF Unsworth, had admired.

Perhaps we can view the churches of the Edwardian period as loosening previous architectural shackles and representing a beginning of the less regimented and more individualistic architecture with which the modern period presents us.

■ **References**
Dixon, p 76; Gray, AS, *Edwardian Architecture* (London, 1985), pp 37–42.

CRESCENT CHRISTIAN BRETHREN CHURCH
University Road, Belfast

Christian Brethren

THIS CHURCH was built between 1885 and 1887 for a Presbyterian congregation, and since 1977 it has been the place of worship for the Assembly of Christian Brethren which previously met in the old music hall in May Street. The situation at the Crescent church is an ideal example of the re-use of a redundant church building.

It was designed by the Glasgow architect John Bennie Wilson, who utilised a fourteenth-century Gothic style, mixing English and French influences. The building is constructed of grey rubble stone, said to have been salvaged from ships' ballast carried from Scotland, and has ashlar dressings. The church, and indeed the whole surrounding area, is dominated by the superb lofty square campanile with its pyramidal slated cap. The most interesting aspect of this structure is the fact that the belfry openings occupy almost half of its height. On the other side of the building is an octagonal projection with a slated roof. Each bay of the nave is divided into two storeys of paired lancets, with the upper windows having the added embellishment of rose windows. The stylised transepts have larger windows. Originally the main entrance door was surmounted by the words 'until He cometh' in Greek, but this has been removed and replaced by a mosaic.

Internally the church is a tall and bright building, with a compartmented roof filled with stencil-work motifs. The side windows are now clear, their stained glass having been wrecked by an explosion. However, there is bright stained glass in the rose window at the east, while the west windows depict saints Peter, Paul and John, and Faith, Hope and Charity. A gallery occupies three sides of the interior and is supported on ten slender round columns which then continue up to the roof. The prominent Gothic pulpit is approached on each side by a flight of steps and is placed in front of the very attractive traceried case of the former organ. The mechanism of this instrument has been removed, but it still has a fine visual impact.

This has been described as one of the best churches in Belfast and it is good that it is once again cared for and used by a vibrant body of Christians.

■ **References**
Larmour, p 51; UAHS (Queen's University area), p 11.

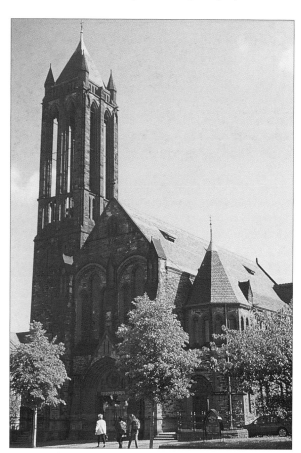

Crescent Christian Brethren Church, Belfast.

CHURCH OF THE IMMACULATE CONCEPTION, STRABANE
Barrack Street, Strabane, County Tyrone   *Catholic*

THIS COUNTY Tyrone church by the inventive William
Hague dates from 1895. Twelfth-century French Gothic
in style, it is cruciform with nave aisles and a rather
original facade, dominated by the western tower and
spire, and flanked by two-bay gabled wings. The west
door has a tympanum depicting the Virgin Mary
attended by angels. Above this is a broad three-light
window with elaborate tracery which illuminates the
internal gallery. Buttresses run up the sides of the tower
and develop into tall pinnacles which stand attendant at
the foot of the spire. As Alistair Rowan points out, this
treatment is reminiscent of William Burges' spires on St
Finbarre's Church of Ireland Cathedral in Cork. At the
corners of the second stage of the tower are rather
ferocious gargoyles which look as though they are about
to spring to the ground and the facade is well-endowed
with creative carving. The body of the church is of five
bays, with the nave abutted by side aisles. There are two
lancet windows on the gable wall of each transept.

The west gallery has decorative tracery taking the
form of trefoil-pointed arches. There are four arches on
each side of the nave, supported on circular polished
granite columns with round capitals. There is also a
clerestory level. The timber roof is trussed and filled with
rich tracery, whereas the chancel ceiling is vaulted in
timber. At the crossing are carved saintly heads. The
sanctuary has been well re-ordered utilising the original
altar of white marble enriched with gold mosaic.
The pulpit is very fine, with carved marble figures set
within ogee arches. The richness of this area of the
church, along with the baptistry and Lady chapel, is
enhanced by the use of mosaic. Of the stained glass,
the most striking is that in the east window, illustrating

Catholic church of the Immaculate Conception, Strabane.

the life of Christ.

■ **References**
Rowan, p 493.

ALL SOULS' NON-SUBSCRIBING PRESBYTERIAN CHURCH, ELMWOOD AVENUE
Elmwood Avenue, Belfast   *Non-Subscribing Presbyterian*

ALTHOUGH THE present Episcopalian-looking church was
built in 1896, the congregation which worships within its
walls can trace its history back to 1709 when the
congregation of Belfast's First Presbyterian Church
divided into two because it had outgrown the original
meeting house. The newly formed Second Belfast

Congregation worshipped in a meeting house in
Rosemary Street, which was rebuilt in 1789. The work to
build a new church was due to the inspired leadership of
Rev Edgar Innes Fripp, who felt that the future of the
congregation lay in the suburbs of the ever-increasing city
of Belfast. The new church of All Souls was completed in

Elmwood Non-Subscribing Presbyterian Church, Belfast.

1896 to the designs of Walter Planck of London, and cost £14,000 to build. It is a remarkable building and has all the appearance of an Anglican church, reflecting a move in the direction of Anglican liturgy by the congregation at that time. The inspiration for the design of the building came from the fourteenth-century Croyland Abbey in Lincolnshire and strong resemblances can be seen in the tower and gable windows at All Souls. Scrabo stone with Doulting dressings has been used throughout and the miniature flying buttresses, on the angles of the tower just below belfry level, are especially pleasing. The tower is a low, sturdy structure, pleasantly covered in ivy and crowned by a rather stumpy spire. Indeed, the church would be as fitting in a rural English setting as in Belfast's busy university area.

All Souls comprises a rectangular nave with flanking aisles, with a clerestory above, and is entered through a very English-looking open timberwork porch. Internally the nave is divided by four arches carried on octagonal columns with foliated capitals, and a continuation of wall and roof flows on into the chancel. The pews within the church were originally in the Second Meeting House in Rosemary Street and stand as a reminder of the continuity of worship by the congregation. These are not the only reminders of the old place of worship, as it is also recalled in the table of the vestry room, which was once the sounding board of the Rosemary Street pulpit. The brass collecting shovels (dated 1789) are also now in All Souls. A memorial board on the back wall was illuminated by Charles Braithwaite in 1908 and it gives information regarding the history of the congregation and its ministers. Recalled here is the Rev James Kirkpatrick

(minister 1708–43), who wrote an *Essay upon the Loyalty of Presbyterians in Great Britain and Ireland from the Reformation to this present year 1713*. The Reverend William Hamilton Drummond (minister 1800–15) is also remembered and he appears to have been an enlightened man, taking a deep interest in natural history, philosophy and poetry. Above the memorial board is a large traceried window, which is reflected by an identical window in the chancel.

The chancel bears the impress of Anglican liturgy, with the Gothic pulpit placed on the left side of the chancel and mirrored by a fine brass eagle lectern at the other side. The Compton organ of 1928 sits within an arched opening on the right-hand wall of the chancel, in a position formerly occupied by an organ acquired for the congregation in 1806 by the musician and antiquarian Edward Bunting. Legend claimed that this earlier instrument had come from St George's Chapel in Windsor and that the ghostly figure of Handel could sometimes be seen at the console! Next to the communion table, which is sited under the chancel window in the Anglican manner, is a chair in which John Wesley is thought to have sat. Given the size of the chair, Wesley must have been a diminutive man even by eighteenth-century standards. There are a number of monuments in the church, some of which found their way here from the old meeting house, but the finest is the First World War Memorial bronze crafted by Rosamund Praeger.

'Wesley's chair' in Elmwood Non-Subscribing Presbyterian Church.

■ References
Larmour, p 58; Millin, SS, *History of the Second Congregation, Belfast, 1708–1900*, (Belfast, 1900), pp 20, 41–4; 77–9.

LITURGICAL OBJECTS

THE CONDUCT of worship entails the use of objects such as crosses, chalices, collecting pans, and these are often of great interest and value.

Chalices are used to contain consecrated wine during communion. The earliest chalices in Ulster probably date from the seventeenth century. Of particular interest within the Catholic church is the chalice at Newtownards and the 'Russell-Taafe' chalice, made in Dublin in 1641. Many Church of Ireland chalices date from the period of the Restoration, such as the chalice given to Dromore Cathedral in 1659–60 by Joanna Taylor, wife of the bishop. The Colville plate in St Mark's, Newtownards, was made by John Cuthbert of Dublin in the late seventeenth century. A fine example of eighteenth-century silver is seen in the flagons given to Bright and Ballee churches in County Down by Dean Patrick Delany, the friend of Jonathan Swift. Unlike the Catholics and Anglicans, Presbyterians usually made their communion-ware from pewter, which

Chalice given to Bright Parish Church by Dean Patrick Delany in 1785.

Traditional collecting shovel, also from Bright church, the gift of the curate, Dr Thomas Kennedy, 1783.

probably reflected the simplicity of their services. The six pewter communion cups from Ballycarry, County Antrim, can be seen in the Non-Subscribing Presbyterian Church in Rosemary Street, Belfast.

Another feature of communion within the Presbyterian church was the issuing of communion tokens. The possession of one of these allowed the holder to receive communion, as they were considered to lead a consistent Christian life. These tokens were made of lead or pewter and bore the name of the church, the minister's name or initials and the date. A collection of these tokens can be seen in the museum at the Presbyterian Assembly Buildings in Belfast.

Lifting the collection was a task assigned to laymen – usually a warden or elder and although it is now the norm to use collecting plates, many churches used collecting pans or shovels in the past. These were plates connected to long-handled shafts, which allowed the collector to reach them under the worshippers' noses across the length of a box pew. A large number of these still exist in the Presbyterian and Anglican churches of Ulster, although, sadly, few, if any, are still used. Crumlin Non-Subscribing Presbyterian Church has a fine set of nineteenth-century collecting shovels mounted in the church porch.

BALLYNAFEIGH METHODIST CHURCH, BELFAST
Ormeau Road, Belfast
Methodist

ALTHOUGH THERE had been a Methodist presence in the area for some time, it was not until 1893 that the congregation purchased a corrugated iron church at a cost of £456. However, within four years plans were being made to build a larger place of worship. So, in December 1897 Messrs Forman and Aston were invited to design a church holding 600 people, but costing no more than £2500. In the event, the cost ran to £3000. The foundation stone was laid by Sir J Henderson, Lord Mayor of Belfast, on 28 May 1898. At the same time four memorial stones were laid and these can still be seen in the porch. The church was opened for worship on Sunday 15 January 1899.

The completed church was certainly very individualistic both inside and out. The exterior originally had a more vertical thrust, with a spire on the tower and a spirelet on the roof of the church. The walls had areas of exposed red brick, which have since been plastered over and painted. The church is basically a rectangular shape with diagonally placed extensions at the angles. The architect has employed a number of architectural idioms; there are Gothic elements, Romanesque and Renaissance. To the road, the facade presents a low square tower which has a hooded group of three windows, with semicircular openings on the uppermost stage, all under an undulating parapet. On the gable is a large semicircular-headed

Ballynafeigh Methodist Church, Belfast.

window which, judging by old photographs, once held stained glass. To the right of the facade is a turret, capped by a copper-clad dome. The two entrance doors are semicircular-headed, flanked by chubby columns with triangular hoods.

The interior of the church remains very much as designed by Forman and Aston, having something of the air of a Tudor theatre. Six columns support the curving raked gallery and are carried upwards beyond this level to support the roof. The gallery seats at the very top of the building have a fine view of the interesting roof structure, which is composed of dark timber trusses against timber infill sheeting. The trusses are ornamented with fretwork arcades. The auditorium feel of the interior is increased by the progressive decline in the floor level as the pulpit is approached down the two aisles. The pulpit, which is a war memorial, stands in front of a raised apse, designed to accommodate the choir. This opening is flanked by two archways containing the organ pipes. The windows have clear glazing and so the interior is extremely light. This airiness, coupled with the fine acoustic qualities appears to have been a trademark of the architects' church work. The dramatic internal use of angles and raked seating give the church a rather jaunty appearance and one can just as easily imagine a play being enacted here, as a church service.

■ **References**
Brett (Belfast), p 42; de Breffny, p 166; Larmour, p 59; Smyth, R, *Ballynafeigh Methodist Church Jubilee Reflections 1899–1949* (Belfast, 1949), pp 3–4.

CHURCH OF THE SACRED HEART, OMAGH
Brook Street, Omagh, County Tyrone   *Catholic*

THIS IMPRESSIVE church succeeds in dominating the town of Omagh and this is perhaps because its style of architecture is so different from its surroundings. With its two spires of unequal height, the church would be just as at home in, for example, Chartres. This asymmetrical feature of the building was intentional, and was not, as fable has suggested, due to a sudden exhaustion of building funds.

On the south side of the south tower are two stone plaques which reveal the age of the church. The first plaque says, 'Cornerstone laid 1892', while the other proclaims, 'Dedicated 1899'. The Sacred Heart church was designed by William Hague, who has provided a magnificent French Gothic facade with a more conventional structure behind. The main east door has a fine tympanum displaying the Sacred Heart of Jesus with an image of the Virgin and Child to the left and St Joseph, the sub-patron of the church, to the right. On either side of the central door are canopied niches containing statues of St Joseph and Jesus of the Sacred Heart. These niches are supported by the symbolic representations of Matthew, Mark, Luke and John. Above the door is a massive Decorated window with a central wheel. This is flanked by the north and south towers, which are clasped by buttresses. The towers are identical as far as belfry level, where they terminate in crocketed gables above the pointed sound windows. At the angles of each tower are rather puzzling protruding rough-hewn blocks. It is easy to suppose that these were simply never carved, but if these were intended to have been gargoyles, then it is likely that they should have been carved on the ground. The spires are fourteenth-century in style, with the southern one being considerably shorter than the northern one. Both spires have lucarnes and crockets at angles. Despite the oft-repeated tale that the southern spire is shorter due to financial difficulties, it is actually more elaborately detailed than its loftier sister.

The church is of seven bays, plus the two-bay sanctuary. The arches of the nave are carried on circular polished granite columns with foliated capitals. There are seven clerestory windows and above is a hipped hammerbeam roof, which is enriched with carved wooden angels. The corbel stops in the nave represent Irish saints, with Sts Patrick and Brigid at the chancel

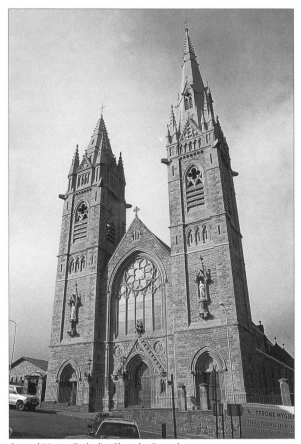

Sacred Heart Catholic Church, Omagh.

arch. The aisles have lean-to roofs and are lighted by six windows filled with coloured glass. Within the sanctuary are two narrower arches supported on columns topped by foliated capitals beneath two clerestory windows. An angel is perched above each capital. The five-light sanctuary window is filled with stained glass depicting, at the bottom, the Last Supper; above is the adoration of the Sacred Heart; in the wheel is a depiction of the Crucifixion. The inscription modestly announces that the window is 'A memorial of Edward Boyle the greatest benefactor of this church'. The front of the high altar shows Jesus being laid in the tomb, while the rather individualistic reredos carries a representation of the Holy Spirit in the tympanum and has Christ and the Apostles arranged along the archivolt. Like the altars in the side chapels, the high altar is made of marble. In the south chapel the windows depict scenes from the early life of the Virgin Mary, while the childhood of Christ is recalled by those in the north chapel. Much of the carving, in stone and wood, is of high quality and originality of design. The very fine pulpit is square, and its main faces are carved with biblical scenes: it is framed by corner niches accommodating small statues. The free-standing confessionals are rather good, made entirely of wood with elaborate pinnacles and scaled pitched roofs.

■ **References**
Rowan, pp 444–5.

HOLY CROSS PASSIONIST MONASTERY, BELFAST
Crumlin Road, Belfast
Catholic

THE ROMANESQUE monastic buildings here were designed by O'Neill and Byrne and predate the church by twenty years. However, the church itself is more rigidly Romanesque in style than its neighbours and is by Doolin, Butler and Donnelly of Dublin, and was built in 1900–2. The facade is dominated by the twin towers, each of which is capped by a pyramidal copper-clad spire. Many parallels can be drawn with the earlier Passionist Monastery at Mount Argus, Dublin, which came from the drawing board of JJ McCarthy. The tympanum over the main door is the work of James Owens and depicts the Descent from the Cross. Angels manage to weave their way through the carved foliage of the capitals by the door. In a niche on the gable stands a statue of Christ. The Lady chapel, which has its own access by a Romanesque doorway, was built in 1902 by John Taggart,

JP, in memory of his wife, Cecilia and the windows in the chapel invite prayers for the souls of the couple.

There is some superb decorative work in the nave and sanctuary of the church. The nave is of five bays with a clerestory, while the sanctuary is of three bays. Four polished columns and two pilasters with massive foliated capitals support the arches of the nave. These divide the nave from the aisles,

Holy Cross Passionist monastery, Crumlin Road, Belfast.

beyond which, on the south, are two chapels of the Passionist Fathers. In the larger chapel, the stained glass depicts the progress of the order at the time of its foundation by Paul Francis Massari in 1720. This chapel, which manages to integrate well into the building, dates from as recently as 1961, and was designed by WD Bready. On the other side of the church, the Lady chapel (RM Butler, architect) has a very fine altar, which is pedimented and has two Corinthian columns flanked by pilastered doorcases.

The decoration of the nave consists of painted roundels at clerestory level, filled with images of the saints. Above is a beautifully painted ceiling, showing the heavenly host. On the walls of the sanctuary are frescoes illustrating the crucifixion and the crusades. The particular interest of these lies in the fact that they are the work of Brother Mark, a member of the Passionist Order. The very rich mosaics in the sanctuary and Sacred Heart chapel are by JF Ebner of London. Christ in the Tomb is the subject of the carving on the front of the altar.

With its prominent towers, the church is a familiar landmark in this part of the city and is well worth a visit to see its interesting and varied internal decoration.

■ **References**
Brett (Belfast), p 62; Larmour, p 68.

HILLHALL PRESBYTERIAN CHURCH
Hillhall road between Lisburn and Belfast, County Antrim   *Presbyterian*

THE FOUNDATION stone of this rather jaunty church was laid on 14 December 1901 and the building which emerged was designed by the firm of Blackwood and Jury. Their design utilises the Art Nouveau idiom which Vincent Craig had dabbled in at Ballywatt and more particularly at Portstewart. At Hillhall even the gate piers are in the Art Nouveau style and the whole building is reminiscent of the work of the Arts and Crafts movement.

The facade is composed of a broad five-light window placed above two smaller windows separated by a single buttress. A chequered pattern occupies the crest of the gable, while the undulating tops of the pinnacles of the tower add to the Art Nouveau feel of the church. These pinnacles cut into the slated pyramidal roof of the tower, which culminates in a weather-vane. The body of the church is of three bays of three-light windows, while the transepts have five-light windows and oculus windows above. With the obvious exception of these, all the

Hillhall Presbyterian Church.

windows have cusped heads. The roof has bands of lighter slates and has a pagoda-like ventilator perched on its summit.

The interior of the church is rather traditional in the Presbyterian manner, being dominated by the pulpit and organ. There is a very sturdy trussed roof rising from stone corbels, while the shallow transepts are divided from the nave by pointed arches. The windows have little touches of Charles Rennie Mackintosh in the floral designs of the glazing, and especially pleasing are the transept windows filled with flowing foliage patterns.

A brass plaque in the porch recalls the work of Rev Robert Robson, who was instrumental in the construction of the present church and even this has Art Nouveau script.

■ **References**
Dixon, p 76.

Art Noveau window in Hillhall Presbyterian Church.

CARLISLE ROAD METHODIST CHURCH, DERRY
Carlisle Road, Derry, County Londonderry   *Methodist*

ALTHOUGH METHODISM was first established in Derry in about 1753 by Thomas Williams, a preaching-house was used in Linenhall Street only from 1789, until a new church was built at the East Wall in 1835. With the industrialisation of the city in the mid nineteenth century, the Methodists, along with all the other denominations, experienced a marked increase in numbers.

To meet this demand, work on a new church on the Carlisle Road began in 1901 when the Duchess of Abercorn laid the foundation stone. The architect was Alfred Forman of the firm of Forman and Aston, who had also designed Ballynafeigh Methodist Church in Belfast. A common feature of both these churches, and one for which the architect was noted, is the excellent acoustics. It has been said that Alfred Forman's interest in auditorial forms and good sound qualities arose from his passion for amateur dramatics. Carlisle Road church was dedicated on 8 May 1903, when the mayor of the city, Marshall Tillie, opened the door using a gold key.

Forman's building makes imaginative use of Gothic Revival elements and the church is an important part of the streetscape. The main entrance is through a pointed doorcase in the foot of the tower. Buttresses run up the side of the tower and culminate in crocketed pinnacles. Flying buttresses run from these to the octagonal spire. The body of the church is of four bays and has a hexagonal baptistry with a slated pyramidal roof at the opposite end to the tower. At clerestory level each window sits within its own gable, and these are echoed by smaller, though similar, windows on the aisle below. Again, Forman employs flying buttresses, which rise on the aisle parapet and abut the wall above. A decorative ridge finial runs along the roof, which terminates in a spirelet.

As at Ballynafeigh, the interior is very light, with a slight slope in the two aisles and a very deep gallery running around three sides of the church, ending a bay short of the pulpit wall to allow for two semi-hexagonal projections. The openings for these projections, and those of the organ gallery, are flanked by tall columns with Romanesque capitals. The pew arrangement on the ground level runs on a concave curve. The ceiling, which is of dark timber, has highly decorative fretwork trusses, again reminiscent of the roof at Ballynafeigh. Having compared their similarities in structure, it must be

Carlisle Road Methodist Church, Derry.

said that the two churches are certainly vastly different in style.

In the porch is a reminder of the old church on the East Wall, in the form of a monument to Rev Thomas Robinson (died 1881), brought here when this church was opened.

■ **References**
de Breffny, p 166; Doak, JC, *Carlisle Road Methodist Church, 1903–1978* (Derry, 1978).

PORTSTEWART PRESBYTERIAN CHURCH
Enfield Street, Portstewart, County Londonderry   *Presbtyerian*

THE PREVIOUS Presbyterian church in Portstewart was a Georgian T-shaped structure and old photographs of it survive. One of these shows a notice in front of the church informing passers-by that the building was due to be demolished and a new church erected. It also informs the reader as to how to make a financial contribution.

Vincent Craig, the brother of Northern Ireland's first prime minister, James Craig, designed this quirky church, with its Art Nouveau overtones. Portstewart Church was completed in 1905, but Craig had earlier had a little excursion into the genre at his Presbyterian Church of Ballywatt, County Antrim, which was built in 1895. Craig provided a cruciform church for Portstewart, with a tower and squat spire at the north-west corner. The building is roughcast, but is enlivened by red sandstone dressings and a red Ruabon tiled roof. The lancet windows of the church are divided by a series of buttresses, and on the facade one of these actually breaks through the west window and its Art Nouveau tracery. At the first stage of the tower is a cheeky little square window filled with star-shaped tracery, while the sound windows above have shallow arched hoods. The parapet of the tower is undulating and the use of curves reminds us the work of Charles Rennie Mackintosh, an influence which is certainly present here.

The aisled interior of the church is lined with columns of Bath stone and the ceiling is of timber, supported on corbel stops. The stained glass is quite fine, especially that in the semi-hexagonal sanctuary which is by Ward and Partners and Clokey. Some of the other windows have plain glass interwoven with Mackintosh-like patterns.

Parallels can be drawn between this church, and that at Hillhall, which was designed by Blackwood and Jury.

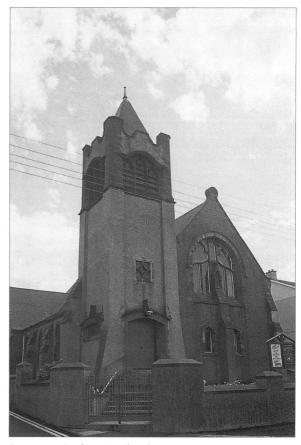

Portstewart Presbyterian Church.

■ **References**
Builder, 27 August 1904, p 233; Rowan, p 460; UAHS (Coleraine and Portstewart), p 35.

CHURCH OF THE GOOD SHEPHERD, SION MILLS
Main Street, Sion Mills, County Tyrone   *Church of Ireland*

THE VILLAGE of Sion Mills owes its existence to the purchase of a mill building by James Herdman in 1835. To operate the mill, the Herdman family required workers, and they created a model village to house their staff. The parish church of St Saviour was completed in 1895 and this still exists as the present church hall: like the rest of the village, it was built in a Tudoresque style. Although St Saviour's was used as the chapel-of-ease to the parent

Church of the Good Shepherd (C of I), Sion Mills.

church at Urney, it was never actually consecrated and, proving too small, was succeeded by the present church in 1909. A bible from St Saviour's can be seen in the present church.

The driving force behind the construction of the new church, dedicated on 15 May 1909, was the rector, Canon J Olphert, with the help of Brigadier-General Ambrose St Quentin Ricardo, whose classical table-tomb is placed outside the front door of the church. The architect of the church was WF Unsworth, a London-based architect, who was the brother-in-law of Emerson Tennent Herdman. Unsworth had designed a number of other buildings in the village, but is principally remembered as the architect of the Royal Shakespeare Theatre at Stratford-upon-Avon. In a daring move away from the Tudoresque architecture of the rest of Sion Mills, Unsworth based his church on one he had seen at Pistoia in Florence. Such a remarkable piece of architecture would be sufficient to ensure that the architect was remembered locally, but at the building's completion he presented a chalice inscribed, 'Of your charity remember in God WF Unsworth, architect of this church 1909'.

The Italianate Romanesque building is essentially a rectangle with apsidal projections on the front, sides and east end. On the front, two lean-to entrance porches abut

the semicircular projection which accommodates the staircase to the gallery, the window pattern indicating the internal presence of the stairs. There are square eastern campaniles, the northern one being taller and capped by a belfry stage. The nave proper is a five-bay hall lighted by Diocletian windows.

On entering the church, the visitor is struck by the lightness of the interior. There is a spacious baptistry area under the west gallery, with a circular font which carries a ewer presented by the children of the parish on the day of the church's dedication. The nave has an almost clinical appearance, with its clear glazing, parquet flooring and cream-coloured walls, spanned by a timber roof. The light pendants throughout were designed by Unsworth and based on the plan of an Orthodox cross. The gallery at the west end holds the Conacher organ and has a drum attached to the front which belonged to the 9th Battalion Royal Inniskilling Fusiliers. On either side of the nave are arched openings with small galleries behind, which are accommodated by the apsidal projections. There are blank niches to the left and right of the chancel arch, which would have been filled with statues in the church's Italian counterpart. Given the relative simplicity of the nave, magnificent emphasis is given to the apsidal chancel, which is raised by a flight of seven steps. On either side of these steps are matching ambos, executed in grey marble and trimmed with Connemara marble. The apse has a barrel-vaulted ceiling which ends in a semi-dome, above a row of eleven clerestory windows. The communion table itself rests on three more steps and is placed immediately in front of a set of dorsal curtains. To the right is a fine piscina made from marble and used for the cleansing of communion vessels.

On the north wall is a memorial to the local employer and landlord, Emerson Tennent Herdman and his wife Fanny Alice (both died 1918), and, on the opposite wall, one commemorating Ambrose St Quentin Ricardo (died 1923), who was a prime mover in the building of the church. Among the other fittings of the church is a very solid early eighteenth-century chalice, with the Irish silver hallmark.

■ **References**
de Breffny, p 165; Rowan, pp 486–7.

12
Modern Developments in Church Architecture

THE TWENTIETH CENTURY saw great diversity in church architecture and the most dramatic change to date in the form and decoration of church buildings. The competent, but architecturally timid, Gothic churches still being built right up to the Second World War could not contrast more sharply with the churches at Creeslough or Steelstown, built only thirty years later. These new and inspiring churches reflect changes in society and liturgy.

The early years of the century saw little change in the accepted architectural genres, with a retention of the Gothic idiom, which was seen as broadly representing church architecture. As noted earlier, there were splashes of colour, such as the Presbyterian churches of Hillhall and Portstewart, which were designed by Blackwood and Jury and Vincent Craig respectively, and both of which have Art Nouveau influences. Despite this apparent foray into a modern art style, there is an air of restraint, as these buildings still have the standard Presbyterian form, and there is little or no innovation in their interiors. The Catholic church had, since the Celtic Revival in the nineteenth century, employed Romanesque architecture with some enthusiasm, and this trend continued into the twentieth century. Indeed, further impetus was added by the gaining of independence for the twenty-six southern counties of Ireland. Here there was a cultural reaction against all things English and this resulted in a move towards an Irish identity linguistically, artistically and architecturally; thus churches were built in an Irish or Hiberno-Romanesque style. This trend was to bring to the fore the array of talented architects whose work unites the story of modern Irish (and Ulster) church

architecture. Parallel to this was the flowering of Irish artists whose contribution to ecclesiastical art continues to the present time. The development of new and unique styles in stained glass was nurtured by Sarah Purser, who founded An Túr Gloine (the tower of glass) in 1903. Evie Hone belonged to that studio and, along with Harry Clarke, is representative of a highly productive and imaginative period in Irish stained glass. In Ulster there is an example of Purser's work at the Convent of Mercy Chapel in Enniskillen, while Hone windows can be seen at St John's, Malone; the Dominican Convent on Belfast's Falls Road; and Fahan Church of Ireland Church, Donegal. Harry Clarke windows are to be found at Carrickmacross, Letterkenny, Lough Derg and also at the Falls Road convent.

The churches designed by Padraic Gregory should be examined, as his work stands at the threshold between church architecture employing Gothic and Celtic traits and truly modern ecclesiastical architecture. A particular feature of Gregory's work is the provision of a baldacchino, as at St Peter's Cathedral, in the Dominican Convent in Belfast and at St Malachy's, Coleraine. Gregory was an accomplished poet, and the architecture that he produced reflects the same artistic talent which so expressively commanded the written word. He was versatile in presenting familiar architectural styles with flair and individuality, and this ability manifested itself in his Romanesque churches at Coleraine and Ederney, County Tyrone, and at the Gothic buildings at Aghagallon, County Antrim and St Anthony's, Belfast. His Coleraine church, described at the time as being

The Catholic cathedral at Cavan. Ralph Byrne, the architect, based his design on the facade of Francis Johnston's church of St George in Dublin.

'Hiberno-Romanesque', was selected to represent Ireland at the International Exhibition of Sacred Art in Rome in 1950. Not all the churches built using this idiom were as outstanding and paler examples of Romanesque are the McCracken Memorial Presbyterian Church and Stormont Presbyterian Church, both in Belfast. Interesting and rather surprising amongst the plethora of Romanesque churches, is the Catholic cathedral at Cavan, built in 1942. Rather than gleaning its inspiration from Irish precedent, it takes its inspiration from the early nineteenth century and the work of Francis Johnston. Cavan Cathedral utilises many essential elements of Johnston's Anglican church of St George in Dublin, grafting a neo-classical portico and steeple onto a large basilica church.

Austerity imposed by the Second World War, both north and south of the border, hindered church building for the duration, but the years which followed have been a highly productive period for the development of modern ecclesiastical architecture. New churches were required where vast suburbs had developed around Belfast, and population shifts, which are still continuing, left churches in the city centre without congregations, but spawned new ones on the periphery. An example of this is the Third Congregation in Rosemary Street, which had seen its old church destroyed in the Blitz, and chose to relocate itself in a new church in the suburbs.

With the increased need for more churches, bodies were set up within the various denominations to address the situation. The Presbyterian church established a Church Extension Committee and the Assembly's Committee on Church Architecture issued a booklet entitled, *The House of God*, which gave guidelines on what was required of a church building and stating that

'function should determine form'. This emphasis on the relationship of liturgy to church design was a factor which applied equally to all denominations.

Within the Church of Ireland the architect Denis O'D Hanna promoted modern architecture with traditional traits. This can perhaps be best seen in his church of St Comgall at Rathcoole, Belfast, completed in 1955. The church has neo-Georgian features and a steeply-pitched roof broken by five bays of tall dormer windows, the whole perched high above the ground-floor church hall. Hanna's greatest contribution to church architecture was his appreciation of the role which good representational art could play in enhancing a building. At St Molua's, Stormont, there is a series of stone plaques by David Pettigrew, along with a mural by Desmond Kinney and a bronze by James McKendrie. At the Church of the Pentecost, Cregagh, there is a representation of the dove of the Pentecost by Elizabeth Campbell, as well as a bronze and a group of stone plaques by Desmond Kinney and David Pettigrew respectively. This drive to include art within the setting of modern ecclesiastical building was to prove important, and is a feature that continues to the present day.

Perhaps the greatest contribution to modern ecclesiastical architecture has come from the Catholic church. Its need for new churches arose due to the fact that many of the buildings, dating from penal times, had reached the end of their useful lives, being either too small or ill-suited to the sweeping liturgical changes which the church sought to implement after the Second Vatican Council. The council's work on the development of the Catholic liturgy had far-reaching consequences for the design of that denomination's churches; relieving the act of worship from the restraints of the past, it effectively did the same for church architecture. The Constitution on the Sacred Liturgy was promulgated on 4 December 1963, and was the most extensive reform of liturgy in the church since the Council of Trent, which held its last session on 4 December 1563. There was a drive towards increasing congregational participation, and it was felt that this could best be done by 'the grouping of the assembly around the altar', as well as 'the provision of a worthy space for the administration of Baptism and Penance'. With such proposals it became clear that the traditional pattern of a sanctuary placed at the end of a long nave was not ideal for the universal witness of the mass. The Constitution of 1963 sought to give more importance to the 'people of God', and it was felt that every architect's brief should reflect this. The central position of the altar was emphasised by the *Pastoral*

Directory on the Building and Reorganisation of Churches. In some instances all that was done was to move the altar forward, while others could see that an opportunity had been presented to build new churches more attuned to the liturgy.

This change within the Catholic church could not have come at a better time in architectural terms. Although there were architects who had sought to innovate and create imaginative buildings, there were those who clung to the more traditional idioms which had really run out of steam. Patrick Haughey's striking church of St Theresa in Sion Mills, County Tyrone, was begun in 1962, just before the Second Vatican Council, and completed after it, and represents a crossroads in Ulster church architecture. It can claim to be the province's first truly modern church, for it bears few if any of the restrictions of tradition. The church is a simple rectangle, but what is really important is its decoration with notable art works, mostly from Irish sources. Within St Theresa's are works by Oisin Kelly, Patrick Pollen, Ray Carroll and Patrick McIlroy; a selection of artistic talent which may reflect the establishment in 1956 of the Church Exhibitions Committee of the Royal Institute of the Architects of Ireland. Biannually this committee supervised the selection of works by Irish artists to be sent to the Salzburg Biennale of Sacred Art. The good judgment and success of their work can be gauged by the almost immediate honours that were gained: a gold medal for Oisin Kelly in 1958, and one for Patrick McIlroy in 1960. In the use of modern art within the church there

Oisin Kelly's sculpture of St Peter at Milford

was proof that mediocrity could be avoided, and that well-conceived artworks could help to elevate a building. With this in mind an Advisory Committee on Sacred Art and Architecture was formed in 1965. One of the first members was the architect, Liam McCormick, and this was to bode well for the future of ecclesiastical art and architecture. Fr Donal O'Sullivan, the then chairman of the Arts Council of Ireland, was in no doubt as to the importance of art as a medium of worship, speaking of it as having an 'elevated task' to aid the praise of God and for the edification of His people. This was why good artists were to be employed; imagination, taste and quality were all that would be fit for the house of God.

Brian de Breffny, in his book *The Churches and Abbeys of Ireland*, makes the point that while all denominations built new churches, it was the Catholic church which produced the most innovative and interesting. He also writes that, 'The most beautiful new churches in Ireland are those designed by Liam McCormick and Partners of Derry'. This statement does not decry the work of others, but underlines Liam McCormick's pivotal position in the development of modern Irish church architecture.

A native of Derry, with the best examples of his work found in north-west Ulster, his importance in this study of the subject cannot be over-emphasised. Dr Paul Larmour, in writing an appreciation of McCormick's work, refers to the architect as the 'father of modern church architecture in Ireland'. This is not over-stating the case, for McCormick churches are unashamedly modern, but not just for the sake of being so, for each one has a sense of individuality, and respects and enhances its surroundings. The architect realised that, particularly in a rural setting, a visit to the place of worship was often the only true encounter with architecture for most people. It had, therefore, to be an uplifting experience that would enrich worship and not have the jarring effect which bad modern architecture could so often have. McCormick commented of modern churches that 'It is important that they be right and correct.' The fact that no two McCormick churches are the same is striking testimony to his innate ability to react to a site. His churches are not imposed on the landscape, rather they react to, reflect and contribute to it. The most outstanding example of this is St Michael's Church at Creeslough. Described by Hugh Dixon as 'topographical sculptural', its undulating form is a man-made reflection of the majestic mountains which loom nearby. Many common elements can be seen in Creeslough and Le Corbusier's famous church at Ronchamp, but although McCormick had studied Le Corbusier's work and was inspired by his Pavillon Suisse during a 1937 visit to Paris, this was not the true influence for the Creeslough church. Liam McCormick had a gift that he perhaps could not have put his finger on himself. He would look at a site and what was to be built there developed, by instinct or intuition. He could visualise the drama of the future occasion when the congregation would open their new spiritual home.

At Burt his circular church of St Aengus took its form from the ancient Grianan of Aileach, and once again this speaks of McCormick's ability to react to a site; the whole area is dominated by the hill-fort, so why break the hold of the circular form by introducing a new shape? Liturgically too, the architect was able to utilise the circular form to give the altar a more central position, as at his churches at Creeslough, Clogher and Carrickfergus. McCormick's selection of materials for his churches also underlines his understanding of each site, for he employed materials common to the area. This is seen in the churches in the 'princely county' (his own words) of Donegal; the white roughcast walls of the churches of Desertegney, Donaghmore, Glenties, Creeslough and Milford all have the same finish as the rural buildings which surround them. Timber, slate, stone and water are all integrated into the designs and their creative manipulation serves to form true and original architecture. Important in relation to modern church architecture is the encouragement that Liam McCormick gave to local artists. Talents such as Helen Moloney, Partick McIlroy, Oisin Kelly, Patrick and Nell Pollen and Imogen Stuart found excellent scope for their gifts within the walls of McCormick churches. Their use of symbolism and visual imagery echoed that sensitive imagination which had created the church buildings where their works are to be found.

Looking at the development of modern church architecture in Ulster, an evolutionary path can be traced: the twentieth century dawned with rather traditional forms of churches; then came a linking of traditionalism and modernity in the works of Gregory and Hanna; and finally the ground-breaking work of Liam McCormick. Reference to the past is still employed – witness, for example, St Columba's Church of Ireland Church in Portadown, which was completed in 1970 and employs the ancient cruciform shape.

In embracing the modernity of every other aspect of life, the church has succeeded in proving itself, and its message, to be a living body. Significant changes in church architecture have been effected due to developments in liturgy within the Catholic church, and in other cases due to practicality. This is evident in buildings such as St Columba's in Lisburn, County Antrim, where the Methodists and Presbyterians share a modern church building.

■ **References**

de Breffny, p 189; Dixon, p 89–90; Evans, p 57; Hurley, pp 23–9; Kidder Smith, GE, *The New Churches of Europe* (London, 1964), pp 86–96; McCormick, WHD, 'Building Churches, 1947–75: A Personal Recollection', in *RSUA Yearbook*, 1976, pp 44–9; Rothery, S, *Ireland and the New Architecture* (Dublin, 1991), pp 157–77; Snoddy, T, *Dictionary of Irish Artists: the Twentieth Century* (Dublin, 1996), pp 62–4, 197–200, 406–9.

FIRST CHURCH OF CHRIST SCIENTIST, BELFAST
University Avenue, Belfast

Christian Science

DESIGNED BY Clough Williams-Ellis of Cushendun and Portmerion fame, this complex of church and ancillary buildings took fifteen years to design and complete, beginning in 1922. In terms of design and fittings the buildings bear very strongly the impress of the architect, and recall his delight in neo-Georgian architecture.

Christian Science first came to Belfast in 1898 when Miss Lillian Riddell, along with a small number of other people began to hold meetings in her home in Great Victoria Street. These meetings gathered momentum until the need for premises was such that a church and reading room were opened in 13 Lombard Street. Following a move to Royal Avenue, it was eventually decided to settle in University Avenue where a school was built in 1923 which also served as a church until the erection of the church proper in 1936–37. The school is well provided with windows, as indeed is the entire complex, and has scriptural panels on the walls flanking the platform. A feature of the interior is the open truss-work of the roof.

Externally, the church appears as a substantial hall ending in an apse, lighted by very tall semicircular-headed windows. The front facade seems to borrow from a number of architectural elements; there are three of the above-mentioned windows; the roofline seems reminiscent of the Dutch gable and is embellished with urns and surmounted by a Tuscan columned cupola. To either side of the facade are extensions to accommodate the internal staircases. The caretaker's house is a pleasant neo-Georgian building of two storeys with a steeply-pitched roof, connected to the church and school by an arcade running round three sides of a well-maintained garden. All painted white, the entire group would seem entirely appropriate sited on some Mediterranean hilltop, rather than in the midst of Belfast's expanses of red brick.

The church is entered from the side, up a flight of steps leading into a spacious lobby which gives access to the main body of the church, or, by further stairs, to the gallery and upper rooms. Five bays in length with two aisles leading to a central platform positioned within an apse, the interior is a mixture of Art Deco and more traditional elements. Above the entrance is a raked gallery with a bow front, while the ceiling is a shallow barrel-vault, its plainness relieved only by three wooden chandeliers, each with eight lights. These, like the unusual star-shaped lights elsewhere in the church, serve to show the individuality of Williams-Ellis' designs. The side walls of the church have quotations from Christ and Mary Baker Eddy, the founder of Christian Science. The two abstract wooden lecterns on the platform were designed and made by Purdy and Millard and stand in front of two doors leading to the readers' rooms.

Behind all of this is a maze of small rooms, but most surprising of all is the room at the very top of the building which is something of a 'star chamber', due to the astronomical details painted on the ceiling.

A visit to a building such as this is a good introduction to the neo-Georgian/neo-classical architecture that was to be employed in a good number of sacred and public buildings in Ulster from the 1920s to the 1950s.

Christian Scientist church, Belfast.

■ **References**
Historical Sketch of First Church of Christ Scientist, Belfast (Belfast 1955), pp 3, 8, 14–18; Haslam, R, *Clough Williams-Ellis* (London, 1996), pp 13, 59, 105; Larmour, p 80; UAHS (Queen's University area), p 24.

ST ANTHONY'S CHURCH, WOODSTOCK ROAD, BELFAST
Woodstock Road, Belfast   *Catholic*

THIS GOTHIC church is the work of the poet/architect Padraic Gregory and was built between 1936 and 1939. It bears many physical similarities to his churches at Aghagallon and Coleraine, particularly in the handling of the tower.

The facade has a broad Gothic pointed doorcase, the hood of which is carried on clustered columns. In the tympanum is a statue of St Anthony, who is invoked in the inscription which reads: 'Sancte Antoni Ora Pro Nobis'. The church is built of Ballycullen stone from Scrabo, whereas the dressings, which include a corbel table, are of pre-cast stone. The tower incorporates a side porch in its foot and is situated on the south side of the church. The tracery of the east window incorporates a

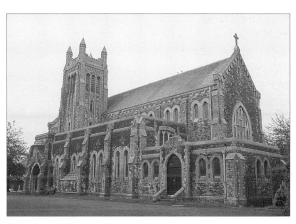

St Anthony's Catholic Church, Belfast.

Latin cross, and as the subject matter of the glass is the Crucifixion, the effect of this clever design is fully appreciated from inside.

The interior is bright and inspiring, especially in the sanctuary where the purples, blues and greens of the east window (the work of Earley of Dublin) radiate colour onto the crisp white walls. At the west end, above the gallery, the stained glass depicts the four evangelists. The Last Supper is the subject of the window in the Lady chapel. Five pointed arches with a smaller arch at each end divide the side aisles from the nave. These arches are carried on clustered columns, and a clerestory rises above, composed of eight pairs of windows. Between these sets of windows are colonettes supporting the ribs of the ceiling. As with the Gregory church at Coleraine, the sanctuary area has been sensitively reordered, retaining the veined marble Gothic arcading on the walls. The overall impression of the interior is quite refreshing given the grey solidity of the exterior.

■ **References**

Larmour, p 91.

ST MALACHY'S CHURCH, COLERAINE
Nursery Avenue, Coleraine, County Londonderry

Catholic

THIS FINE Hiberno-Romanesque church in large and beautiful surroundings was completed in 1937 to the designs of Padraic Gregory, and has many features akin to his church of St Anthony in Belfast.

The church is a rectangular structure of undressed sandstone dressed with cement trim, with a square tower and Lady chapel on the west and a narrow aisle to the east. The facade is approached by a flight of steps and is dominated by the large round-headed doorcase and massive rose window incorporating a Celtic cross. The arch of the doorcase is decorated with a chevron pattern and springs from clustered columns. The tympanum incorporates the Chi Rho, which is reflected by the motif under the baldacchino in the sanctuary. The rose window on the facade radiates from a central cross and there is a corbel table running the entire circuit of the eaves-line. The nave and aisles are of seven bays of paired round-headed windows, with another bay beyond. Placed halfway down the west side is the tower with a round-headed Romanesque door at its foot. The tower itself is buttressed with three belfry windows on each face.

St Malachy's Catholic Church, Coleraine.

The interior of the church has been criticised for the use of lined cement to simulate masonry, but the present colour scheme of pinks and whites gives the church an airy spaciousness. The six semicircular arches on each side of the nave rest on scalloped capitals on stout square columns. The gallery has a rather attractive convex front. The ceiling is barrel-vaulted and compartmented with Celtic crosses worked into the decorative square bosses.

Great credit must go to the church authorities for the imaginative and sensitive manner in which the recent reordering of the sanctuary has been handled. This area of the church is dominated by the fine baldacchino, a favourite device of Gregory, which now gives cover to the tabernacle, sitting above the Chi Rho symbol taken from the old altar frontal. The present altar is of polished marble and was cleverly made from older altar fronts placed back-to-back. The ambo is made from a section of the old high altar. Placed to the left of the sanctuary is an object that must be unique in an Irish church. It is a depiction of the Madonna and Child from the Umbrian School. It is of oil, painted on wood, and can be dated to the fifteenth century, having once been the central section of a triptych. The historical value of this piece (which was given to the church in 1960) is increased by the fact that it once belonged to Mary, Queen of Scots. The glass throughout the church is of coloured querries incorporating cross motifs.

At the head of the aisle is the foundation stone of the former St Malachy's Church, which was closer to the town centre. It is inscribed: 'The Church of St Malachy. Erected AD 1837'.

■ **References**

Rowan, p 206; UAHS (Coleraine and Portstewart), p 21.

STRABANE FIRST PRESBYTERIAN CHURCH
Derry Road, Strabane, County Tyrone *Presbyterian*

THIS CONGREGATION was originally founded in 1659, and worshipped in a Victorian Gothic church which was destroyed by an accidental fire on Christmas Day 1938. The foundation stone for the present building was laid on 19 May 1955 by Lord McDermott, the Lord Chief Justice of Northern Ireland, and son of a former minister. The new church was designed by Thomas T Houston and completed in 1957. In the intervening years the congregation held joint services with another Presbyterian congregation in the town.

The church is a large hall-like structure of pink brick, built in a sparing Scandinavian style. The main gable wall is dominated by the large mullioned window, which incorporates a wooden door carved with a representation of Christ. The flanking doors sit within recessed stone frames. To one side of the facade is a tall brick campanile with a bell perched on top.

Light streams through the large front window, lighting the generous vestibule and the church beyond. The interior is lighted by segmental-headed windows, as well as a clerestory of eleven slit windows. Like the gallery above, the floor of the church is raked, giving something of the air of a lecture theatre. Although, as in many Presbyterian churches, there are three aisles, the east end has a rather Anglican layout. Rather than being centrally placed, the wooden pulpit is set to the left of the communion table and, remarkably, considering the age of the church, it has a sounding board. The east wall is built of brick, but there is a recessed sanctuary lined with cut-stone. The east window depicts Christ with the little children, and is signed by the artist, William Morris of Westminster. The font is circular, of polished and unpolished marble, and has a copper cover, surmounted by a dove.

■ **References**
Killen, p 232; Rowan, p 493.

First Presbyterian Church, Strabane.

ST PETER'S CHURCH, MILFORD
Milford, County Donegal

Catholic

THE SELECTION process for the site of this church serves to show the importance which Liam McCormick placed on this aspect of his church design. He said himself that on such a site 'a church designed with a slender tower gives a focal point to the town'. And indeed it does, placed on its elevated position.

Dedicated to St Peter and opened in 1961, the church has a number of visual references to the fisherman apostle. A bronze figure of the saint with his keys to the kingdom is placed over the entrance door, and this

St Peter's Church, Milford.

was made by Oisin Kelly. On the sacristy roof is a weather-vane made by Ian Stuart, and the cockerel recalls Peter's denial of Christ. Internally, the pews are laid in a herringbone pattern, as is the sheeted ceiling. The fishing allegories are continued in the reredos tapestry by Colin Middleton, which depicts the Miraculous Draught of Fishes and dominates the sanctuary. Structurally, the church is laid out longitudinally, with angled walls at the west end. The independent tower is a flattened hexagon, with a long opening to accommodate the three bells. In its pristine white, the building clearly shows a Swiss influence. The wooden entrance doors are carved with religious images of Alpha and Omega, the keys of Heaven, a dove, the Agnus Dei, St Brigid's cross, grapes, corn and flames.

Internally, the church is lined with brown brick, and the wall spaces are dominated by the fine stained glass windows. The large window at the west end streams light through the gallery, and is predominantly green with an abstract plant-like design. The stained glass in the south wall is by a variety of talents and depicts Irish saints. The window showing saints Columcille, Adhamhnain and Comgall is the work of Patrick Pollen; saints Brendan, Patrick and Eunan are by Patrick Pye; saints Malachy,

Brigid and Attracta are by Phyllis Burke, while Imogen Stuart designed the St Garvan window. On the opposite wall are the ceramic stations, also by Imogen Stuart. McCormick's firm achieved a Royal Institution of Architects of Ireland commendation for 1961–63 for the design of this church.

The original design has been altered by the re-designing of the sanctuary in 1987 and the construction of an oratory in 1992. Both these works were at the hands of Tom Mullarkey, but being from the McCormick studio, the integrity of the original concept is maintained.

■ **References**
Rowan, p 420.

ST MOLUA'S PARISH CHURCH, STORMONT
Upper Newtownards Road, Belfast

Church of Ireland

THE DECORATION and fittings of this church, designed by Denis O'D Hanna and consecrated in November 1962, serve as a fine representation of the architect's interest in visual symbols of faith. The building itself is basically a large hall with an apse and flanking apsidal chapel and vestry room. Of red brick construction inside and out, with ten angled windows running the full height of the walls, it is easy to appreciate Dr Paul Larmour's comparison with Coventry Cathedral. The windows on the north side are clear, but those on the south are glazed with the liturgical colours.

The facade has a very striking vertical emphasis, dominated by a large window of plain glass and crowned with a tall slated finial, flanked by two thinner finials. The panels immediately above the doors are filled by representations of angels, symbolising the protection of heaven. The external stone plaques are the work of David Pettigrew and each has a symbolic meaning. One carving represents the Word of God showing an eagle strangling Satan and an open book with Alpha and Omega. On another, the Holy Spirit descends into the sacramental symbols – bread, wine and a font. Jesus is symbolised through the rose of Sharon, the Agnus Dei, the pelican in its piety, the crown of thorns and Calvary. The Saviour is also seen in images of fish and the tree of life. The Creation and Fall are depicted on stone plaques on the other side of the building. This series concludes with the hand of Christ offered to Adam and Eve, giving them, and the believer, fresh hope. The hand of God is also shown protecting man and lifting him from the flames of Hell. There are two carvings depicting scenes from the life of St Molua – one where he heals his father's cancerous foot, and another where, as a bishop, he supervises the building of a church. This series of panels is interesting not only for the fine artwork involved, but for the way in which it recalls the time when visual imagery was one of the church's strongest evangelising tools.

The main theme of the interior of the church is God's

St Molua's (C of I) Church, Stormont.

A stall frontal in St Molua's.

plan for the redemption of man and the illustrative panels on the ceiling relate the life of Christ and ultimately His offer of salvation. The ceiling shows the Annunciation; the Nativity; the baptism of Christ in the river Jordan; the Last Supper and the kiss of betrayal by Judas Iscariot in Gethsemane. By following these scenes along the nave, the visitor is led to the chancel where the canopies above the choir stalls represent Calvary, with three crosses surrounded by the spears of the Roman soldiers. The organ came from the closed church of St Matthias in Dublin. The mural, painted by Desmond Kinney, shows Jesus Christ ascended and enthroned with the orb of majesty; the light of God is depicted as a great sunrise, and the dove symbolises the Holy Spirit.

The woodwork throughout the church is of light oak, and is simple and appropriate. The carving on the front of the pulpit represents the Four Gospels – the lion, ox, man and the eagle, and on the lectern is seen the Word of

God in the form of an eagle carrying the torch of truth and smiting Satan. In the chancel are canopied decani and cantoris desks made on the lines of traditional canopied thrones, but simplified in design to the basic structural shapes. In the baptistry area is the stout font and cover which represents of the orb of the world surmounted by the Cross.

At the rear of the church is a hall which was also designed by Hanna. Above the door is a bronze by James McKendrie depicting Christ as the master-carpenter, exceptionally appropriate in a church where various skilled craftsmen have worked in His service.

■ **References**
Larmour, p 112; anonymous unpublished notes about the artistic symbolism in the church.

BAPTISMAL FONTS

FONTS WERE placed near the door of a church to indicate symbolically the entrance to the Christian life and the beginning of a spiritual journey. Although the New Testament has no indication of infant baptism, this is the most common form practised by churches. In the days of high infant mortality it was of particular importance that a child be baptised as soon as possible.

Like so many other ecclesiastical objects, the shape and size of fonts has changed through the centuries. One of the most ancient still in use in Ulster is the granite font in the Church of Ireland cathedral at Downpatrick, which possibly dates from the tenth century. It was not until the early years of the twentieth century that this was once again used as a font, having spent many years elsewhere, possibly being used as a horse trough. The font at the Church of Ireland church at Saul is also of ancient origin, although it was brought here from a church in County Kilkenny. That in Armagh Church of Ireland Cathedral is octagonal, with fine carving on each of its faces. However, despite its appearance, it dates only from the 1834–41 restoration of the cathedral. It is a relatively close copy of a piece of medieval stonework which was found outside the west door of the church. The architect, Lewis Cottingham, made a copy for use as a font and kept the original stonework for his own collection.

At the time of Jeremy Taylor, the font was usually a stone basin mounted on a stout wooden pedestal, and examples of these exist at Taylor's churches at Ballinderry and Dromore. There are also seventeenth-century fonts at Loughilly (1637) and Enniskillen (1666) which have a similar appearance, but are entirely of stone.

Simple, yet elegant, eighteenth-century fonts can be seen in the Anglican churches at Hillsborough and Lisnadill, both of which have basins mounted on a tall fluted column. The font which is displayed at the old Drumcree Chapel at the Ulster Folk and Transport Museum provides us with an indication of what a font looked like in a Georgian Catholic church. It is a basin and pedestal carved from stone, very similar to the font which, before its destruction, could be seen in the Catholic church at Aldergrove.

In the nineteenth century, the Tractarian movement within the Anglican church placed great emphasis on the sacramental and visual nature of baptism and provision was made for this within a number of High Victorian churches. At St Mark's, Dundela, William Butterfield placed the font in a large baptistry under the west tower. This was intended to mirror the sanctuary, the other sacramental focus, at the east end. A

The font at St Luke's Ballymoyer, designed by William Butterfield.

similar arrangement exists at St Luke's Church of Ireland at Ballymoyer, County Armagh. Here the font is also the work of Butterfield and it stands in its own chamber beneath the tower, the walls being lined with encaustic tiles. Of particular interest is the iron canopy for the font, suspended from the ceiling on a counter-weight. It is known that during the nineteenth century at Hillsborough Parish Church, the rector, Archdeacon Walter Mant, moved the font to the crossing of the church in order to allow the congregation to witness properly the act of baptism.

In more recent times, the desire that worshippers should see the baptism more clearly was met by placing the font at the front of the church. Such is the case in Presbyterian churches and many Catholic churches following Vatican II. A fine example of a modern font can be seen in the sanctuary at St Theresa's Catholic church in Sion Mills. This is the work of Oisin Kelly and is circular, of dark marble with biblical scenes carved and picked out in white.

The Baptist Church has had a presence in Ireland since the seventeenth century and practises 'believer's baptism' rather than infant baptism, where those being baptised affirm their personal faith in Christ. The service involves total immersion and provision is made for this in Baptist church buildings.

ST THERESA'S CHURCH, SION MILLS
Main Street, Sion Mills, County Tyrone   *Catholic*

St Theresa's Church, Sion Mills.

THE REMARKABLE exterior of this striking church, although unlike the rest of Sion Mills, seems fitting in a street which is already full of architectural surprises. St Theresa's was designed by Patrick Haughey in 1962 and was completed in 1965. Its layout is longitudinal, and indicates that the church was designed before the Second Vatican Council's move towards increased congregational witness of the mass.

On the whole, the design is uncomplicated, and it is the use of works by talented Irish artists which really elevates the building. The church, sitting on a podium of steps, is steel-framed and constructed of grey brick with a low-pitched roof clad in copper. On the facade is a large and inspiring depiction of the Last Supper. This is incised on slate, the full width of the front, and is an outstanding example of the work of Oisin Kelly, whose work is also represented elsewhere in the church.

Again, Irish talent is to be seen in the stained glass throughout the church, which is the handiwork of Patrick Pollen. A continuous clerestory runs along three sides of the church, terminating at the altar wall with windows the full height of the building. St Theresa of Lisieux is illustrated in the clerestory just above the gallery, while a chalice and a cross are worked into the glass at the altar end. In the porch the glass depicts Christ's parents: Mary is seen spinning, while Joseph labours at his carpenter's bench. Internal decoration is sparing, the walls being of grey brick and the ceiling sheeted. It is left to the liturgical furnishings, all the work of skilled artists and craftsmen, to inspire the worshipper. The altar furniture was designed by Werner Schurmann, and the original sanctuary cross, which has been replaced with a more traditional one, was the work of Patrick McIlroy. The carved stations are by Ray Carroll. Next to the altar is the circular font, carved with biblical images by Oisin Kelly. We are shown the Good Shepherd with his flock, the wise virgins, Noah in his ark, and an angel slaying a winged beast.

St Theresa's Church stands as an excellent example of the integration of art into modern ecclesiastical architecture, as well as making a very positive contribution to the streetscape of Sion Mills.

■ **References**
de Breffny, p 184; Hurley, pp 60–1; Rowan, p 487.

STAR OF THE SEA CHURCH, DESERTEGNEY
Desertegney, north of Buncrana, County Donegal

Catholic

MOUNTAINS BEHIND, Lough Swilly in front, this gleaming white church of 1964 is best seen on a clear sunny day, when its clinical external colour sparkles against a blue sky, and the full impact of its setting can be appreciated.

Appropriately, given the church's dedication, the body of the building has been likened to an upturned boat. Perhaps most striking is the manner in which the tower resembles a lighthouse in its positioning, overlooking the sea. Indeed, on one occasion the church's architect,

Star of the Sea Church, Desertegney.

Liam McCormick, had to use the tower as a navigational point while sailing during a heavy mist. The body of the church is roughcast, being oblong with gently curving ends, while the pitched roof is shallow with over-hanging eaves. On the end wall is a mural of Mary, Star of the Sea by Imogen Stuart. Very idiosyncratically, the windows have curved tops and bottoms. The tower is of two tall solid sections joined by three 'platforms' and a flat roof, crowned by a cross. Walking under the tower the visitor moves through a clear-glazed passageway and into the church. Hit by the profusion of colour from the stained glass windows on the white surfaces, the contrast with the pristine starkness of the exterior could not be more marked. The shallow curve of the ceiling is supported on fourteen pillars, which drip from the roof like giant stalactites; the effect is almost surreal. The positioning of the pillars allows for an ambulatory which progresses from the baptistry under the gallery, right round the church, behind the altar and back to the baptistry. The effect of Helen Moloney's windows is memorable, shooting light across the expanse of ceiling and pouring it down the walls. At the rear of the church, cool colours such as blues and greens predominate, but as the altar is reached, vivid reds and purples take control and give this pivotal section of the church a certain visual intensity.

The content of the windows reflects the building's dedication and proximity to the sea, with visual reference to boats and fishing. The sanctuary windows powerfully represent the four evangelists. A semicircular podium of three steps holds the very wide granite altar which has a bronze strip by Patrick McIlroy, employing the emblems of the evangelists and fishing imagery, reflecting Christ's words regarding the disciples as fishers of men. Similar workmanship can be seen on the font in the church's baptistry, which is placed behind a set of white gates under the gallery. The window here shows Christ's baptism in the River Jordan by John the Baptist.

Some see this church as having Cubist traits; others see Expressionist qualities, and it is possible to detect a thread of Surrealism. The impact which it created at the time of its opening can be gauged by the fact that it won a Civic Trust Award in 1966.

■ **References**
Rowan, p 230.

ST AENGUS' CHURCH, BURT
At Burt outside village of Burnfoot, County Donegal   *Catholic*

SUPERBLY SITED below the looming ring-fort of the Grianan of Aileach and overlooking Lough Swilly, this modern church combines imagination and astute appreciation of the importance of good positioning. The church replaced an earlier building, and was completed in 1967 to the designs of Liam McCormick. The architect was anxious that the church should be sited here rather than simply utilising the site of its predecessor. By choosing to give the church a circular form inside and out, the architect drew his inspiration from the ancient seat of the O'Neills which dominates the local landscape, but he also reminds us of the importance which the circular shape had in Ireland's ancient architecture, in the form of raths, crannogs, monastery enclosures and round towers.

The church is built as a rotunda of rubble-stone, surmounted by a continuous clerestory and a copper-clad conical roof, with an off-centre lantern spire. The entire circuit of the building is surrounded by a moat, bridged in four places to give access to the interior. The existence of this moat, as with the use of water at other McCormick churches, is suggestive of his appreciation of the power of symbolism; water representing baptism and spiritual renewal, and the worshipper having to bridge this physically, reflects his need to embrace it spiritually. To the left of the entrance is a wall mounted with visual representations of the history of the site by Oisin Kelly.

The entrance doors to the church are sheeted in copper and riveted and have circular handles decorated in a 'Newgrange' fashion with concentric lines. Stone walling accommodates the porch with its engraved glass, and guides the visitor into the interior. What is not readily apparent is that the architect has enclosed a separate circle tangentially within a larger one to create a crescent-shaped space for a sacristy and offices. The only break in the internal ellipse is to allow for a circular top-

St Aengus' Church, Burt.

The interior at Burt.

lit baptistry. The architect's manipulation of light is highly dramatic. We leave behind the light which is admitted by the glass doors and our eyes meet the richly-coloured glass of the continuous clerestory. Incorporating arabesque designs and the symbols of the fish and the Chi Rho, the windows are ablaze with yellows, greens, blues and reds. This glass was made by Helen Moloney, at the behest of the architect. The ceiling rises smoothly to be channelled towards the lantern which splashes light onto the altar. Ten circular pillars support the edges of the ceiling.

The pews are arranged as segments of a circle to underline the curvilinear thrust of the church and to emphasise the liturgical centrality of the altar. The altar, by Imogen Stuart, is placed on three concentric circular steps, and bears the symbol of the fish. Particularly striking of the fittings is the frontal of the ambo, which is boldly embroidered in strong colours with the symbols of the four evangelists. The tabernacle on the wall behind the altar is guarded by six angels of beaten copper and was the work of Patrick McIlroy, while the crucifix is of wood and silver. The stations are expressed as plain crosses, nothing detracting from the spatial qualities of the structure.

Travelling towards this church, its presence in the landscape and its almost mystical appearance catches and fires the imagination to the same degree as its ancient forebear on the hill-top above. By capturing the form of the ring-fort, harnessing the shape which inspired our ancestors, Liam McCormick has created what must be one of the most exciting and dramatic modern churches in Ulster, if not in Ireland. The widespread approval with which the design met is evidenced by the fact that it won the Royal Institution of Architects of Ireland Triennial Gold Medal in 1971; the first time that this had been won outside Dublin, and was also the first award for a church.

■ References
de Breffny, p 189; Hurley, pp 65–6; Rowan, pp 157–8.

ST MICHAEL'S CHURCH, CREESLOUGH
Creeslough, County Donegal
Catholic

PERHAPS MORE than any other, this building of 1971 demonstrates Liam McCormick's superb ability to site a church. Not only does it make its own impact on its surroundings, but it is integrated into the rugged natural setting of Creeslough. The roof of the church is suppressed, and it is the undulating form of the white roughcast walls which grabs the attention and follows the flow of the rolling hills and Muckish Mountain beyond. McCormick was deeply moved by Le Corbusier's Notre Dame du Haut at Ronchamp, France, and parallels can be drawn between the two buildings even though McCormick did not physically see Le Corbusier's masterpiece until some years later. It is, perhaps, testimony to the man's creativeness that his church was visualised independently, but should emerge with the

The sanctuary at St Michael's Church, Creeslough.

same remarkable vision. GE Kidder Smith says that the church at Ronchamp 'commands the rolling countryside', and exactly the same can be said of McCormick's church here. The metalwork cross which stands at the entrance to the church reminds us of the ancient Irish practice of delineating 'God's Acre' with decorated stone crosses. The bell of the old church is hung at the entrance in an open metalwork structure. The window of the baptistry looks out onto a circular pool, the water symbolising baptism and the use of white roughcast, stone, heavy timber doors and water all reflect, by their simplicity, the nature of rural life in Donegal.

There is a sense of drama upon entering the church, for the worshipper comes into a dark enclosed space, but turning to the left the whole airy interior of the church opens up. The plan is fan-shaped with roughcast walls and a broad expanse of flat ceiling. The three blocks of pews follow the curve and close in upon the altar, with light provided from behind by a clerestory. A circular roof-light is placed directly above the altar to heighten the sense of its pivotal position within the church. Simplicity can be seen in the stations, which are expressed only as numbered crosses.

The church also presents us with a powerful utilisation of space. The Blessed Sacrament chapel is a dark, intimate space, its only natural light being that admitted from above the altar. Colour seeps into the darkness through six vibrant windows designed by Helen Moloney. These have representations of fruit, fish, loaves, a dove, an eagle and the elements of the eucharist, and their physical arrangement on the wall once again

Liam McCormick outside St Michael's, Creeslough.

reminds us of Ronchamp. The baptistry is a tall oval space entered through another break in the wall, and the font is decorated with the symbol of the fish (icthus). The Lady chapel represents the part of the church where man-made architecture and nature seem to merge. There is a clear ceiling-to-floor window which gives worshippers a view of the garden and the hulking mass of the mountains beyond. Ivy has been allowed to grow on one of the interior walls here, so nature has actually entered the church.

The contractor for the building was John Hegarty, with artistic contributions from Helen Moloney, Veronica Rowe, John Behan and Ruth Brandt.

■ **References**

de Breffny, pp 189–90; Hurley, pp 71–2; Kidder Smith, GE, *The New Churches of Europe* (London, 1964) pp 86–96.

ST CONAL'S CHURCH, GLENTIES
Glenties, County Donegal

Catholic

AS WITH all of Liam McCormick's churches, that at Glenties (built in 1974) has an air of drama, with its steep sloping roofs which thrust it into its hillside setting. The building is rectangular and is composed of two gabled triangular sections, one bigger than the other, placed together. The longest side of each triangle forms the roof of the church, a massive slope covered in slates, stopping just short of ground level to allow for windows and entrance doors. Water from the roof is, as at the similar church at Steelstown, directed into a pool running the length of the building. Here McCormick uses the device of a physical bridging of the water to gain entrance to the

church. This is a reminder of the symbolic use of water at baptism, the point of spiritual admission into Christ's church. Glimpses of the water at St Conal's and the planting beyond are very attractive from inside the church. On the eaves are a row of animal-head gargoyles, reminiscent of their use in medieval church building. These were made by Imogen Stuart.

Internally, the architect has employed a number of devices to heighten the sense of drama, particularly in the form of the entrance and the dual-level flooring. The church is entered from the side and the worshipper can either turn left into the daily chapel or to the right, to face

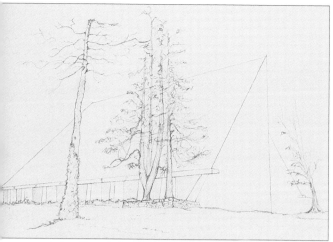

St Conal's Catholic Church, Glenties.

straight up the central aisle of the church. The rectilinear interior is perhaps more traditional in feel than the architect's excursions into the curvilinear, as at Burt and Creeslough. However, the use of materials and manipulation of space places the church well above the strictures of traditional church architecture. Geometric shapes dominate the interior, and the choice of materials (white plastered walls, concrete slabs and sheets of timber) serve to highlight the angular qualities of the building. The three aisles are flagged with concrete slabs and lined

with timber pews, reflecting the vast expanses of Western Hemlock timber sheeting on the ceilings. The use of timber is more subdued than at the later church at Steelstown and the end walls are roughcast and painted. The left aisle sits higher than the rest of the church and is divided from it by a kind of retaining wall, which follows the line of the division between the two triangular sections of the building. This split-level arrangement reflects the church's position, as the raised aisle is built on a shelf of natural rock. The clerestory windows at the top of the higher section of ceiling throw a stream of light down onto the shorter section.

As with other McCormick churches, the fittings are the work of an impressive array of artists, including Imogen Stuart, Ruth Brandt and Michael Biggs, who was responsible for the altar fittings. There are three wall-mounted figures representing Sts Conal, Columcille and Our Lady, which are the work of Nell Pollen, as are the stations of the cross. The architect's wife, Joy, contributed to the church by her involvement in the making of the clergy vestments. St Conal's received a commendation from the Royal Institution of Architects of Ireland in its Triennial Gold Medal Award for 1974–76.

■ References
Evans, p 61; Hurley, p 88; Rowan, p 309.

OUR LADY OF LOURDES CHURCH, STEELSTOWN
Steelstown Road, Derry, County Londonderry
Catholic

COMPLETED IN 1976 to the designs of Liam McCormick and Partners, this church has many similarities to the firm's church at Glenties, County Donegal. On viewing this church, one observer claimed, 'Liam McCormick is the kind of architect who can make a little go a very long way'. Indeed, there was a restricted budget of £104,000 to provide a church for what was then a new parish. The design earned a Royal Institution of Architects of Ireland commendation in 1978.

Externally, the church is an aggressively angular structure, composed of three massive graduated sloping roofs, covered with asbestos slates. These roofs stop just short of ground level to allow for narrow strip windows. A series of pools run along below these windows and serve to catch rainwater from the roof and to enhance the view from inside.

The overall effect of the interior, sheeted entirely in rough-sawn deal timber, is akin to the ancient Scandinavian wooden churches. The windows at the foot of each slope of the roof are too low to admit light, and are really there to provide reflective sights of the outside. Lighting comes from strips which run up one slope of the roof and down another, as happens at four stages on the roof. Excellent use has been made of the church's rectangular floor plan, with an enclosed area which is both the daily and the crying chapel for children. Beyond this is the roughcast sacristy block. On the wall of this is displayed Oisín Kelly's wood carving of St Bernadette and Our Lady of Lourdes. The vast triangular timber wall of the west end is enhanced by the cleverly angled organ case, while the altar wall is graced by a large and colourful crucifix, painted by Helen Moloney. She was also

Our Lady of Lourdes, Steelstown.

responsible for the inventive symbolic images on the ambo and altar. The ambo frontal shows a dove, the symbol of peace, carrying an olive branch in its beak, reminding us of God's message to Noah. On the altar is a representation of a fish (an early symbol for Christianity), the body of which incorporates a boat shape, recalling the fact that Christ's first disciples were fishermen.

The tabernacle, candlesticks, sanctuary lamp, holy water stoups and font lid are by Patrick McIlroy and make great use of metal and enamel. In recent years McIlroy was commissioned to design and make a new monstrance for the church. This magnificent piece is laden with symbolic imagery, depicting God's people in Celtic idiom surrounding the Host, indicative of the centrality of the sacrament. Saints are worked into the patterns around the base. The church's font is set next to a symbolic pool in the sanctuary area.

The stations of the cross were painted by Sister Aloysius McVeigh and are striking and well-conceived pieces, each full of symbolism and powerful imagery. On each station the shape of the cross is actually cut out to give it emphasis. The Pietà is particularly evocative, as its background includes buildings from the city of Derry; the suffering of Christ and His mother, reflecting the city's suffering communities during the height of the Troubles.

As the architect intended, this church possesses a sense of drama: its vast sloping expanses of roof rise up in the midst of a residential area, and it is approached through a simplified form of lychgate, topped by a cross.

■ References

Church of our Lady of Lourdes, Shantallow, Souvenir of the Opening (Derry, 1976), p 6; Hurley, p 100.

DONAGHMORE PRESBYTERIAN CHURCH
Donaghmore, County Donegal

Presbyterian

THE CONGREGATION can trace its history back to 1658 and this building was built in 1977, to replace an earlier church which was destroyed by fire. It is the only Protestant church to have been designed by Liam McCormick and, although simpler by virtue of Presbyterian liturgical tradition than his well-known Catholic churches, McCormick has managed to add his touch of individuality and imagination to this pleasing church building.

Donaghmore Presbyterian Church.

The church is rectangular with white roughcast walls, and the main facade has a roundel bearing the inscription: 'Donaghmore Presbyterian Church 1977'. The roof is slated and sports a thin slated spire. The foundation stone indicates that it was laid by Rev John Sproule on 20 November 1976. The building is entered from the side, and, as with so many McCormick churches, the entrance to the church proper is cleverly handled. The visitor goes into a circular vestibule and turns 90 degrees to the right to enter the church. On the other side of the vestibule is the minister's room. Light is admitted into the vestibule by a window representing Christ as the light of the world. The church has a central aisle running through the timber pews towards the broad, centrally-placed pulpit. There are four colourful stained glass windows in the other long wall, one of which has a representation of the burning bush, so important in Presbyterianism. Motifs in the windows, which are the work of Helen Moloney, represent God's creation, presence, guidance, covenant and word.

The curves and undulations of the walls are reflected by the sweeping sheeted ceiling which rises in the centre. The fittings are simple but appropriate, such as the light-coloured wooden communion table by Derry O'Connell,

the front of which says: 'Do this in remembrance of me'. The burning bush tapestry behind the pulpit was presented to the church by the contractor, John Hegarty, and was designed by Helen Moloney.

Donaghmore Presbyterian Church is an extremely important building in that it demonstrates Liam McCormick's versatility as a church architect, and it must be regretted that his skills were not employed by other Protestant denominations.

■ **References**
Killen, p 118.

ST PATRICK'S CHURCH, CLOGHER
Clogher, County Tyrone

Catholic

St Patrick's Church, Clogher.

THIS IS a fine modern church, completed and dedicated to St Patrick in 1979, having been designed by Liam McCormick. It replaced the church of St Mary, Augherdrummond, of 1802, the gable cross of which is preserved at the door of the present church.

The architect has utilised a circular plan for the church, its battered walls being built of brown brick, while the low conical roof is slated and crowned with a slender cross-adorned spire. Particularly inventive is the 'gargoyle' near the main door, which is made from two metal sections and has a decorative chain falling from its mouth to the ground. The colourful doors by Helen Moloney have a representation of the Good Shepherd and the Tree of Life; these were originally made for the now much-altered McCormick church at Toomebridge.

There is a striking use of fresh and inspiring complementary colours in the interior; green carpeting, pale grey walls and the white expanse of roof. The tabernacle, which depicts the Angus Dei, is set in a recess behind the altar, which has light admitted by a side strip

window, lending emphasis to the tabernacle's position. The roof is carried on twelve square roughcast piers which rise upwards and divide the ceiling into segments. The segment above the altar has a thin vertical louvred strip which directs light onto the altar itself. Liam McCormick was excellent at manipulating natural light to enhance the interiors of his churches, and here he also allows light to enter the building by a continuous concealed window which runs around the circumference of the base of the roof. By having no windows on the walls, as at Burt and Creeslough, the worshippers can scan the circuit of the church and have their attention captured principally by the altar. The arrangement of the pews in graduated segments also serves to make the altar the focal point of the interior.

Nell Pollen's very sparing and appropriate stations of the cross are of ceramic and complement the other artworks in the church; the altar, ambo and font being designed by the architect himself, while the metalwork is by David King.

ST BRIGID'S CHURCH, BELFAST
Derryvolgie Avenue, Belfast

Catholic

THIS IS a much-admired modern church, completed in 1995 to the designs of Kennedy Fitzgerald Associates, who won the contract by an architectural design competition. It replaced a Romanesque-style church which dated from 1891 and was designed by James J McDonnell.

The new church is constructed of York brick and roofed with Welsh slate, presenting its apse and slender bell tower to the Malone Road. Externally, the church is an interesting array of shapes, the purpose of which are more apparent from the inside. The area at the front door of the church is attractively covered by a loggia, made from cedar, which leads into the porch. A Latin inscription stone in this porch relates the history of the building, and above this is a carved copy of a penal cross by Ken Thompson of Cork. To the left of the porch there is a side chapel which retains stained glass windows from the original church, depicting Sts Augustine, Gregory, Jerome and Ambrose.

The church proper is arranged longitudinally, with the central aisle raking towards the sanctuary and the side aisles divided from the nave by stone columns which carry the ash trusses of the roof, which is in fact one of the best features of the interior. Natural light is admitted at roof level throughout the entire church as the nave has a clerestory. The internal walls of the church are of brick and have very pleasant inset stations, beautifully carved and lettered from dark polished stone by Ken Thompson. The convex gallery at the back of the church is reflected by the concave sanctuary space at the other end of the building. The positioning of the side chapels help to create interest as the expanses of wall are punctuated with glimpses of the intimate spaces of the side chapels and their coloured windows. St Brigid's chapel has a statue of the saint holding her interlaced cross, while a modern interpretation of the St Brigid's cross can be seen woven into the carpet at the foot of the sanctuary steps. The baptistry is treated in a highly individualistic manner, incorporated into a sunken circular space which is approached by descending steps. The limestone font and the sanctuary fittings were designed by Richard Hurley.

There are modern depictions of St Columban and St Oliver Plunkett in the circular stairwells on the south side of the building, while the southern side chapel has a window in memory of the martyred Bishop Conor O'Devanney (1533–1612), which is the work of Lua

St Brigid's Catholic Church, Belfast.

Breen. St Malachy is also shown in one of the windows.

Among the awards won by the church are the 1995 Royal Institution of Architects of Ireland regional award for the best building in the northern region and the 1996 Royal Institute of British Architects regional award for architecture.

■ **References**
Perspective, Vol 5, No 2, p 2.

Conclusion

CHRISTIANITY HAS evolved greatly in 2000 years and many people in our community have seen vast changes in patterns of worship and church attendance within their own lifetimes. In a world in which we are constantly being offered choice, it is of little surprise that the number of Christian denominations has expanded in the last fifty years. The new churches of these denominations are now as much a part of our surroundings as the longer-established churches. Sadly, as patterns in society change, new problems have surfaced which directly affect both congregations and the buildings in which they worship. Population shifts, along with declining church attendance, have placed many old inner-city churches at risk of closure. Church authorities now find themselves facing problems that have confronted their counterparts in Dublin and London for some time. Churches were built to serve a vibrant part of community life and the challenge of preserving the architectural integrity of a church, while making it useful to the community, is enormous.

In Dublin and London, closed inner-city churches have been converted for cultural use. This is of little help in a city like Belfast, which is almost over-subscribed with cultural venues. Solutions can be found, but the sheer size of a former church will present difficulties which require imagination to surmount. The former church halls of the old Carlisle Circus Methodist church now provide a centre for Belfast's Indian community, while the former Duncairn Presbyterian Church is an antiques shop. In both cases the public has access to these buildings. Less happy is the fate of Donegall Square Methodist Church, now incorporated into commercial premises and reduced to a two-dimensional facade.

To the average church-goer the closure and subsequent re-use (if any) of churches represent a sad sign of the times when traditional religious observances and reverence for consecrated property are in decline. Church authorities, however, would point out the futility of clinging to large empty buildings which invariably drain much needed resources. They would highlight the development of congregations in newer residential areas as the positive aspect of inner-city decline. The sad reality is that if a closed church is allowed to remain vacant, it very quickly degenerates and becomes an eyesore in the midst of the very community it once served.

Throughout the Troubles, political events have heightened inter-community tensions and churches have suffered as a consequence. Sectarian arson attacks have too frequently robbed a congregation of their spiritual home and the rest of us of structures of architectural value. A sad example of this is the early nineteenth-century Catholic church at Aldergrove, County Antrim, which has been restored following an arson attack. However, the survival of the Christian spirit in the face of such adversity serves to remind us that, ultimately, the work of the church is not to maintain historic buildings. Despite a desire to maintain their architectural heritage, many congregations find this a great burden and a distraction from their fundamental purpose. Those of us interested in our ecclesiastical heritage should strive to find creative solutions to the problem when church buildings can no longer fulfil their original function for practical reasons.

Each generation has left its mark on the physical and spiritual landscape of Ulster and we have already traced that development up to the present, but simply to look at those churches which we regard as 'historic', is to fail to appreciate their religious context. While some of the larger denominations have left us our 'historic' churches, generations of other Christians have worshipped God in their own way and in their own surroundings, and they continue to do so. The number of simple gospel halls in the Ulster countryside demonstrates the personal relationship with God which many people have developed without the urge for liturgical or physical ostentation. This form of Christianity also finds expression in the tradition of missions and itinerant preachers (going back to the time of John Wesley and George Whitefield) and the gospel tents which are still a feature of the religious landscape of Ulster. In his book, *Buildings of County Armagh*, CEB Brett gives honourable mention to the well-maintained corrugated iron gospel hall at Glenanne, County Armagh. The inclusion of this little building highlights the fact that the 'iron hall' is part of the Ulster countryside which is rapidly disappearing and should also be cherished.

Not all gospel halls are structures of iron, but make use of buildings which once served a different function. The gospel hall in the Mall at Armagh was formerly a masonic hall and is a very jaunty little building, not really at all matching the sobriety one usually associates with a meeting house. It has been described as 'vaguely Venetian Gothic' built in polychrome brick and has a rose window and slated spirelet. Paul Larmour points out the neo-Georgian gospel hall on Belfast's Albertbridge Road, designed by John MacGeagh, the architect of the south transept of St Anne's Cathedral and the library block at Queen's University.

By the 1950s and 1960s it was becoming commonplace to see newer denominations building substantial church buildings, and this trend continues to the present time. An examination of the architecture of these buildings reveals a move from traditional themes towards more adventurous designs. The Elim Ulster Temple on the Ravenhill Road, which was completed in 1931, has an air of neo-classicism about it, with pilasters imposed on a brown brick facade. Further along the same road is the Martyrs Memorial Free Presbyterian Church, which once again is of brick. The facade has a very interesting window pattern, with a number of segmental-headed windows and a large central rose window beneath a clock. Interest is added to the interior with a series of

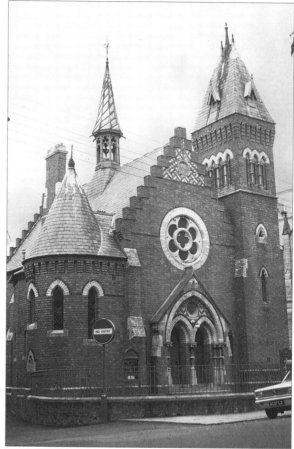

The gospel hall in Armagh's Mall.

images of Reformation martyrs. Once again, the internal emphasis is on the pulpit, reflecting the centrality of the word of God.

One of the most commented-upon church buildings constructed in recent years has been the Whitewell Metropolitan Tabernacle, completed in 1994. Inspiration for this huge structure came from the vast American evangelical churches. Whereas previously, ecclesiastical buildings have tended to spread their communal activities between church, church hall and ancillary facilities, the tabernacle has all of its facilities under the one roof. These include a restaurant, creche, kitchen and counselling rooms.

The building has a simple external appearance, being constructed of brick with a sheeted roof topped by a glass lantern, with the suggestion of a cruciform plan, as prominence is given to the gable walls. Internally the church has the primary function of an auditorium. It was felt to be important that everyone should have an uninterrupted view of the preacher (just as in the

Whitewell Metropolitan Tabernacle.

nineteenth-century meeting houses) and so a trussed roof is employed to avoid the use of columns. The interior is large and bright, the only concession to past architectural idioms being the pulpit, which is a replica of the pulpit built for the London Metropolitan Tabernacle 130 years previously.

Denominations with smaller numbers appreciate the impracticality of large church buildings and have to find methods of accommodating their members in line with their resources. The members of the Orthodox community in Ulster actually belong to the parish of Dublin, while Belfast's Lutheran congregation meet in the Moravian Church on University Road. Some groups of Christians believe the way forward to be the development of 'house churches', where the priority is meeting for worship and fellowship, irrespective of the physical surroundings. This situation is particularly suitable for groups whose numbers are too small to allow a church building to be an option and it may well represent an alternative for declining congregations right across the denominations.

A survey of Ulster churches from the medieval period reveals the adaptability and versatility of Christians throughout the ages, with worship having taken place in fields, barns, timber yards and even in a sandpit. There is, therefore, every reason to expect that Christians will continue to tailor their worship to meet changing circumstances and this in turn will dictate the future development of Ulster churches.

■ References
Brett, CEB, *Buildings of County Armagh* (Belfast, 1999) p 63.

Appendix 1:
Alphabetical List of Churches

Aldergrove; St James' Church
Antrim; All Saints' Parish Church
Ardkeen Catholic Church
Armagh; Abbey Street Presbyterian Church
Armagh; former chapel of the Church of Ireland Archbishops of Armagh
Armagh; Scotch Church
Armagh; St Patrick's Church of Ireland Cathedral

Balligan; St Andrew's Parish Church
Ballinderry Lower; Moravian Church
Ballinderry; The Middle Church
Ballycastle; Holy Trinity Church
Ballycastle; St Patrick's and St Brigid's Church
Ballykelly Presbyterian Church
Ballykelly; Tamlaghtfinlagan Parish Church
Ballymena; Faith Mission Hall
Ballymoney Methodist Church
Ballymore; St John's Parish Church
Banagher Presbyterian Church
Banbridge; Downshire Road Non-Subscribing Presbyterian Church
Belfast; All Souls' Non-Subscribing Presbyterian Church
Belfast; Ballynafeigh Methodist Church
Belfast; Carlisle Memorial Methodist Church
Belfast; Crescent Christian Brethren Church
Belfast; Elmwood Presbyterian Church
Belfast; First Church of Christ Scientist
Belfast; former Donegall Square Methodist Church
Belfast; Holy Cross Passionist Monastery
Belfast; May Street Presbyterian Church

Belfast; Rosemary Street Non-Subscribing Presbyterian Church
Belfast; Sinclair Seamen's Presbyterian Church
Belfast; St Anthony's Church
Belfast; St Brigid's Church
Belfast; St George's Parish Church
Belfast; St Malachy's Church
Belfast; St Mark's Parish Church
Belfast; St Molua's Parish Church
Belfast; St Patrick's Church
Belfast; University Road Methodist Church
Benburb; St Patrick's Parish Church
Brookeborough Methodist Church
Buncrana; St Mary's Oratory
Burt; St Aengus' Church

Carrickfergus; St Nicholas' Parish Church
Castlecaulfield; St Michael's Parish Church
Castlewellan; St Paul's Parish Church
Cavan Parish Church
Clogher; St Patrick's Catholic Church
Clonoe; St Michael's Parish Church
Clough Non-Subscribing Presbyterian Church
Coagh Presbyterian Church
Colebrooke; St Ronan's Parish Church
Coleraine Methodist Church
Coleraine; St John's Church
Coleraine; St Malachy's Church
Coleraine; St Patrick's Parish Church
Cookstown Methodist Church
Cookstown; Holy Trinity Church

Creeslough; St Michael's Church
Crumlin Non-Subscribing Presbyterian Church
Cultra; Catholic Church of St John the Baptist
  (formerly of Drumcree)

Derriaghy; Christ Church
Derry; Carlisle Road Methodist Church
Derry; Great James Street Presbyterian Church
Derry; St Columba's Church, Long Tower
Derry; St Columb's Cathedral
Desertegney; Star of the Sea Church
Donaghmore; Donaghmore Presbyterian Church
Donegal Methodist Church
Donegal; St Patrick's Church
Downpatrick; Holy Trinity Parish Church
Downpatrick; Stream Street Non-Subscribing
  Presbyterian Church
Dromara; Ardtanagh Presbyterian Church
Drumbanagher; Tyrone's Ditches Presbyterian Church
Dungannon; St Patrick's Church
Dunlewey; Sacred Heart Church
Dunmurry Non-Subscribing Presbyterian Church

Enniskillen Methodist Church
Enniskillen; St Michael's Church

Gilford Free Presbyterian Church
Glaskermore; Glascar Presbyterian Church
Glenties; St Conal's Church
Gracehill; Gracehill Moravian Church
Grange; St Aidan's Parish Church

Hillhall Presbyterian Church
Hillsborough; St Malachi's Parish Church
Hilltown; St John's Parish Church

Islandmagee; St John's Parish Church

Jordanstown; St Patrick's Parish Church

Kilwarlin Moravian Church
Knockbreda Parish Church

Lisbellaw Parish Church
Lisnadill; St John's Parish Church

Maghera Parish Church
Magheralin; St Patrick's Church
Magherally Presbyterian Church
Milford; St Peter's Catholic Church
Moira; St John's Parish Church
Monaghan; St Patrick's Parish Church
Moyallon Friends Meeting House

Newry; St Mary's Parish Church
Newtownards Methodist Church
Newtownards; St Mark's Parish Church
Newtownards; St Patrick's Church

Omagh; Church of the Sacred Heart

Portadown; Thomas Street Methodist Church
Portaferry; Ballyphilip Parish Church
Portaferry Presbyterian Church
Portstewart; Adam Clarke Memorial Methodist Church
Portstewart Presbyterian Church
Poyntzpass; St Joseph's Church

Rademon Non-Subscribing Presbyterian Church
Randalstown 'Old Congregation' Presbyterian Church
Rosslea; St Tierney's Church

Saul; St Patrick's Memorial Church
Sion Mills; Church of the Good Shepherd
Sion Mills; St Theresa's Church
Steelstown (Derry); Our Lady of Lourdes
  Catholic Church
Strabane; Church of the Immaculate Conception
Strabane First Presbyterian Church

Tamlaghtard; St Cadan's Parish Church
Tandragee Methodist Church

Waringstown; Holy Trinity Parish Church

Appendix 2:
Architects of Ulster Churches

BARRE, William Joseph (1830–67)

Barre was articled to Thomas Duff at the age of seventeen and moved to Dublin a year later to complete his training following the death of Duff. At twenty he set up in practice in his native Newry and his first commission was the Non-Subscribing Presbyterian Church in the town. This building is seen as marking the change from classical to Gothic in nonconformist church architecture. Barre worked with flair and individuality and these attributes earned him a number of high profile commissions such as the Ulster Hall and the Albert Clock in Belfast. Seen as a pioneer of High Victorian architecture, his biographer (Dunlop) said, 'Mr Barre was exceedingly partial of the noble and inexhaustible Gothic, if he could be justly classed as belonging to any particular school it would be the Eclectic'. A remarkable aspect of his work is the fact that he designed churches for five different religious denominations, quite unusual for the time. The richness of his work, both sacred and secular, emphasises the great loss caused by his early death at the age of thirty-seven. WJ Barre is buried in the graveyard of St Patrick's Church of Ireland Church in Newry.

Ulster churches designed by Barre:

Ballymoyer Church of Ireland Church,
  County Armagh (chancel designed by Barre)
Ballynahinch Catholic Church, County Down
(additions to the existing building and design
  of the tower)

Belmont Presbyterian Church, Belfast
Crossgar Presbyterian Church, County Down
Duncairn Presbyterian Church, Belfast
Dungannon Church of Ireland Church, County Tyrone
Drumbanagher Church of Ireland Church,
  County Armagh
Enniskillen Methodist Church, County Fermanagh
Newry Non-Subscribing Presbyterian Church,
  County Down
Portstewart Methodist Church, County Londonderry
Riverside Presbyterian Church, Newry, County Down
Rockcorry Church of Ireland Church,
  County Monaghan
University Road Methodist Church, Belfast

BUTTERFIELD, William (1814–1900)

One of the most outstanding High Victorian architects, Butterfield began his training in 1831 under Thomas Arber. He then served three years articled to EL Blackburne and worked in Worcester for a time, before establishing an independent practice in 1840. Butterfield's own high church beliefs are conveyed by much of his ecclesiastical work, with a strong relationship between architecture and liturgy. His most famous works are All Saints, Margaret Street, London, and Keble College Chapel. In addition to his surviving work in Ulster, he was also consulted regarding the construction of St Comgall's Church of Ireland Church in Bangor.

Ulster churches designed by Butterfield:

Ballymoyer Church of Ireland Church,
  County Armagh (font designed by Butterfield)
Lambeg Church of Ireland Church (this work
  was subsequently removed)
St Mark's Church of Ireland Church, Dundela, Belfast

COOLEY, Thomas (c1740–84)

Cooley was born in England and served his apprenticeship in London under a carpenter called Mr Reynolds, before becoming a pupil of the architect Robert Mylne. Cooley came to Ireland when he won the competition to design the new Royal Exchange in Dublin and following this was appointed to the position of Clerk and Inspector of Civic Buildings. His connection with Ulster was established when he was employed by Archbishop Richard Robinson to design the archiepiscopal palace, library and Royal School in Armagh. He provided the archbishop with a series of pattern book church designs and a number of churches in the archdiocese of Armagh are derived from these. Francis Johnston received his training from Cooley and completed work left by his master at the time of his death in 1784.

Ulster churches designed by Cooley:

Chapel of the Church of Ireland Archbishops of
  Armagh, Armagh
Grange Church of Ireland Church, County Armagh
St John's Church of Ireland Church, County Armagh

DREW, Sir Thomas (1838–1910)

Eldest son of Rev Dr Thomas Drew, a founder member of the Down and Connor Accommodation Society, Drew has been called one of the most distinguished architects of the nineteenth century. At the age of sixteen he entered the practice of Sir Charles Lanyon, before going into partnership with Thomas Turner in 1861. The following year he entered the office of William Murray, whose daughter he married. In 1868 he set up his own practice, and built a very fine reputation for himself. He served as President of the Royal Hibernian Academy and of the Royal Society of Antiquaries. His interest in, and knowledge of, antiquities was well-known and is reflected in the sensitivity with which he treated older buildings upon which he worked.

Ulster churches designed by Drew:

Clanabogan Church of Ireland Church, County Tyrone
Eglantine Church of Ireland Church, County Down
Kilmore Church of Ireland Church, County Down
St Anne's Church of Ireland Cathedral, Belfast
St Jude's Church of Ireland Church, Belfast

Sympathetic restoration work at Hillsborough, Knockbreda, Raphoe, Waringstown and St Mary's, Newry.

DUFF, Thomas (1792–1848)

Duff was a native of Newry and is principally remembered for his Catholic churches designed in a Tudor Gothic idiom, in particular the church at Dundalk and the cathedral at Newry. He was also responsible for the initial design of the Catholic cathedral at Armagh, although the design was altered dramatically by JJ McCarthy who completed the cathedral following Duff's death. Duff worked in partnership for a time with Thomas Jackson, the architect of St Malachy's in Belfast, and it is possible to see a close stylistic connection between the work of the two men.

Ulster churches designed by Duff:

Armagh Catholic Cathedral (initial design)
Newry Catholic Cathedral, County Down

GREGORY, Padraic B (1886–1962)

Gregory was born in Belfast, but spent a part of his childhood in Colorado before returning to Belfast to study under JJ O'Shea. While studying architecture he also developed a love and talent for poetry, which is demonstrated in works such as *The Ulster Folk* and *Ulster Love Songs and Ballads*.

Early ecclesiastical architectural commissions included the extension to the Dominican Convent on the Falls Road and the sanctuary fittings for St Malachy's in Alfred Street. During the 1930s he worked on some of his most outstanding works, such as Coleraine, Aghagallon and St Anthony's, Woodstock Road. Photographs of St Malachy's, Coleraine, were selected to represent Ireland at the 1950 International Exhibition of Sacred Art in Rome. Gregory frequently added interest to his churches by the use of a baldachino or by incorporating religious symbols such as a Latin or a Greek cross into the tracery of windows.

Ulster churches designed by Gregory:

Aghagallon Catholic Church, County Antrim
St MacNissi's College Chapel, Carnlough,
  County Antrim
Carryduff Catholic Church, County Down
Coleraine Catholic Church, County Londonderry
Creggan Catholic Church, County Tyrone
Dominican Convent Chapel, Belfast (extension)
Drumaness Catholic Church, County Down
Ederney Catholic Church, County Fermanagh
St Anthony's Catholic Church, Belfast
St Colmcille's Catholic Church, Belfast
  (chancel extension)
St Thérèse de L'Enfant Christ Catholic Church, Belfast
Tullyallen Catholic Church, County Tyrone

HAGUE, William (1840–99)

Hague was born in County Cavan and was the son of a builder. He went on to design a number of churches in his native county, as well as designing the French Gothic churches of Strabane and Omagh. He was in partnership with TF McNamara, who completed Letterkenny Cathedral following Hague's death in 1899.

Ulster churches designed by Hague:

Ballyboy Catholic Church, County Cavan
Butlersbridge Catholic Church, County Cavan
Kingscourt Catholic Church, County Cavan
Letterkenny Catholic Cathedral, County Donegal
Monaghan Catholic Cathedral, County
  Monaghan (spire only)
Sacred Heart Catholic Church, Omagh, County Tyrone
Strabane Catholic Catholic Church, County Tyrone
Swanlinbar Catholic Church, County Cavan

HANNA, Denis O'Donaghue (1901–71)

The son of an architect, Denis O'D Hanna had a particular knowledge of Ulster's architectural heritage, as demonstrated in his book *The Face of Ulster*. However, he was an exponent of good modern architecture and was concerned with integrating the best aspects of Ulster vernacular tradition into it – an idiom he called 'National Modernism'. He was also at pains to promote the position of the artist in architecture, and this is seen primarily in his churches at Mount Merrion and Stormont. Hanna was also responsible for the restoration of the early

eighteenth-century church of St Andrew at Balligan, County Down, and presented it with furnishings appropriate to a church of that era. He had a great interest in Irish churches in general and regularly wrote and illustrated articles on the subject for the *Church of Ireland Gazette*. Hanna served as architect to a number of Church of Ireland dioceses.

Ulster churches designed by Hanna:

Mount Merrion Church of Ireland Church, Belfast
Rathcoole Church of Ireland Church, Belfast
Seymour Hill Church of Ireland Church, Belfast
  (now the church hall)
Stormont Church of Ireland Church, Belfast
Sydenham Church of Ireland Church, Belfast
  (since rebuilt)
Hanna was also responsible for the belltower at Carrickfergus and the transeptal screens at Hillsborough, as well as the porch fittings of Shankill Parish Church, Lurgan (all C of I).

HANSOM, Joseph A (1803–82)

The inventor of the Patent Safety Cab (Hansom Cab), and architect of Arundel Cathedral, his only Ulster work was commissioned by the Marchioness of Londonderry.

Ulster church designed by Hansom:

Newtownards Catholic Church, County Down

HEVEY, Timothy (1845–78)

A native of Belfast, Hevey served his articles with Boyd and Batt of Belfast. At the age of twenty-one he went to Dublin and worked as an assistant to Pugin and Ashlin, specialising in ecclesiastical work. He drew many of the illustrations for the *Dublin Builder*. Hevey set up his own practice in Belfast in 1869, and was in practice with James F McKinnon for the duration of 1873. In 1874 he joined with Mortimer H Thompson, who carried out much church work. Thompson completed some of Hevey's unfinished work, following his death in 1878, at the age of 33.

Ulster churches designed by Hevey:

Dunlewey Catholic Church, County Donegal
Gweedore Catholic Church, County Donegal
Holywood Catholic Church, County Down
  (tower only surviving)
Raphoe Catholic Church, County Donegal
St Joseph's Catholic Church, Belfast
St Patrick's Catholic Church, Belfast
Warrenpoint Catholic Church, County Down
  (tower and spire only)

JACKSON, Thomas (1807–90)

Born of Quaker parents, Jackson worked in partnership with Thomas Duff until 1835. Jackson's best-known work is St Malachy's Catholic church in Belfast, and it is thought that his inspiration came from William Cavalier's *Specimens of Gothic Design*. Jackson was also an inspiration to the cleric/architect Fr Jeremiah McAuley.

Ulster churches designed by Jackson:

Faith Mission Hall, Ballymena, County Antrim
Reformed Presbyterian Church, College Square
  North, Belfast (now demolished)
St Malachy's Catholic Church, Alfred Street, Belfast

JOHNSTON, Francis (1760–1829)

One of the most famous architects of his age, Johnston was a native of Kilmore, County Armagh, and received his education in the world of architecture through the good offices of Archbishop Richard Robinson. At the age of eighteen he was sent by Robinson to work in Dublin under Thomas Cooley and Samuel Sproule. With Cooley's early death in 1784, Johnston became architect to Robinson, completing his ecclesiastical works in and around Armagh, most notably the Primate's Chapel. Johnston's drawings for this and for a new tower for the cathedral still exist. His career led him to become architect of the Office of Public Works in Dublin, where his finest buildings are the General Post Office, the Chapel Royal and the church of St George. Among Johnston's many interests was his great love of campanology and he regularly took part in bouts of bellringing at Hillsborough Parish Church. The bell at Clare Church of Ireland Church, County Armagh, bears his name, while the bells at Holywood Parish Church came from Johnston's own private bell-tower. They came

into the architect's possession having hung in the tower of Dublin's Crowe Street Theatre.

Ulster churches designed by Johnston:

Armagh Church of Ireland Cathedral (tower)
St Mark's Church of Ireland Church, Armagh
  (of his work, only the tower survives)
Primate's Chapel, Armagh (completion of work)

LANYON, Sir Charles (1813–89)

A native of Eastbourne in Sussex, Lanyon became articled to Jacob Owen at the Irish Board of Works in 1832, before being appointed as County Surveyor of Antrim in 1836. He was extremely versatile and during the course of his career was responsible for bridges, railways, roads, mansions, colleges, public buildings and churches. In Belfast he was responsible for Queen's College (now Queen's University Belfast) and the Customs House. He kept himself in the public eye, serving as Mayor of Belfast and as a Conservative member of parliament. He also gave his services free to a number of smaller architectural projects, which often earned him larger lucrative commissions. He offered his services free to the Down and Connor Church Accommodation Society. Lanyon was the head of the firm of Lanyon and Lynn, and his son, John, later entered this and designed the Church of Ireland churches of St Thomas', Belfast, and Willowfield.

Ulster churches designed by Lanyon:

Ballyclug Church of Ireland Church, County Antrim
Craigs Church of Ireland Church, County Antrim
Glynn Church of Ireland Church, County Antrim
Groomsport Church of Ireland Church, County Down
Hollymount Church of Ireland Church, County Down
Holywood Non-Subscribing Presbyterian
  Church, County Down
Killagan Church of Ireland Church, County Antrim
Lower Kilwarlin Church of Ireland Church,
  County Down
Muckamore Church of Ireland Church, County Antrim
Raloo Church of Ireland Church, County Antrim
Trinity Church of Ireland Church, Belfast
  (destroyed in the Blitz)
Upper Kilwarlin Church of Ireland Church,
  County Down
Waringstown Presbyterian Church, County Down
Whitehouse Church of Ireland Church, County Antrim

LYNN, William Henry (1829–1915)

Although born at St John's Point, County Down, Lynn was educated at Bannow in County Wexford. With its wealth of medieval ruins, the 'Irish Herculaneum' was to prove very influential on Lynn's work. At the age of seventeen he was an assistant in the office of Charles Lanyon, and in this capacity he worked as the clerk of works during construction of Queen's College, Belfast, and Crumlin Road Court House. Lynn was subsequently to become Lanyon's partner and was an imaginative designing force in the business until the split of the partnership in 1872. Moved by John Ruskin's *Stones of Venice*, Lynn was to utilise the Lombardic style for the first time in Ireland when he designed Sinclair Seamen's Church in Belfast (1856–57). Lynn was a noted antiquarian, and his appreciation of ancient Irish ecclesiastical architecture finds itself manifested in Jordanstown Parish Church, County Antrim (1866–68). He continued to design buildings right up to the end of his long life, most notably by being involved in the work at St Ann's Cathedral, Belfast. The *Irish Builder* said of him: 'In the days of the Gothic Revival Lynn was a keen and brilliant student of medieval work, his ecclesiastical designs having a scholarly and refined flavour and perfect mastery of Gothic detail'.

Ulster churches designed by Lynn:

All Saints' Church of Ireland Church, Derry
Belfast Castle Chapel (Church of Ireland)
Ballymena Presbyterian Church, County Antrim
Carlisle Circus Methodist Church, Belfast
Castlewellan Church of Ireland Church, County Down
Gilford Church of Ireland Church, County Down
Jordanstown Church of Ireland Church, County Antrim
St Ann's Cathedral, Belfast (baptistry)
St James' Church of Ireland Church, Belfast
  (tower and spire only surviving)
St Pauls' Church of Ireland Church, Belfast
Sinclair Seamen's Presbyterian Church, Belfast

McAULEY, Fr Jeremiah Ryan (1829–73)

This cleric/architect was born in Belfast and received his architectural training under Thomas Jackson. Having practised as an architect for a time, he decided to join the Passionist order, and subsequently trained for the priesthood. McAuley was ordained in Dublin in 1858, and designed St Peter's Pro-Cathedral (as it then was) in

Belfast before going to study in Salamanca. He returned to be the curate of Belfast and from 1871 he was the administrator of St Patrick's Church in the city.

Ulster churches designed by McAuley:

Aughlishnafin Catholic Church, County Down
Ballycastle Catholic Church, County Antrim
Ballykinlar Catholic Church, County Down
Dervock Catholic Church, County Antrim
St Peter's Catholic Cathedral, Belfast
Saul Catholic Church, County Down

McCARTHY, James Joseph (1817–82)

The 'Irish Pugin' was born in Dublin and learnt his profession at the Figure and Ornament Schools of the Royal Dublin Society, and served his apprenticeship under William Farrell. It is thought that he was associated in England with Charles Hansom, one of Pugin's rivals. In 1851 McCarthy published a paper, 'Suggestions on the Arrangement and Characteristics of Parish Churches'. He felt a strong need for a return to medieval principles in architecture and said, 'A Catholic architect must be a Catholic in heart. Simple knowledge will no more enable a man to build up God's Material than His spiritual temples'. McCarthy's work reflects a religious and a national renewal. In 1849 he was one of the three joint secretaries of the Irish Ecclesiological Society, founded to encourage the study of the relationship between the ancient ecclesiastical architecture of Ireland and the contemporary church. His desire for a resurgence in the fortunes of the Irish nation, and the fact that he was an architect working with his faith, secured for him a large number of commissions. Although the bulk of his work is outside Ulster, we do have some fine examples.

McCarthy's Ulster Churches:

Armagh Catholic Cathedral
Carrickmacross Catholic Church, County Monaghan
Cookstown Catholic Church, County Tyrone
Dungannon Catholic Church, County Tyrone
Mayobridge Catholic Church, County Down
Monaghan Catholic Cathedral
St Columb's Catholic Church, Derry

McCORMICK, William Henry Dunlevy (Liam) (1916–96)

Born into a family long prominent in the affairs of Derry, Liam McCormick was educated at Greencastle in County Donegal, where he lived for the larger part of his life, and at St Columb's College in Derry. He graduated with a Diploma in Architecture from Liverpool in 1943 and worked for a time in the City Surveyor's office in Derry, and then spent a year as architect to Ballymena Council. The first church which he designed was the award-winning Ennistymon Church, County Clare, in 1947, which was a joint effort with Frank Corr. After setting up a practice in Derry with Corr, McCormick carried out design work for a number of school-building schemes for Bishop Farren of Derry. Another church commission was that for the Church of the Holy Rosary in Limerick, which was completed in 1951. Ulster church commissions started to appear in the form of the Good Shepherd Convent Chapel, Nazareth House Chapel and St Mary's Church, all in Derry. These were followed by the churches at Milford and Murlough, both in County Donegal. In 1968 the firm of Liam McCormick and Partners was established with Tom Mullarkey and Joe Tracey, fine church architects in their own rights. Work with churches resulted in awards and commendations from the Royal Institution of Architects of Ireland; the gold medal in 1971 for Burt; commendations for the Glenties and Steelstown churches. Recognition of McCormick's skill and judgment came through appointments such as the chairmanship of the Northern Ireland committee for the 1975 Architectural Heritage Year; trustee of the Ulster Museum; High Sheriff of Derry, a position which his grandfather had held. In 1978 he was awarded an honorary doctorate by the University of Ulster.

As well as his very obvious gifts as an architect, Liam McCormick had a deep love for and knowledge of the sea, having made many voyages to the Continent, witnessing European architecture on the way. He retired from the firm of McCormick Tracey Mullarkey in 1982, and was made a Knight of St Gregory in 1984. Liam McCormick continued to design churches and domestic buildings throughout his retirement, and died in August 1996.

Ulster churches designed by McCormick, arranged chronologically:

St Mary's Church, Creggan, Derry (1954–59)

Chapel of the Convent of the Good Shepherd, Waterside, Derry (1956–58)

Nazareth House Chapel, Bishop Street, Derry (1957–62)

St Peter's, Milford, County Donegal (1961)

St Patrick's, Murlough, County Donegal (1962–64)

Star of the Sea, Desertegney, County Donegal (1964)

St Aengus', Burt, County Donegal (1964–67)

St Michael's, Creeslough, County Donegal (1970–71)

St Mary's, Maghera, County Londonderry (demolished) (1973–74)

St Conal's, Glenties, County Donegal (1974–75)

Our Lady of Lourdes, Steelstown, County Londonderry (1975–76)

St Oliver Plunkett, Toomebridge, County Antrim (altered) (1975–76)

Donaghmore Presbyterian Church, County Donegal (1976–77)

St Patrick's, Clogher, County Tyrone (1979)

St Nicholas', Carrickfergus, County Antrim (destroyed by fire) (1980–81)

Designed by the firm of Corr and McCormick:

St Clement's Retreat Chapel, Antrim Road, Belfast (1966–67) by Frank Corr

Designed by Liam McCormick and Partners:

St Mary Queen of Peace, Garrison, County Fermanagh (1972) by Joe Tracey

MILLAR, John (1811–76)

Although a native of Belfast, Millar trained in London under Thomas Hopper, before winning the competition for the design of the Third Presbyterian Church in Belfast's Rosemary Street when he was just eighteen. He was renowned as a classicist, being particularly influenced by the publication of *The Antiquities of Athens*. He did also design in the Gothic style, as at the Presbyterian church in Crumlin. Never a very sharp businessman, he died in New Zealand after a period of some financial difficulty.

Ulster churches designed by Millar:

Antrim Presbyterian Church, County Antrim
Castlereagh Presbyterian Church, County Down
Crumlin Presbyterian Church, County Antrim
Kircubbin Church of Ireland Church, County Down
Malone Presbyterian Church, Belfast (demolished)
Portaferry Presbyterian Church, County Down
Rosemary Street Third Presbyterian Church,
  Belfast (destroyed in the Blitz)

MULHOLLAND, Roger (1740–1818)

Considered the first native architect of Belfast, Mulholland was born in the diocese of Derry, and it is conjectured that he worked under the influence of Derry's Michael Priestley. Stylistic links, particularly a liking for Gibbsian surrounds, seem to add weight to this argument. Secular buildings in Belfast designed by Mulholland included the development of the area around St Anne's Parish Church, which included the vicarage. The design of the town's White Linen Hall is also attributed to him, as is the 'House of Correction', which stood in Howard Street.

Ulster churches designed by Mulholland:

Dunmurry Non-Subscribing Presbyterian
  Church, County Antrim (attribution)
Rosemary Street Non-Subscribing Presbyterian
  Church, Belfast

WELLAND, Joseph (1798–1860)

Born in Midleton, County Cork, Welland received his early training from John Bowden. By 1826 he was working under John Semple, and from that year until 1833 he worked for the Board of First Fruits as the architect for the archdiocese of Tuam. Following this he was appointed architect to the board's successor, the ecclesiastical commissioners, and he was their sole architect from 1843 to 1860, after which the firm of Welland and Gillespie was architect to the commissioners.

Ulster churches designed by Welland:

Annahilt Church of Ireland Church, County Down
Ballymena Church of Ireland Church, County Antrim
Lisnaskea Church of Ireland Church,
  County Fermanagh
Magherafelt Church of Ireland Church,
  County Londonderry
Ramoan Church of Ireland Church, County Antrim

Ulster churches designed by the firm of Welland and Gillespie:

Ballyclog Church of Ireland Church, County Antrim
Camlough Church of Ireland Church, County Armagh
Clanabogan Church of Ireland Church,
  County Londonderry
St Matthew's Church of Ireland Church, Belfast
Tullylish Church of Ireland Church, County Down

WILLIAMS-ELLIS, Clough (1883–1978)

Born in Northamptonshire, Williams-Ellis trained at the Architectural Association School in London. Much of his work had a very firm foundation in traditionalism and he was responsible for the picturesque villages of Portmerion in Wales and Cushendun in County Antrim. Although he designed only one Ulster church, his school at the Giant's Causeway has a rather church-like appearance.

Ulster church designed by Williams-Ellis:

First Church of Christ Scientist, Belfast

Bibliography

Architecture in the Irish Presbyterian Church

Atkinson, ED, *An Ulster Parish: A History of Donaghcloney* (Belfast, 1898)

Atkinson, ED, *Dromore: an Ulster Diocese* (Dundalk, 1925)

Anderson, M, *St Joseph's, Poyntzpass* (Newry, 1996)

Bailie, WD, *Portaferry Presbyterian Church, 1642–1992* (nd)

Barr, WNC, *Derriaghy: a Short History of the Parish* (Belfast, 1974)

Barry, J, *Hillsborough: a Parish in the Ulster Plantation* (Belfast, 1982)

Beckett, JC, *Innishargy through the Ages* (Belfast, 1966)

Beckett, JC, *St Mark's, Dundela, 1878–1978* (Newtownards, 1978)

Blaney, R, *Presbyterians and the Irish Language* (Belfast, 1996)

Bolton, FR, *The Caroline Tradition of the Church of Ireland with Particular Reference to Bishop Jeremy Taylor* (London, 1958)

Breakey, JC, *Presbyterian Church Architecture in Ireland* (nd)

Brett, CEB, *Buildings of Belfast*, revised edition, (Belfast, 1967)

Brett, CEB, *Buildings of County Antrim* (Belfast, 1996)

Brett, CEB, *Roger Mulholland, Architect, of Belfast* (Belfast, 1976)

Brett, CEB, *Buildings of County Armagh* (Belfast, 1999)

Builder, The 1843 onwards

Burges, YA, *History of St Michael's, Castlecaulfield,* (Dungannon, 1966)

Carmody, WP, *History of the Parish of Knockbreda* (Belfast, 1929)

Cassidy, H, *St Patrick's Cathedral, Armagh* (Derby, 1991)

Chapman, GR, *Historical Sketch of Moyallon Meeting* (nd)

Church of Our Lady of Lourdes, Shantallow, Souvenir of the Opening (Derry, 1976)

Craig, MJ, *The Architecture of Ireland* (London, 1982)

Curl, JS, *Classical Churches in Ulster* (Belfast, 1980)

Curl, JS, *The Architecture and Planning of the Estates of the Drapers' Company in Ulster* (Belfast, 1979)

Curl, JS, *The History, Architecture and Planning of the Estates of the Fishmongers' Company in Ulster* (Belfast, 1981)

de Breffney, B, and Mott, G, *Churches and Abbeys of Ireland* (London, 1976)

Day, A, and McWilliams, P, (eds) Ordnance Survey Memoirs of Ireland, 40 vols, (Belfast, 1990–98)

Dewar, J, *A History of Elmwood Church* (Belfast, 1900)

Dixon, H, *An Introduction to Ulster Architecture* (Belfast, 1975)

Doak, J, *Carlisle Road Methodist Church, 1903–1978* (Londonderry, 1978)

Drew, T, *The Ancient Church of St Nicholas, Carrickfergus* (Dublin, 1872)

Drew, T, *A Brief History of the Church of St Patrick, Coleraine, with some account of its proposed restoration* (Dublin, 1883)

Dukes, FE, *Campanology in Ireland* (Dublin, 1994)

Dunlop, D, *A Memoir of the Professional Life of William J Barre Esq* (Belfast, 1868)

Dwyer, F, *Georgian People* (London, 1978)

Eastlake, CL, *A History of the Gothic Revival* (London and New York, 1872)

Ellwood Post, W, *Saints, Signs and Symbols* (London, 1964)

Evans, D, *An Introduction to Modern Ulster Architecture* (Belfast, 1977)

Form and Function in Vernacular Church Buildings of Ulster (nd)

Fleming, J, Honour, H, Pevsner, N, *Penguin Dictionary of Architecture* (London, 1991)

Fothergill, AB, *The Mitred Earl: An Eighteenth Century Eccentric* (London, 1974)

Foy, JH, *Moravians in Ireland* (Belfast, 1986)

Galloway, P, *The Cathedrals of Ireland* (Belfast, 1992)

Godkin, J, *Ireland and her Churches* (London, 1867)

Gray, AS, *Edwardian Architecture* (London, 1985)

Green, WJ, *Methodism in Portadown* (Belfast, 1960)

Greer, RF, unpublished historical notes on the church of St Paul, Castlewellan

HMSO, *Archaeological Survey of County Down* (Belfast, 1966)

HMSO, *Historic Monuments of Northern Ireland* (Belfast, 1987)

Hanna, D O'D, *Ulster Barn Churches: their Origin and Development* (Belfast, 1952)

Harbinson, P, Potterton, H and Sheehy, J, *Irish Art and Architecture from Prehistory to the Present* (London, 1993)

Harris, W, *The Antient and Present State of the County of Down* (Dublin, 1744)

Haslam, R, *Clough Williams-Ellis* (London, 1996)

Historical Sketch of First Church of Christ Scientist, Belfast (Belfast, 1955)

Holmes, F, *Our Presbyterian Heritage* (Belfast, 1985)

Hurley, R, and Cantwell, W, *Contemporary Church Architecture* (Dublin, 1985)

Johnston, EM, *Ireland in the Eighteenth Century* (Dublin, 1974)

Killen, WD, *History of the Congregations of the Presbyterian Church in Ireland* (Dublin, 1886)

Kidder Smith, GE, *The New Churches of Europe* (London, 1964)

Larmour, P, *Belfast: an Illustrated Architectural Guide* (Belfast, 1987)

Leask, HG, *Irish Churches and Monastic Buildings* (Dundalk, 1955)

Lewis, S, *Topographical Dictionary of Ireland* (London, 1837)

Loane, E, 'Architectural Drawings by Thomas Cooley in the Public Library, Armagh', undergraduate thesis, Dublin, 1983

Methodist Churches of Newtownards and Comber (Newtownards,1954)

McAdoo, HR, *Jeremy Taylor: Anglican Theologian* (Omagh, 1997)

McCappin, W, *St Patrick's Church, Jordanstown* (Belfast, 1993)

McBride, S, 'Bishop Mant and the Church Architecture Society Influences on the Nineteenth Century Ecclesiastical Architecture of Ulster', unpublished paper presented to the Church of Ireland Historical Society, May, 1997

McCormick, WHD, 'Building churches: 1947–75. A personal recollection', *RSUA Yearbook*, 1976

McCormick, WHD, 'Memories wise and otherwise', *RSUA Yearbook*, 1990

McCullough, N, and Mulvin, V, *A Lost Tradition: the Nature of Architecture in Ireland* (Dublin, 1987)

Millan, SS, *A History of the Second Congregation, Belfast, 1708–1900* (Belfast, 1900)

Mitchell, G, *A Guide to St Nicholas' Church, Carrickfergus* (Carrickfergus, 1962)

Moore, T, *First Presbyterian Church, Belfast: a Chronological History 1644–1994* (Belfast, 1994)

Mullan, D and Donnelly, P, *St John's, Coleraine* (Coleraine, 1992)

Myles, J, *LN Cottingham 1787–1847: Architect of the Gothic Revival* (London, 1996)

O'Laverty, J, *An Historical Account of the Dioceses of Down and Connor* (Dublin, 1878)

Ó Saothraí, S, *An Ministir Gaelach Uilliam Mac Néill (1774–1821)* (Belfast 1992)

Patton, M, *Central Belfast: a Historical Gazetteer* (Belfast, 1993)

Perspective, the journal of the Royal Society of Ulster Architects

Presbyterian Historical Society of Ireland, *A History of the Congregations in the Presbyterian Church in Ireland*

Potterton, H, *Irish Church Monuments 1570–1880* (Belfast, 1975)

Rankin, P, *Irish Building Ventures of the Earl-Bishop of Derry* (Belfast, 1972)

Reside, SW, *St Mary's Parish Church, Newry* (Newry, 1933)

Richardson, DS, 'Gothic Revival architecture in Ireland', unpublished doctoral thesis, Yale University, 1974

Richardson, N, *A Tapestry of Beliefs: Christian Traditions in Northern Ireland* (Belfast, 1998)

Rogers, E, *Memoir of Armagh Cathedral* (Belfast, 1888)

Rothery, S, *Ireland and the New Architecture* (Dublin, 1991)

Rowan, A, *North-West Ulster* (London, 1979)

St Malachy's Church, Belfast, Centenary Record (Belfast, 1948)

Sheehy, J, *JJ McCarthy and the Gothic Revival in Ireland* (Belfast, 1977)

Sheehy, J, *The Rediscovery of Ireland's Past: the Celtic Revival 1830–1930* (London, 1980)

Smyth, R, *Ballynafeigh Methodist Church Jubilee Reflections 1899–1949* (Belfast, 1949)

Snoddy, T, *Dictionary of Irish Artists: the Twentieth Century* (Dublin, 1996)

Solemn Dedication of St Patrick's Church, Newtownards (Belfast, 1978)

Stevenson, J, *A Boy in the Country* (London, 1912)

Stuart, J, *Historical Memoirs of the City of Armagh* (Newry, 1819)

Thompson, P, *William Butterfield* (London, 1971)

Ulster Architectural Heritage Society, surveys of towns and areas of architectural importance, 1969–present

Ulster Architectural Heritage Society, *The Buildings of Armagh* (Belfast, 1992)

Ulster Historical Society, *Clergy of Down and Dromore* (Belfast, 1996)

Ulster Journal of Archaeology, second series (Belfast, 1897)

Ulster Times, (p 163)

Walker, BM, and Dixon, H, *In Belfast Town: Early Photographs from the Lawrence Collection 1864–1880* (Belfast, 1984)

Wesleyan Historical Society, *Donegall Square and Belfast Methodism* (Belfast, 1994)

Whyte, J, and Wynne, M, *Irish Stained Glass* (Dublin, 1963)

Williams, J, A Companion Guide to Architecture in Ireland 1837–1921, (Dublin, 1994)

Williamson, HR, *Jeremy Taylor* (London, 1952)

Young, A, *A Tour through Ireland in 1776, 1777 and 1778* (London, 1780)

Glossary

ACANTHUS A plant represented in classical and Renaissance ornament and particularly in the Corinthian and Composite Orders.

AISLE A passageway running parallel to the main span of a church.

ALTAR Table of stone used for the celebration of the Eucharist.

AMBO Podium or pulpit.

ANGELUS A devotional prayer, based on the annunciation to the Virgin Mary. This is observed at 6 am, 12 noon and 6 pm and may be signalled by the ringing of a bell.

ANGUS DEI Christ was often symbolised as the Lamb of God and this is an image often found on the front of altars or communion tables. It is the particular image of the Moravian Church, depicting a lamb with a flag.

ANTAE In early Irish churches, a prolongation of the side walls in advance of the gable walls.

APSE A projection, semicircular or polygonal in plan, from the walls of a church or other building.

ARCADE A series of arches carried on piers or columns. **BLIND ARCADE**, a series of arches carried on shafts or pilasters against a solid wall.

ARCHITRAVE A moulded enrichment to the sides or head of a door or window opening; the lowest member of an entablature.

ARCHIVOLT The continuous architrave moulding of the face of an arch, following its contour.

ASHLAR Masonry wrought to an even face and squared edges.

BALDACCHINO Canopy over an altar or tomb.

BALUSTER Pillar or post supporting a rail or coping. A series of these form a **BALUSTRADE**.

BAPTISTRY Area of a church where baptism is performed.

BARLEY-SUGAR COLUMNS Columns decorated in the manner of sticks of barley-sugar, ie, twisted down the length of the column.

BARN CHURCH The term used to refer to Ulster churches which have the proportions and external appearance of a barn, eg, they may have a hipped roof. These tend to be nonconformist churches of the eighteenth and nineteenth centuries.

BATTER The inclined face of a wall.

BATTLEMENT A parapet with alternating indentations or embrasures and raised portions or merlons; also called **CRENELLATION**.

BAYS The main vertical divisions of a building or feature. The division of a roof, marked by its main trusses.

BELFRY/CAMPANILE Accommodation for bell or bells.

BELL CAPITAL A capital which the appearance of an upturned bell.

BELLCOTE A frame on the gable of a roof in which a bell is hung.

BOARD OF FIRST FRUITS The Board of Fruit Firsts existed to provide finance for church building using a proportion of the income of the first year of an ecclesiastical living. This was often augmented by grants from parliament.

BOSS Ornamental knob or projection covering the intersection of ribs in a vault or ceiling.

BRACE In roof construction, a subsidiary timber inserted to strengthen the framing of a truss.

BROACH-SPIRE In a broach-spire, the angles of the tower are surmounted by half-pyramids (broaches) to effect the change from the square(of the tower) to the polygon (of the spire).

BULLS-EYE WINDOW A small circular window.

BURNING BUSH The symbol of Presbyterianism, which recalls the bush witnessed by Moses which burned, but was not destroyed. This is thought to symbolise the indestructability of the church.

BUTTRESS A mass of masonry or brickwork projecting from or built against a wall to give it additional strength.

CANOPY A projection or hood over an opening; the covering over a tomb or niche.

CAPITAL Head or top part of a column.

CARDINAL FACES The surfaces of a building facing towards the points of the compass.

CARTOUCHE An ornamental panel with scrolling edges, often carrying an inscription.

CASTELLATION See **BATTLEMENT**.

CHAMFER The surface created by cutting off a square edge, usually at an angle of 45 degrees.

CHANCEL The east end of a church. In medieval times reserved for the clergy and choir.

CIBORIUM The sacred vessel used in the Eucharist to contain the Host (consecrated bread).

CLERESTORY An upper storey, pierced by windows, in the main walls of a building.

COFFERED Decorated ceiling or vault, composed of sunken square or polygonal sections.

COLONETTE Small column or shaft.

COMMUNION TABLE In the Anglican, Presbyterian and Methodist churches, where the communion elements of bread and wine are consecrated.

COMMUNION TOKENS Tokens, often made of pewter, which were distributed to communicants in the Presbyterian church. They were stamped with the name of the congregation and the minister's initials.

CONFESSIONAL Free-standing or integral booth found in Catholic (and some Anglican) churches in which confessions can be heard.

CORBEL A projecting stone or timber for the support of a superincumbent weight. **CORBEL TABLE**, a row of corbels supporting a projection.

CORBEL STOP The carved projection at the termination of a corbel.

 CORINTHIAN The Corinthian order developed in the fifth century BC. A Corinthian capital is characterised by decoration with acanthus leaves.

CORNICE The crowning member of an entablature.

COURSE A continuous layer of stones or bricks in a wall.

COVE A concave under-surface in the nature of a moulding but on a larger scale.

CRENELLATION See **BATTLEMENT**.

CROCKETS Gothic decoration on the edge of a sloping feature.

CRUCIFORM Church built in the shape of a cross.

CRUCK A roof having a truss with principals (crucks) springing from below the level of wall-plate. The timbers are usually curved.

CUSPS The projecting points forming the foils in Gothic windows, arches, panels, etc.

DADO The finishing of the lower part of an interior wall from floor to waist height, terminated by a dado rail.

DECORATED English Gothic architecture, c 1290–c1350.

DENTILS The small rectangular tooth-like blocks used decoratively in classical cornices.

DIOCLETIAN WINDOW Semicircular window, often divided by two uprights.

 DORIC The earliest of the classical architectural orders. Doric columns have very simple turned capitals.

DRESSINGS The stone or brickwork used around an angle, window or other feature when worked to a finished face, whether smooth, tooled or rubbed, moulded or sculptured.

DRIPSTONE Projecting moulding which throws off or carries away water.

EARLY ENGLISH English Gothic architecture, 1200–50.

EAVES The lower part of a sloping roof overhanging a wall.

EMBRASURE Splayed opening.

ENTABLATURE In classical or Renaissance architecture, the moulded horizontal superstructure of an opening, wall or colonnade, consisting of an architrave, frieze and cornice.

EUCHARIST Also known as Holy Communion, Mass, the Lord's Supper.

FACADE The front or face of a building.

FANLIGHT A window, often semicircular, over a door. Particularly common in Georgian buildings.

FENESTRATION The arrangement of windows on a building.

FLUTING Shallow concave grooves running vertically on the shaft of a column or pilaster.

FINIAL An ornament at the top of a gable, canopy, pinnacle, etc.

FOIL (trefoil, quatrefoil, cinquefoil, multifoil, etc) A leaf-shaped space defined by the curves formed by the cusping in an opening or panel.

FOLIATED Carved with leaf ornament.

FONT Mounted vessel containing water used in the sacrament of baptism. Holy water fonts or stoups are placed near the door of Catholic churches for those entering to make the sign of the cross as a reminder of their baptism.

FRIEZE The middle of an entablature or the decorated band along the upper part of a wall.

GARGOYLE A water spout projecting from a roof, often carved in the form of a grotesque.

GIBBS SURROUND Surround of door or window designed by James Gibbs (1682–1754) which has blocks interrupting the architrave.

GOTHIC The architecture of the pointed arch. Gothic architecture developed from the twelfth century.

GOTHICK The spelling of Gothic in the eighteenth century, which has tended to lend itself to the Gothic architecture of the period.

HAMMERBEAMS Horizontal brackets of a roof projecting at wall-plate level and resembling the two ends of a tie-beam with its middle part cut away; they are supported by braces and help to diminish lateral pressure by reducing the span.

HARLED Roughcast.

HIPPED ROOF A roof with sloped instead of vertical ends.

HOOD-MOULD A projecting moulding on the face of a wall above an arch, door or window.

IN ANTIS Flat pilasters placed at the short projecting walls of a portico or colonnade.

 IONIC The Ionic order originated in the sixth century BC. An Ionic capital will be recognised by ornamentation with scrolled decoration or volutes.

JAMBS The vertical straight sides of a door or window or other opening.

KEY-BLOCK Block of stone at the centre of the head of a door or window.

KEYSTONE The middle stone of an arch.

KING-POST The middle vertical post in a truss-roof.

LANCET A tall, narrow window with a pointed head.

LECTERN Reading stand to hold a copy of the Bible.

LIGHT Compartment of a window.

LINTEL A horizontal beam or stone over an opening.

LOGGIA A gallery or room, open on one or more sides.

LOMBARDIC A style of twelfth-century architecture derived from the Lombardy region of Italy.

LOUVRE A lantern-like structure surmounting the roof of a hall or other building, with openings for ventilation or the escape of smoke, usually crossed by sloping slats (called louvre-boards) to exclude rain. Louvre-boards are also used in church belfries instead of glazing, to allow the bells to be heard.

LUCARNE Dormer window on a roof or spire.

MARGIN-PANED WINDOWS Sashed windows with narrow side lights incorporated within the frame.

MODILLION A small bracket or console, a number of which can support a cornice.

MONSTRANCE In the Catholic church a monstrance is used to display the Host (consecrated bread) on the altar during periods of Exposition.

MOULDING Ornament of continuous section.

MULLION A vertical post or upright dividing an opening with lights.

NAVE The western section of a church, often flanked by aisles.

NICHE Recess in a wall, often containing a statue or a decorative object.

OCULUS A circular opening in a wall.

OGEE A compound curve of two parts, one convex, the other concave.

PATEN Plate or shallow dish, usually made of silver, to contain consecrated bread or wafer during communion.

PEDIMENT A low-pitched gable used in classical and Renaissance architecture above a portico or feature, at the end of a building or above doors, windows, niches, etc; sometimes the apex is omitted, forming a **BROKEN PEDIMENT** or the horizontal members are omitted, forming an **OPEN PEDIMENT**.

PERPENDICULAR The last of the Gothic styles, c 1400–1550.

PILASTER A shallow pier of rectangular section attached to the wall.

PINNINGS Small stones used to fill irregularities in masonry.

PISCINA A basin in a church used for washing the sacred vessels.

PLINTH The projecting base of a wall or column.

PODIUM In classical architecture, a basis, usually solid, supporting a superstructure.

POLYCHROMATIC The use of many colours, usually for external architectural decoration, often describing brickwork in Victorian buildings.

POPPYHEAD Carved pew finial.

PORTICO A covered entrance to a building, colonnaded, either constituting the whole front of a building or forming an important feature.

PRECENTOR Clergyman or lay-person charged with the conduct of church music.

PRINCIPALS The main, as opposed to the common, rafters of a roof.

PULPIT An elevated stand of stone or wood for a preacher.

PURLINS A horizontal longitudinal timber in a roof structure.

QUOINS The stones, generally dressed, at the angles of a building.

RAFTERS Inclined timbers supporting a roof covering.

REREDOS A wall or screen of stone or wood, rising behind an altar or communion table.

ROMANESQUE Eleventh- to twelfth-century architecture, which preceded Gothic architecture, characterised by round-headed doors and windows.

RUBBLE Walling of rough or unsquared stones.

RUBRICS Liturgical instructions, literally printed in red.

RUSTICATION Masonry cut in blocks and separated by deep joints, often of V-section.

SACRED HEART The Sacred Heart of Jesus is a Catholic form of devotion recalling the suffering of Christ as witnessed in the visions experienced by Margaret Mary Alacoque in the seventeenth century. Many Catholic churches have a Sacred Heart chapel.

SACRED MONOGRAM The letters IHS, found on altars and communion tables in Catholic and Anglican churches, denote the first three letters in Greek of Christ's name.

SACRISTY A room in a church (usually Catholic) for sacred vessels and vestments.

SANCTUARY Area around the altar or communion table of a church.

SCAMOSSIAN Named after Vincenzo Scamozzi (1552–1616), who presented his architectural ideas in his work *L'idea dell'architettura universale* (1615), which provided a codification of the architectural orders.

SCHIST A shale-type stone.

SEGMENTAL-HEADED The head of a door or window with an arc substantially less than a full circle.

SHAFT A slender column.

SHINGLES Wooden tiles for covering roofs, walls or spires. Could also be made from other materials.

SOLE PIECES Sole or wall-plate upon which a truss rests.

SOFFIT The under side of an arch, lintel, vault, staircase, etc.

SOUND WINDOWS The windows on the upper section of a tower, often protected by louvres, which allow the sound of bells to escape.

SPANDREL The triangular-shaped space above the outside curve of an arch, sometimes enclosed by a rectangular framework or moulding.

STAGES The divisions (eg, of a tower) usually marked externally by horizontal string-courses.

STATIONS OF THE CROSS Fourteen images recalling the death and passion of Christ.

STOUP Vessel for holy water.

STRING-COURSE A projecting horizontal band in a wall, usually moulded.

STRUT A timber forming a sloping support to a beam, etc.

STUCCO Smooth plaster finish on a building. A compound of gypsum, sand and lime.

TABERNACLE An enclosed chamber behind an altar holding the sacred vessels which contain the bread and wine for Eucharist.

TIE-BEAM The horizontal transverse beam in a roof, tying together the feet of pairs of rafters to counteract thrust.

TRACERY The ornamental work in the head of a window, screen, panel, etc, formed by the curving and interlacing of bars of wood or stone, grouped together, generally over two or more lights or bays.

TRANSEPT The arms of a cross-shaped church.

TRANSOM An intermediate horizontal bar of stone or wood across a window opening; also the member separating a door and fanlight.

TRIGLYPHS Blocks with vertical channels placed at intervals along the frieze of the Doric entablature.

TRIPTYCH A three-sectioned altar-piece or religious image.

TRUSSED ROOF Roof supported by timbers.

TYMPANUM The triangular or semicircular field in the face of a pediment or in the head of an arch.

VAULT An arched ceiling or roof of stone or brick, sometimes imitated in wood and plaster. Also used to refer to a place of burial beneath a church or a structure in a churchyard, ie, a burial vault. **BARREL VAULTING** is a continuous vault unbroken in its length by cross-vaults.

VENETIAN WINDOW A three-light window with a tall round-headed middle light and shorter lights on either side, the side lights usually with flanking pilasters and small entablatures forming the imposts to the arch over the central light.

VESTRY The Anglican term for a **SACRISTY**.

WALL-PLATE A timber laid lengthwise on the wall to receive the ends of the rafters and other joists.

Sources of Illustrations

Unless otherwise stated, the photographs and drawings are by the author. The remaining illustrations are reproduced by kind permission of the following people and institutions, or come from the following published sources: p. 17 from an engraving by Peter Lombart in *Ductor Dubitantium* (London, 1660); p. 67 (upper) from a painting by Sir Joshua Reynolds reproduced by permission of the governors and guardians of Armagh Public Library; p. 43 from *Belfast Literary Society* (Belfast, 1902); p.114 from *The Builder;* p. 5 from *The History of the Town of Belfast* by George Benn (Belfast, 1827); p. 14, Mr Samuel Campbell; p. 79 from *The Life and Times of Henry Cooke, D.D, LL.D.* (London, 1871); p. 89 from *The Journal of John Wesley, A.M.,* Vol III, ed. N Curnock (London, 1909); pp. 2, 3, 10, 21, 24, 26, 29, 32, 67 (lower), 82, 83, 117 (lower), 132, 176, Department of the Environment for Northern Ireland, Environment and Heritage Service; p. 120 from *A Memoir of the Professional Life of William J Barre Esq* by D Dunlop, (Belfast, 1868); p. 156, drawing by Ms Rita Harkin; p. 25, Hillsborough Parish Church Bellringers; p. 8 from *The Church of Ireland in Belfast* by JF MacNeice (Belfast. 1931); p. 6 from a gouache by William Miller (d. 1779) and p. 131, a photograph from the Welch Collection, the trustees of the National Museums and Galleries of Northern Ireland, Ulster Museum (the Welch Collection); p. 147, Mrs Kathleen E Milligan/Crown Copyright; p. 70 the National Trust, Ickworth House, England (painting by Vigée Le Brun, 1790, photographed by Jeremy Whitaker); p. 25 from *Bells Thro' the Ages: the Founders' Craft and the Ringers' Art* by JR Nicholls (London, 1928); p. 177, *Northern Builder* magazine; p. 123 from *The History of the Parish* [Holywood] *from the Earliest Times* by J O'Laverty (Belfast, 1893); p. 7, PRONI, D/2886/A/2/12/1/6, the Deputy Keeper of the Public Record Office of Northern Ireland, reproduced in *The Way We Were: Historic Photographs from the Allison Collection* by Desmond Fitzgerald and Roger Weatherup (Belfast, 1993); p. 59, *Historic Memorials of the First Presbyterian Church* (Belfast, 1887); pp. 38 (upper) and 55 (lower) *Saints, Signs and Symbols* by W Ellwood Post (London, 1964 rev. 1975) by permission of the SPCK; pp. 68 and 164, Mrs Primrose Wilson.

Index